The
one-state
solution

New Approaches to
Conflict Analysis

Series editor: Peter Lawler, Senior Lecturer in
International Relations, Department of Government,
University of Manchester

Until recently, the study of conflict and conflict resolution remained comparatively immune to broad developments in social and political theory. When the changing nature and locus of large-scale conflict in the post-Cold War era is also taken into account, the case for a reconsideration of the fundamentals of conflict analysis and conflict resolution becomes all the more stark.

New Approaches to Conflict Analysis promotes the development of new theoretical insights and their application to concrete cases of large-scale conflict, broadly defined. The series intends not to ignore established approaches to conflict analysis and conflict resolution, but to contribute to the reconstruction of the field through a dialogue between orthodoxy and its contemporary critics. Equally, the series reflects the contemporary porosity of intellectual borderlines rather than simply perpetuating rigid boundaries around the study of conflict and peace. *New Approaches to Conflict Analysi*s seeks to uphold the normative commitment of the field's founders yet also recognises that the moral impulse to research is properly part of its subject matter. To these ends, the series is comprised of the highest quality work of scholars drawn from throughout the international academic community, and from a wide range of disciplines within the social sciences.

PUBLISHED

Eşref Aksu
The United Nations, intra-state peacekeeping and normative change

M. Anne Brown
*Human rights and the borders of suffering:
the promotion of human rights in international politics*

Lorraine Elliott and Graeme Cheeseman (eds)
*Forces for good:
Cosmopolitan militaries in the twenty-first century*

Richard Jackson
*Writing the war on terrorism:
language, politics and counter-terrorism*

Tami Amanda Jacoby and Brent Sasley (eds)
Redefining security in the Middle East

Jan Koehler and Christoph Zürcher (eds)
Potentials of disorder

Helena Lindholm Schulz
*Reconstruction of Palestinian nationalism:
between revolution and statehood*

David Bruce MacDonald
*Balkan holocausts?
Serbian and Croatian victim-centred propaganda and the war in Yugoslavia*

Jennifer Milliken
The social construction of the Korean War

Ami Pedahzur
*The Israeli response to Jewish extremism and violence:
defending democracy*

Maria Stern
*Naming insecurity - constructing identity:
'Mayan-women' in Guatemala on the eve of 'peace'*

Tarja Väyrynen
*Culture and international conflict resolution:
a critical analysis of the work of John Burton*

The one-state solution

A breakthrough
for peace in the
Israeli-Palestinian
deadlock

Virginia Tilley

Manchester University Press
Manchester

Copyright © by the University of Michigan 2005

Published in the United States of America by
The University of Michigan Press
Manufactured in the United States of America

This edition published in the UK, Ireland, Europe, the Middle East and the Far East
by Manchester University Press
Oxford Road, Manchester M13 9NR, UK
www.manchesteruniversitypresss.co.uk

British Library Cataloguing-in-Publication Data
A catalogue record for this book is available from the British Library

ISBN 0 7190 7336 7 *hardback*
EAN 978 0 7190 7336 6

First published 2005

14   13   12   11   10   09   08   07   06   05   10   9   8   7   6   5   4   3   2   1

TO THE PALESTINIAN & JEWISH PEOPLES

"Zion shall be redeemed through justice,
and her returning ones by doing what is right."
                                          —*Isaiah 1:27*

Contents

Illustrations

MAPS

Illustrations

x

FIGURE

Acknowledgments

I owe innumerable intellectual debts for the contents of this book—written nineteen years after I first went to Jerusalem in 1985 (then entirely naive), on a study-abroad program from Antioch College. While living nearly two years in the Old City of Jerusalem, El Bireh, Ramallah, and Bir Zeit and working with Israeli and Palestinian peace groups especially in East and West Jerusalem, I had the privilege of working with the most courageous people I have ever known. The capacity of Jewish Israelis, Arab Israelis, Palestinians, and a cluster of foreigners to sustain a moral compass through the most daunting of conditions was a lasting inspiration and left me with a sense of moral obligation to the Israeli-Palestinian conflict, which I hope this book can partly indicate to these people even if it digresses from their views. I could not mention any of them individually without slighting others; a generic thanks is all I can offer.

My capacity to build on that experience in more theoretical ways traces, first, to Professor Hassan Nejad at Antioch College and, later, to graduate study with the outstanding faculty at the Center for Contemporary Arab Studies at Georgetown University. Doctoral work on ethnic conflict with Crawford Young and other faculty at the University of Wisconsin-Madison also infuses this work in ways that they will perceive and that I hope will meet with their approval. In writing much of this book, I also often recalled my work in Washington, D.C., with the remarkable Joseph Schechla, whose insights still hover between many of these lines. My contact through him to Tom and Sally Mallison, Elmer Berger, Roselle Tekiner, and others from the

International Organization for the Elimination of All Forms of Racial Discrimination was a rare privilege and lastingly strengthened my work in the field.

Returning in spring 2004 to the subject of Israel-Palestine, after years of comparative work in Latin America, I relied heavily on the excellent primary documentation now available online from such projects as the Foundation for Middle East Peace and the Jewish Virtual Library. My analysis was also freshly filled out by conversations and correspondence with Avi Shlaim at Oxford University (whose particular generosity is gratefully remembered), Rabbi David Goldberg in London, and 'Azmi Bishara during one important evening. Steven Friedman at the Center for Policy Studies in Johannesburg offered key early insights and ongoing feedback that greatly assisted my analysis. Tony Judt and an anonymous reviewer for the University of Michigan Press provided crucial feedback and immeasurable help in identifying slips and weaknesses in my argument. All these people, each working in a different realm, consistently engaged difficult questions about Israel-Palestine with an exemplary fairness, professionalism, and personal integrity that encouraged my optimism for broader discussions among international networks similarly anxious about the present course of events. These people should not, however, be assumed to agree with me on all points presented here, and certainly no errors here trace to them. Other people who helped with this book, but who are under such political difficulty as to ask anonymity, are quietly appreciated and I hope their role will someday be known.

Finally, for their patient reading of drafts and their very thoughtful comments, which were of immeasurable value in strengthening my discussion in this book, I am grateful to my dear friends Patricia Billings, Meredith Moodie and, not least, my extraordinary editor at the University of Michigan Press, Jim Reische. In their kind assistance, all these friends reflected back to me a sense of their collective care for the project. I hope this book fulfills their expectations and offers some return for their guidance and encouragement.

1. Facing Facts

In the 1960s, U.S. intellectual Izzy Stone used to point out that simply reading the *New York Times* would lay bare the facts behind Nixon's obfuscating murk about Vietnam. He would tear the broadsheet pages in half for easier reading, pull them out at restaurants and talks, and stun listeners with the political picture revealed to have been before their own eyes all along. Today, facts are again sitting right there in the mainstream news which signal that, while all the theater of Middle East conflict has been roiling by, the very terms for peace in the Middle East have inexorably transformed. The Jewish settlements, always recognized by the international community as an "obstacle to peace," have accomplished their purpose: the territorial basis for a viable Palestinian state no longer exists. The premise for all present diplomacy—the two-state solution—has therefore become impossible. The same reality now confronts all parties involved: only one state can viably exist in the land of historic Palestine between the Mediterranean and the Jordan River. And everyone—Israel and its friends, the Palestinians and their friends, and the international community as a whole—must consider seriously what to do next.

The two-state option has been eliminated as a practical solution in two senses. First and most graphically, Jewish settlements have carved Palestinian territory into a vestige too small to sustain a viable national society (see maps 1 and 2). Even a decade ago, the settlements were much smaller and more scattered; their road grid was attenuated, and the settler population was sparse. A meaningful

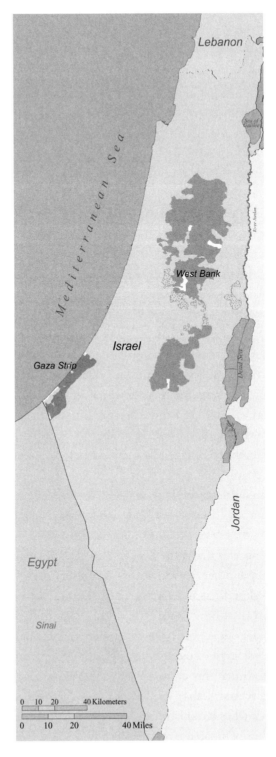

Map 1.   The future Palestinian state as suggested by route of Israel's "security fence" and the settlement grid. (Pal Map, copyright 2003.)

Israeli withdrawal and a viable Palestinian state were still imaginable. By the end of the 1990s, however, the settlements were major urban complexes burrowed deep into Palestinian territory. Their major connecting highways had sliced the territory into chunks, and 230,000 settlers were embedded in the region, with jobs, children, social networks, and full cultural lives. Even if most settlers claimed they would leave in exchange for financial compensation (as some surveys indicated), this massive grid's economic, political, and demographic weight rendered it a politically immovable object. When President George W. Bush publicly affirmed these "realities on the ground" in April 2004, the international community was shocked, shocked, that he had discarded four decades of international diplomacy, which had always held the settlements illegal. But protests had the vaporous character of diplomatic theater, scandalized about protocol rather than substance—for who, staring at the West Bank landscape, could now convincingly disagree?

Any Palestinian state created in the twisted scrap of land remaining is certain to fail Palestinian-national hopes and needs. Indeed, few close observers dispute this much, and international debate still holds that removing the settlements is prerequisite to viable Palestinian statehood and a stable peace agreement. But as this book demonstrates, no power—internal or external—has the political capacity to effect any meaningful withdrawal of these urban communities and their infrastructure, and no such capacity is likely to appear, given constraints operating in the United States. Except for some Gaza settlements and a few token West Bank outposts, the settlement grid therefore now manifests as a permanent part of the landscape, suggesting that most of the West Bank will be formally incorporated as "Israel" within another decade or so. No viable Palestinian state can be constituted in what is left: we have only confounding rhetoric about it.

The second sense in which the two-state solution has died is that even if a Palestinian "state" were declared in this dismembered enclave, it can bring only continuing instability. The resulting Palestinian statelet would be blocked off physically from the Israeli economy, its major cities would be cut off from each other, and its government would be unable to control the territory's water resources,

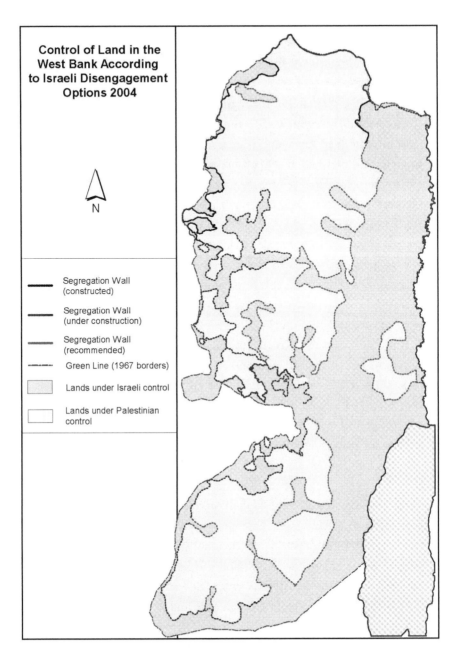

**Control of Land in the
West Bank According
to Israeli Disengagement
Options 2004**

N

Segregation Wall
(constructed)

Segregation Wall
(under construction)

Segregation Wall
(recommended)

Green Line (1967 borders)

Lands under Israeli control

Lands under Palestinian
control

Map 2. Future Palestinian sovereignty in the West Bank as suggested by Ariel Sharon's "unilateral disengagement" policy. (Courtesy the Health Development Information and Policy Institute.)

develop its agriculture, or manage its trade with neighboring states. It would comprise little more than a sealed vessel of growing poverty and demoralization. That portent of Palestinian misery is, of course, no accident; it is a calculated Israeli strategy. Ariel Sharon hopes it will force "soft transfer"—mass emigration of Palestinians to wherever in the world they can find kin or jobs.

In such crippled conditions, no Palestinian government can operate effectively to contain the political fragmentation and extremism that would inevitably result, which suggests dangerous new security risks to Israel. Still, disintegrating Palestinian authority might serve some vision of Israel's interests. It would usefully redirect Palestinian grievances away from Israel and toward the failing Palestinian government, while redefining the Palestinian problem for the international community as bad internal management. More broadly, an enclave of Palestinians squabbling within a claustrophobic territory, under a government unable effectively to meet the needs of its population, could imaginably reduce Palestinian nationalism to a sad parody within two or three decades. Destroying the Palestinian-national movement has been Ariel Sharon's lifelong goal, and all dimensions of the two-state "solution" are now converging toward its realization. That Israel can contain the resulting unrest and extremist terror is Sharon's great gamble.

Israel's great Wall (or "security fence"), under rapid construction at this writing, reflects this strategy. The Wall is designed to seal Israel off from the security and labor pressures of an increasingly ruined and wretched Palestinian society and to force Palestinian emigration— and political aspirations—eastward, toward Jordan and the rest of the Arab world. But the Wall will not secure Israel from the trouble ahead, for the Palestinian nation is unlikely to wither peacefully. Even in Sharon's best-case scenario (mass Palestinian emigration triggered by miserable conditions), many hundreds of thousands of Palestinians would remain in their ancestral land, and their misery and anger in their impoverished national ghetto would still foster unrest that would plague Israeli politics, security, and society. Moreover, as a shocking symbol of racial defense, the Wall itself will crystallize Palestinian and broader Arab grievances against its architects, leaving Israel the ideological and physical target of resentful Arab and Muslim movements and dangerously fueling anti-Western resentments of militant Islamic radicals who view the Palestinian plight as a basic crime. Even if the Palestinian Bantustan gains the diplomatic support of neighboring Arab regimes anxious for any semblance of peace, those movements now bode very ill for Israel, the region, and, indeed, the world. Devastating terror attacks on Western capitals loom in this scenario.

But if the two-state solution now promises only lasting dangers for Israel and unacceptable risks for the international community, what are the alternatives? Three are immediately apparent. The first, nightmarish alternative would be Israel's forced expulsion of the Palestinian population out of the country. Frighteningly, this solution of "hard transfer" reflects one living thread of right-wing Israeli-Zionist thought that has long endorsed the notion that Jordan is the "true Palestinian state,"[1] but a general logic of transfer floats more broadly among Jewish-Israeli thought. Indeed, the idea has fed through Zionism from its beginning; even Zionist founder Theodor Herzl wrote in his diaries of the need to "spirit the penniless population across the border," and David Ben-Gurion fully adopted the logic, ordering the mass expulsion of Palestinians from their cities and villages in the wars of 1948 and effecting the ethnic cleansing that secured a Jewish majority in Israel in the first place.[2]

But the time when such extreme actions could be sheltered from international scrutiny are long past, and even hard-liners like Ehud Olmert have rejected mass expulsion as inhumane and untenable (aside from the purely logistic difficulty of moving over a million people in a region with no trains). Only in some terrible crisis might the effort actually be undertaken—by the brutally shortsighted—as a quick, if dirty, solution to Israel's demographic and security dilemmas. Yet the effort would backfire, for the spectacle of Palestinians forcibly ejected en masse from their ancestral territory would manifest internationally as a human rights violation of such magnitude as to scandalize, radicalize, and destabilize the entire region, greatly worsening Israel's security. The repercussions—the collapse of "moderate" Arab and Muslim regimes and an explosion of Islamic and other militancy—would indeed be unimaginably dangerous to the entire international community. Accordingly, that doomsday scenario is not explored further in this book, except to note that it is a matter of international urgency, as well as enlightened Israeli self-interest, that proponents of "hard transfer" remain firmly contained.

The second alternative is the so-called Jordan option (sometimes referenced by the claim "Jordan is Palestine"), in which Palestinians would find stable lives and political fulfillment through citizenship in the neighboring state of Jordan. This vision, long promoted by Ariel Sharon and wishfully sustained by Israelis in many political camps, entertains the rosy if hazy presumption that Palestinians—whether politically disenfranchised in annexed Israeli territory or facing stifled lives in an unviable Palestinian state—can be induced to seek political rights across the Jordan River and so could cease to be of concern to Israel. This plan, too, therefore aims for "soft transfer."

Differing geographic visions accompany this dream. If the West Bank remained Palestinian territory, it could form a single state straddling the Jordan River, as Transjordan did between 1948 and 1967. But as land left to Palestinians in the West Bank is now far reduced, it is not clear just what chunk of territory might be involved in such a union. For example, Ariel Sharon's annexation strategy, which attaches to Israel a broad buffer zone in the Jordan Valley, places Palestinian West Bank territory entirely within Israel. A "Jordan option" promoted by arch right-wing Israeli cabinet minister Binyamin Elon insists that the entire West Bank be annexed by Israel and that the "State of Palestine" be formed solely on the east bank of the Jordan River, in present-day Jordan.[3] Whatever the territory, all these visions affirm a natural political unity between Palestinians and Jordanians, based on history (the Transjordan experience and some Jordanian and Palestinian rhetoric), present-day demography (Palestinians today comprise about 60 percent of Jordan's population), and the idea that Palestinian political aspirations can be satisfied in Jordan as well as anywhere. All planners hold that any Palestinians remaining in the West Bank and the Gaza Strip will somehow manage their local affairs satisfactorily through long-distance participation in Jordan's political system.

Some Arab and Palestinian rhetoric has indeed affirmed the unity of Jordan and Palestine over the years. But any idea that Jordan can somehow absorb and satisfy Palestinian society and national politics is transparently misguided, as it rests on some basic misconceptions. First, its proponents assume that "Arabs," being one nation, migrate and blend into each other readily and indiscriminatingly—a belief which requires willful blindness to the actual deep cultural divisions in the Arab world. Second, in assuming that Palestine and Jordan naturally form one sociological and politically seamless unit, its proponents rely on a cluster of Zionist fictions: for example, that Palestine was a desert terrain like Jordan prior to the Zionists' arrival, instead of a rich agricultural area with a distinct culture, and that Palestinian national society has no distinct political character of its own (based on a deep history within its ancestral territory) but was invented by architects like Arafat and is artificially sustained by rejectionist Arab states.

None of these beliefs bear scrutiny. As chapter 3 discusses in more depth, the agriculturally based Palestinian society and its merchant classes in the twentieth century had very little cultural concord with the mostly bedouin society in the territory that became Jordan—which was indeed mostly desert prior to its invention as a modern state by Britain in 1923. Jordan does have a large Palestinian population today, reflecting both refugees (from the 1948 and 1967 wars) and Jordanian sovereignty over the West Bank between 1948 and 1967 (which greatly expanded social and business connections between East Jerusalem and Amman). But the Palestinian population in Jordan remains dwarfed by the Palestinian population in the occupied territories and has converted Jordan into Palestine neither socially nor in the Palestinian national imagination. Moreover, Jordan's monarchy—installed by Britain to reward a World War I ally, the Hashemite monarchy based in Mecca—has no legitimacy for Palestinians. Hence, neither the Palestinians' cultural references, their nationalist experience, their economy, nor their present (highly democratic) political culture finds any resonance in Jordan. The Palestinians have therefore always flatly rejected the entire plan. The Jordanian monarchy, knowing itself doomed in this scenario, has also flatly rejected it.[4]

Even more unimaginable is how the whole model would serve the 1.2 million Palestinians in the Gaza Strip. Any idea that they could somehow satisfactorily manage vital local problems (e.g., water management and policing) by long-distance political participation in Jordan is clearly absurd. Belief that their gradual economic ruin under these anarchic circumstances would be politically passive is also recklessly unsound. (The Elon Plan mentioned earlier, which calls for ethnic cleansing to solve these problems, is actually more honest than other versions of the Jordan option, in recognizing its inevitable violence.) Some proponents of the Jordan option therefore suggest a corollary "Egypt option" (or "Sinai option") for the Gaza Strip. But this idea proposes that Palestinian nationalism will somehow evaporate—that Palestinians from the West Bank and the Gaza Strip will simply forget and abandon their myriad family and political ties—which is also clearly a fantasy.

Hence, only in Zionist imagination will rational choice by Palestinians, based on their ruined local lives in the West Bank, somehow readily dissolve the emotional and cultural attachments of some three million highly politicized people to their ancestral homes, lands, communities, and national affinity and send them off peacefully to a different climate and country, seeking political fulfillment under an alien monarchy. A corollary fantasy is that the Jordanian monarchy would view that same prospect with anything but dread. The Jordan option would therefore have to be imposed by Israel by force and thus would reproduce the mass trauma and terrifying implications for regional security generated by "hard transfer." These overwhelming obstacles so cripple the Jordan option that it, too, will not be treated further in this book except to note that it only clouds discussion and distracts thinking to no purpose.

The third alternative solution to the Israeli-Palestinian conflict, the one-state solution, would resolve the entire conflict in one magisterial gesture and is already an impending reality. It would absorb all the entrenched populations between the Mediterranean and the Jordan River into one unified state. Because this would mean an Arab majority, it would also mean that Israel would cease to be a "Jewish state" in the sense commonly understood by most people today. For complicated reasons explored in this book, this solution therefore frightens or even outrages many who understand Jewish statehood as an essential or even sacred Jewish-nationalist mission. But the model is not as bizarre or alien to the conflict as some people believe or argue. The idea of a shared state has floated in and out of Zionist thought and

Palestinian politics for a century, eclipsed, rather than eliminated, by the Holocaust and the subsequent deadly flux of war and terrorism. Today, it has revived, in a range of forums, in the writings and arguments of both Palestinians and Jewish liberals (in Israel and abroad), and, despite vitriolic Zionist denunciations, is growing inexorably in force. The reasons for its expanding influence are equally complicated, reflecting changes in Israeli society as well as the "facts on the ground." For some advocates, weariness with conflict and a liberal distaste for ethnic chauvinism are strongly in play. But all of the advocates take their energy from recognizing the stubborn reality generated by the settlement grid: no other solution, at this point, can work.

The one-state solution clearly raises immense political difficulties, as well as conundrums about exactly how it might be pursued. Most obviously, the one-state solution would force an immediate decision about the fate of Israel as "the Jewish state." Should or could the new polity remain a Jewish state in the sense of sustaining Jewish-national dominion in politics? Or, as some urge, has Jewish nationalism seen its day and become ripe for abandonment? Or can some compromise be wrought, through which the Jewish national home can somehow be preserved in a genuinely civil-democratic system similar to those of Western European states—which do not, at least officially, discriminate among their citizens according to ethnicity or religion?

The first option concerning the fate of the Jewish state defends it in terms cherished by mainstream Zionist thinking for a century, but it promises crippling trouble down the road. If Israel remains democratic, the Arab population would become a majority, and its electoral clout might be sufficient to alter Israel's founding laws, which presently secure privileged standing for Jews and the Jewish nation. Many Zionists view that future with genuine dread and issue dark forecasts of Jewish suffering or even expulsion. But if, on that very apprehension, Israel were to deny Palestinians the vote, excluding over half the country's territorial population from political rights, Israel would become a smaller South Africa. That prospect—even if it remained stable (which is very doubtful)—is morally untenable to many liberal Zionists. The contradictory formula emphasized by pro-Israel lobbyists urging the two-state solution—that Israel must remain "Jewish and democratic"—reflects keen appreciation that the twin perils of Arab domination and apartheid must both be avoided to preserve Israel as they know it, by any measure that will preclude absorbing the Palestinians within Israeli territory. Indeed, Palestinians themselves also reject the option of living within a Jewish state, foreseeing their own subordination as well as the civil strife and ugly confrontations that would inevitably ensue.

The second option, converting Israel into an ethnically neutral secular-democratic state, seems an obvious course to a few liberal thinkers, but it does not strike most people as more promising. Many, if not most, Jews would protest losing the spiritual and nationalist mission that Israel has represented—although mixed feelings about Israel's impact on world Jewry are increasing. Even for many secular Jews now living comfortably in diaspora, the idea of losing the psychological baseline of a Jewish sanctuary against potential anti-Semitic attack strikes a deep chord of fear. Abandoning the Zionist dream of securing a Jewish national home in the biblical homeland would therefore shock and dismay Israel's supporters all over the world, albeit for different reasons.

Although about a quarter of Palestinians indicate that they would prefer a one-state solution (see app. B), they, too, would fear such a transition. Some elements in the present Palestinian Authority (especially those sustaining the legacy of Arafat) would certainly resist this solution, as it would promptly eliminate their atrophied (and lucrative) roles. Others would resist abandoning the dream of Palestinian statehood, which has been cultivated since the early twentieth century. And after the past decade of misery under an increasingly repressive occupation, the general Palestinian population is exhausted but also more angry and suspicious than before. Life in a state still dominated politically by the Jewish society that has demonized them would be a frightening prospect. Any equal distribution of resources would also clearly require years, if not decades, of work—as the South African case is illustrating. Zionist and Palestinian fears therefore react to each other, and those sentiments have hitherto forestalled debate about a one-state solution.

But the one-state solution cannot be dismissed, however overwhelming these obstacles appear, for no other choice remains. A viable Palestinian state has become impossible. The land base is insufficient, Jewish settlements and Palestinian villages are juxtaposed in an intimate patchwork, and the two economies are already fused into one—bound inextricably by trade, labor, and natural resources. The third one-state option must therefore be brought onto the table: some way must be found to make sense of Israeli-Palestinian interdependence by consolidating the land into one democratic state, which will serve all its citizens equally and in which the Jewish national home can find a new and more secure configuration no longer requiring a Jewish majority or Jewish ethnic dominion over the state.

This book explores this option in the spirit of preserving a future for all parties. Discussion of a civil-democratic one-state solution to the Israeli-Palestinian conflict is indeed now of urgent universal concern and requires a fresh look by all. The two-state solution has evolved from promising a stable mutual peace to promising only greater danger—and not only to Israel. Given the Palestinian problem's progressive transmutation into Islamic militancy, now extending into global terror networks, the entire international community is directly implicated in the future of this conflict. The terms of its debate must therefore change—and quickly. For, as Tony Judt has written, "the alternatives are far, far worse."[5]

This book draws heavily on scholarly sources, and owes boundless debt to them, but is not intended to be an academic study. It offers no comprehensive literature review, for example (for overviews of the literature and debates, readers are referred to other sources, such as review essays by Gary Sussman).[6] Rather, this discussion offers an extended essay arguing for one secular-democratic state and exploring some of its implications for Zionism and the Jewish national home. Chapter 2 opens this argument by presenting the "facts on the ground": the scale and character of the settlement grid and the political factors that anchor the settlements as permanent fixtures of the West Bank landscape. Chapter 3 reviews how this politics derails various proposals now being floated for the settlements' "withdrawal" (a problematic term in itself) and various plans for Israeli or Palestinian sovereignty, and illuminates why none of these proposals can generate a peaceful solution. Chapter 4 then lays out why no external actor is likely to change that equation: it examines the U.S. role and why it will not improve, the weakness of the Arab states and the Palestinians, and the more ambiguous role of Europe. These three chapters portray the empirical reality that any new discussion must consider.

What new diplomatic direction should then be taken from the political logjam created by the settlement grid is the question now on the table. I submit here that the one-state solution is the only viable one and that its obstacles therefore require new thinking and frank discussion. Chapters 5 and 6 open that discussion by probing two basic Zionist tenets that obstruct the one-state solution: that Jewish statehood is essential to Jewish national survival and that a Jewish majority is essential to constituting a Jewish national home in the state's territory. These twin tenets have steered the Zionist project to establish a Jewish state in the territory since the early twentieth century. They prescribed the Palestinians' transfer and exclusion in the first place and now preclude the multiethnic civil democracy that can finally provide the conflict's stable resolution. But those tenets are less monolithic and inflexible than they often seem, and identifying their controversies will reveal their actual potential for flexibility. Chapter 5 first highlights the need for that exploration through comparison with the South African and Northern Ireland cases and then explores some hidden inconsistencies within threads of argument defending Jewish statehood. Chapter 6 sketches the spectrum of present debates about the one-state solution and offers an initial exploration of Zionist "principles" and their implications for maintaining a Jewish national home in one multiethnic state.

This analysis ascribes no special sins to Jewish statehood. Ethnic statehood is inadmissible everywhere, because it universally generates the kind of discrimination, inequality, and human rights abuses now shaping the Israeli-Palestinian conflict. For this reason, it has been abandoned—at least, officially—everywhere else. (As this book explains, the Zionist claim that Israel's Jewish character merely replicates other nationalisms, like that of France, is inaccurate in this respect.) But the Jewishness of Israel cannot be lightly discarded as simply one more ethnic nationalism whose time has passed.[7] Everything in the history of this conflict indicates that the Zionist project to rebuild a Jewish national home, in territory now carrying such resonance for Jewish religious and social tradition, is of such compelling psychological and political character that it must remain foundational to any lasting peace.

The very difficult question, then, is how the Jewish national home can be preserved without the bitter trappings of Jewish statehood long deemed essential to it. Recent discussions about a one-state solution have suggested a range of formulas—federal, confederal, consociational, binational, or multiethnic civil-democratic—with various subcategories and variations.[8] All are worth exploring whether as final models or as interim stages, but all suggest difficulties. For instance, any attempt to generate territorial jurisdictions (e.g., joining Jewish and Palestinian states in a federation) would confront the already crippling problem of wildly gerrymandered boundaries. Consociationalism has proved so unevenly successful (e.g., it has worked tolerably well in Holland and Belgium but was a disaster in Lebanon) that its proponents must undertake very cautious comparative analysis. A binational formula, the most common proposal dating to the 1920s, seems most promising to many, but inscribing two national identities in constitutional law might only reify the old ethnic polarity—again, a risk requiring extended comparative study. A unitary civil democracy, such as those sustained by the Western European democracies and ultimately sought by South Africa, may therefore promise the best solution, in which ethnic interests are sorted out through the usual party politics. (South Africans themselves might offer invaluable advice on this trajectory, as well as counsel about navigating the labyrinthine debates that will necessarily precede it.)

Discussing these formulas seriously and sketching a viable "blueprint" might seem incumbent here. Most pressingly, Jewish fears that dissolution of the Jewish state would threaten Israel's Jews with unacceptable dangers—and even imperil Jews everywhere—demand a convincing argument that a unified secular-democratic state will continue to protect Jews and Jewish cultural life. Moreover, some solid proposal may seem necessary to counter the first common objection to the one-state option, which is that it is "unfeasible." Again, the one-state solution cannot be dismissed on grounds of its feasibility. Like a well gone dry, the two-state solution is already obsolete; rejecting the remaining one-state reality as "unfeasible" is therefore pointless. But in calling for serious debate of a solution involving one secular-democratic state, I might be expected to offer some convincing argument that such a state is not beyond the realm of the possible.

That vital discussion is not, however, engaged here in any detail. The design of the unified state will not emerge from isolated writers like myself; it must be debated by the protagonists—the Israeli Jews, Israeli Arabs, and Palestinians—whose lives will be immediately impacted by any resulting formula. I do suggest, in chapter 6, some reforms that seem basic to establishing a stable multiethnic society in any formula; and for readers' historical reference, appendix A offers three solutions imagined in the 1940s. But this book is dedicated to a prior task: identifying the operative values, beliefs, fears, and prejudices that presently impede those very discussions and forestall creative thinking among the conflict's participants toward overcoming the obvious difficulties.

Three dimensions of this effort call for brief advance note. First, although drawing heavily from published scholarly material, analyses, and journalistic commentary, my framework reflects primarily my own nineteen-year experience of polemics and rival narratives concerning the Israeli-Palestinian conflict in local, national, and international forums. Specific Zionist and Palestinian ideas and arguments are annotated to signal where readers might find examples and their context, but most people experienced in these arguments should find their summaries here familiar. Whether my analysis adequately addresses these complex matters is a separate question, but this book is meant to open and encourage their constructive discussion and certainly does not pretend to encapsulate them.

Second, relative to its discussion of Zionism, I skim briefly over problems and challenges regarding Palestinian politics. Several reasons contribute to this neglect, but I do not fail to appreciate either Palestinian-national rights and collective wishes, on the one hand, or bad Palestinian leadership and the impact of terrible terrorist attacks on Israeli civilians, on the other. As this book will make clear, mass Palestinian political views are pivotal to any stable peace and are crucial to any deeper analysis of the one-state solution. At the same time, Palestinian politics is fraught with turbulence, and as chapters 3, 4, and 6 explain, the current two-state trajectory promises only more trouble. Indeed, dire leadership difficulties and internal fragmentation are major reasons why increasing numbers of Palestinians are endorsing the one-state solution, because any Palestinian "state" formed in the crippled enclave now taking shape promises only to reify these debilities and to create a political life not worth achieving.

Still, beyond citing some summary impressions of Palestinian views by observers whom I consider convincing based on my own experience, I leave fuller discussion of Palestinian politics to others—not least because the project is particularly challenging. Under conditions of occupation, comprehensive opinion surveys and a free press are hardly possible, and trends in political views are not easy to document. Palestinian politics is also in rapid flux, having transformed twice since the first intifada (1987) and through the period of the Oslo Accords (begun in the 1990s), in ways that have greatly complicated internal discussions and tensions among its fragmented tendencies. Closer observers intimately familiar with multiple sectors within the occupied territories must flesh out how the one-state solution will engage the complicated inner dynamics of evolving Palestinian political views.[9]

The challenges mentioned so far are not, however, my primary reason for minimizing the vital subject of Palestinian politics in this study of the one-state solution. Rather, I see the present configuration of Palestinian politics as stemming from the generative condition of the Zionist project to create a Jewish state, which has imposed on the Palestinians the distorting effects of a half century of forced relocation, four decades of occupation, and now Bantustanization. Again, this understanding does not imply that Palestinian views are not central to any peaceful future or that the Palestinian's tormented national politics has not contributed to the present predicament. Rather, it assumes that the conditions for Palestinian responses will alter dramatically if Israel's ethnic statehood transforms to a model of civil democracy. International engagement with apartheid in South Africa was made under comparable assumptions, with actors sometimes offering guarded critiques of the African National Congress (ANC) but generally avoiding the subject—not because the ANC lacked serious difficulties but because most people recognized that its problems so heavily reflected distorting conditions generated by apartheid that their true reform could not be undertaken until apartheid was dismantled. The Palestinian movement is no more absolved of addressing its dire internal problems than was the ANC. But for reasons noted briefly in chapter 4, the effort simply cannot progress meaningfully under current conditions. Developing a new framework for all such efforts is my focus here.

Finally, this book interrogates Zionist beliefs which engage very powerful emotions. I intend no disrespect toward those emotions, even if some offense is taken or inevitable. Nor do I mean to disregard in any way the Jewish national experience as I attempt to engage central Jewish concerns for sanctuary and cultural survival. Those concerns must be respected and answered in any discussion of the Jewish state; the history of European Jewry is too compelling for any responsible discussion of this conflict to do otherwise. Still, in this book, I cannot possibly address the fuller body of Jewish feelings and fears that engage Jewish statehood; those sensitivities must be pursued by people better positioned, within the Jewish community, partly by hard discussion of what a single democratic state might actually look like. Instead, I offer evidence that precisely such discussion is now imperative.

In recognizing those sensitivities, however, I draw a boundary when Jewish emotions extend to seeing anti-Semitism in any criticism of Israel or talk of one secular-democratic Israeli-Palestinian state. The international community will also have to muster greater fortitude to confront such attacks. Anti-Semitism is an evil I have fought my entire adult life, but the charge of anti-Semitism can no longer be allowed to intimidate and sabotage principled inquiry into a different future for the Zionist dream—especially as that dream itself now so urgently requires it.

For a new challenge faces Israel and the world after the Oslo decade. The conflict now converges in a territory where two viable nation-states are no longer possible. The Palestinian "state" in the West Bank, with its 1.3 million people, no longer stands beside Israel but is physically embedded within the body of the Jewish state and is doomed to national failure. It cannot be made viable by erecting a wall of ethnic defense in the spirit of apartheid, a wall that today has no parallel in the world. The consequences have become intolerably dangerous. A new vision for the Zionist dream must therefore, finally, come under open and rapid discussion.

2. The Immovable Object

The Settlement Grid

A basic misconception plaguing debate about Jewish settlements in Palestinian territories is that their withdrawal by the Israeli government, if attempted, would entail only a cluster of microstruggles—like those rare moments when Israeli authorities forcibly dismantle the trailers of some settlement "outpost" and zealot settlers are dragged off in theatrical confrontation. But the problem of Jewish settlements is not represented by a few clusters of trailers on windswept hilltops. If we swivel the cameras just a few degrees in the West Bank, a true Jewish settlement is likely to come into view: a two-story town of hundreds or thousands of stone residences draped along a neighboring hillcrest, its outer edifice forming a continuous defensive stone bastion, with tendrils of new construction stretching toward the neighboring settlement. Some of these settlements are small cities: Ariel, in the center of the West Bank, has about twenty thousand residents; Ma'ale Adumim, stretching east from Jerusalem, has over twenty-five thousand. The larger settlements include major shopping malls and cinemas, full school systems, recreation centers and parks, synagogues and cultural centers, and adjacent industrial zones with factories representing hundreds of millions of dollars in investments. Any visitor looking at these massive planned communities (and their huge road network) promptly loses any idea that the Israeli government has any intention of removing them—or that it even has the capacity to do so. The grid is now so embedded in the land—and the Jewish and Palestinian infrastructure is so interwoven, with resources such as water so inseparably bound together—that even a superficial tour suggests that it is inextricable.

But the "facts on the ground" that debilitate any withdrawal are not simply physical and financial. To grasp the actual immobility of the Jewish settlements, we need to appreciate not only the grid's physical weight—its size and infrastructure and its impact on the land and on Palestinian society—but also its political weight. The latter includes not only its off-cited importance to some currents of Zionist imagination but also its less-recognized ties to major state agencies as well as private commercial and industrial investment. These political and economic aspects obviously interplay: evacuating so vast a social infrastructure, including hundreds of thousands of people in full-scale cities, would entail huge costs and therefore require a tremendous political will on the part of any Israeli government. But such will is not simply missing in this case: Israeli public policy has for decades been directed into expanding the settlements, through channels more extensive and complicated than most people realize. While occasionally withdrawing a few outposts (with much public fanfare), the Israeli government has actually been funding and building the settlements and working hard to attract settlers to them (doubling their population in the 1990s), for three decades of (supposed) peace talks and at an accelerating pace since the Oslo negotiations began in the early 1990s. Assumptions that this state policy might be reversed and the settlers withdrawn have gravely underestimated all these dimensions.

THE PHYSICAL GRID

Detailed analyses of the settlements exist elsewhere, so their physical scale will just be summarized here. Jewish settlements in the occupied territories are routinely analyzed as falling into four regions occupied by Israel in the 1967 Six-Day War: the Golan Heights, East Jerusalem, the West Bank, and the Gaza Strip. At this writing, these territories hold some 230 settlements and some four hundred thousand Jewish settlers (about 10 percent of Israel's population). Israel has annexed East Jerusalem and the Golan Heights and considers them part of Eretz Israel (the land of Israel), Israeli sovereign territory. Because Israel took these territories forcibly in the 1967 war, however, international diplomacy considers all four to fall within the general category of "occupied territory," whose final status is still pending. But each territory has a different political profile and presents different challenges to any withdrawal.

The Golan Heights is usually treated apart. Annexed by Israel, it is still disputed by its former sovereign, Syria. Its final disposition therefore remains essential to any comprehensive regional peace. It is a visually compelling region, with thirty-three Jewish settlements sparsely scattered through a craggy moor landscape marked by 131 destroyed Arab villages, which were bombed and/or bulldozed by Israel after the flight in 1967 of some one hundred thousand Arab residents. An Israeli withdrawal from the Golan engages the same questions as other regions—questions of ideology, security, and especially water (the Golan's aquifer is crucial to Israel).

For two reasons, however, the Golan falls outside most discussions of Israeli-Palestinian peace. First, Israel has annexed (rather than merely occupied) the Golan and considers it to fall into a different diplomatic category. Second, its seventeen thousand remaining Druze-Arab residents (clustered in four northern villages) identify politically as Syrians and are therefore not considered part of the "Palestinian problem" or participants in negotiations toward any prospective Palestinian state. The Golan is neglected henceforth in this book solely for this reason, but one prospect can be hypothesized here: the one-state solution would eventually allow normalized relations with Syria, permit more open borders, and lay a basis for negotiations about the return of Golani Arabs to their abandoned villages. Despite hard talk by both sides, quiet diplomatic murmurs suggest that some territorial division of the region might still be negotiated in any comprehensive peace agreement.

East Jerusalem is also often considered apart, partly because it, too, was annexed, but also for other reasons. The eastern half of Jerusalem was not taken by Zionist forces in the 1948 war but was held instead, along with the West Bank, by Jordan. Between the 1948 and 1967 wars, the Green Line (or armistice line) passed through the center of the city, with the Old City and its sacred sites on the eastern Jordanian side. The eastern half of the city was conquered and promptly annexed by Israel after the 1967 Six-Day War, and the Old City, with Judaism's most sacred site, the Western Wall, was seized by Israeli troops with great rejoicing. According to international diplomacy, however, East Jerusalem is still occupied territory.

Loaded with religious significance for all three monotheistic religions, Jerusalem's permanent legal status is one of the principal controversies blocking a permanent peace agreement. It remains the administrative, political, economic, cultural, and religious center for Palestinians: it is still by far the largest Palestinian urban center, with a population (Christian and Muslim) of about 288,000 in 2004—about 40 percent of Jerusalem's total population.[1] The city's disposition is therefore a very hot point for Palestinian diplomacy. No peace agreement can be accepted by any Palestinian leadership without securing permanent Palestinian political rights in East Jerusalem. But Jerusalem's annexation has been declared permanent by a series of Israeli governments, often under the religious-nationalist mantra "Jerusalem will never again be divided." This claim centers emotionally and spiritually on the famous Western, or Wailing, Wall, which is actually one portion of one side of the great Temple Mount, or Haram al-Sharif (Arabic for "Noble Sanctuary"). The Western Wall is indeed composed partly of the enormous stonework, built by King Herod, that once, when the mount's five-acre top was at a lower level, supported the Jewish Second Temple (built in 353 BCE and destroyed by the Romans in 68 CE). Unfortunately for the Israeli-Palestinian conflict, on its present (much higher) platform, the Temple Mount also holds Islam's sacred Al-Aqsa Mosque and the exquisite Islamic eighth-century Dome of the Rock, which surmounts the top of Mount Moriah (from which, according to legend, Muhammad once ascended into heaven). Within a literal stone's throw of each other, the Western Wall and the Islamic structures therefore comprise one of the hottest religious juxtapositions in the world. Even worse for peace, a few blocks away (but also in the Old City), the Church of the Holy Sepulcher stands on the spot where Jesus was supposedly crucified. (Contrary to common stereotypes conflating Palestinians with Muslims, about 7 percent of Palestinians are Christian, although, under occupation, the proportion in the territories has dropped to nearly 2 percent. In Jerusalem, however, the proportion was historically closer to 50 percent. The Old City has a large and ancient Christian-Arab quarter.)[2]

Israel's insistence on an undivided city invokes biblical references centered on Jewish collective mytho-historical memory. The claim is also strategically directed toward Western Christians and particularly toward right-wing fundamentalist Christians in the United States, whose crucial political support for Israel is based on simplistic Bible-story visions of the "Holy Land" and even millennialist ideas that Israel's formation marks the imminent return of the Messiah. But as Israeli policy has vastly expanded the city's borders, the mantra "Jerusalem will never again be divided" is now deployed to consolidate Israel's claims over a geostrategic area far larger than the historical Old City (see map 3).

Israel's unilateral annexation of Greater Jerusalem has indeed been buttressed by a ring of urban Jewish settlements constructed around its much-expanded borders, a bulwark designed to provide a defensive barrier but also to preclude any negotiated return to Arab control. That ring is now so massive—the physical bulk of settlements like Gilo (with a population of twenty-seven thousand) is colossal—that it now comprises one continuous megalopolis, interwoven by major highways, organically integrated into Greater Jerusalem and with nearly two hundred thousand Jewish settlers well entrenched. Most pragmatic analyses therefore accept these settlements' permanency; even recent negotiations toward the establishment of a Palestinian capital in East Jerusalem have not called for their withdrawal. Israel's always-skillful coupling of ideological discourse, demographic and civil engineering, and military geostrategy has been a crowning success in this urban consolidation.

The East Jerusalem settlements are geostrategic also in that they merge seamlessly into the continuous string of Jewish-only construction that stretches eastward through the West Bank all the way to the

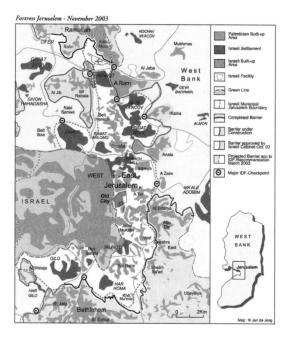

Map 3.   Expanded Jerusalem. (Courtesy Foundation for Middle East Peace.)

Jordan Valley. Hence, the settlement of Ma'ale Adumim—a full-fledged city, with full commercial facilities, an industrial zone, its own cultural life and over twenty-five thousand residents—snakes along the Judean hill ridges and connects with other settlements (and their buffer zones) to bisect the West Bank across its narrowest point. These Jewish "neighborhoods" are not slated for negotiation by Israel; all state energies are instead directed toward their expansion. (In 2004, one official Web site was heavily promoting settlement in Ma'ale Adumim, lauding its new centrally located mall, with four movie theaters, fast-food restaurants, a mega-supermarket "and over 50 other stores," a new library and a new art museum, and a new swimming pool—supplementing the existing retractable-roof pool.)[3]

The West Bank presents a very different political picture. It has not been formally annexed by Israel and is still called "administered territory" in Israeli discourse and "occupied territory" by everyone else. Some Jewish/Zionist sentiment and most Israeli maps have already absorbed it as an intrinsic part of Israel, but other currents of Israeli-Jewish thought consider it expendable in exchange for peace. In practice, however, Israeli state policy has been to embed a grid of settlements throughout the West Bank to preclude any evacuation. Hence, outside of East Jerusalem, the West Bank holds, at this writing, some 141 settlements and some 230,000 Jewish settlers, according to Israeli official figures. Independent surveys have identified 157 "built-up areas" and dozens of additional "outposts."

Viewed as triangles on a map (see map 4), these settlements might imply a scattered array of communities that could conceivably be dismantled—with their Jewish residents removed—in a peace agreement. But such maps fail to convey the settlements' physical impact. As in the East Jerusalem ring of settlements, most West Bank settlements are built in strategic blocs: several settlements are clustered together partly to enhance security, but also to facilitate their gradual linkage and mergence and ultimately their annexation, as a coherent bloc of territory, to Israel (for example, the Ariel bloc, nested deep within the northern West Bank; see map 5). Moreover, through a combination of adjacent military and other closed zones, they command land and transportation for some distance around. Finally, as noted, most settlements are substantial middle-class communities, well built and nicely landscaped, representing billions of dollars of investment. Some consist of a few dozen houses, but many are substantial communities, and eight are small cities, fully adorned with commercial facilities (shopping malls and so forth). Most are primarily residential but are flanked by industrial zones built especially to provide local jobs; all have some version of military defenses and bunkers. Physically dismantling these towns and their infrastructure, in the sense of taking them apart and carrying them away, is impossible. If they were blown up or bulldozed, the damage to the delicate highland landscape would be ruinous.

This archipelago of settlements is truly consolidated as a grid, however, by its major road network, which links West Bank settlements strategically linked to cities (and jobs) inside Israel. Deliberately inaccessible to Palestinian villages, these roads cut off Palestinian villages from their central towns and ruin Palestinian market and other social connections. Some settlement roads are sheltered with elaborate fences to repel stone throwers and more serious Palestinian attacks; all have cleared areas along each side, from which Palestinian use is banned. Various additional zoning—"closed military zones," "nature preserves," and "state land"—expands this exclusionary impact far more broadly, encroaching heavily on Palestinian village land and subsistence. Palestinians shot for trying to harvest from family

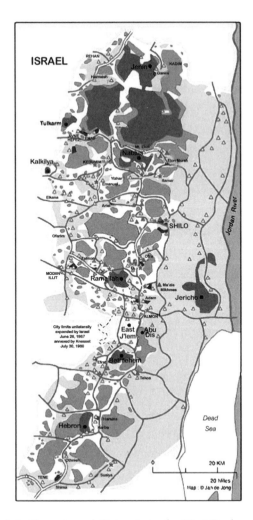

Map 4.   Israeli Settlements and Outposts in the West Bank, 1999. (Courtesy
Foundation for Middle East Peace.)

orchards adjoining a settlement road and the destruction of hundreds
of thousands of olive trees (sometimes of great age) are infamous features of settlement-road construction and related security measures.
From the Palestinians' perspective, it is these highways and the closed
zones that connect and flank the settlements—more than the settlements themselves—that impact their daily lives and slice the West
Bank into chunks. Jewish and Palestinian roads indeed form two
entirely separate grids, on which travelers move through entirely different ethnic landscapes—either the ancient organic array of Arab villages or the geostrategic sequence of Jewish settlements. But as the
Jewish settlement grid has greatly expanded, cutting across Palestin-

Map 5. The Ariel Settlement Bloc with the "Separation Barrier." (Courtesy
Foundation for Middle East Peace.)

ian roads without access junctions and between villages so that travel
between them is impossible, the Palestinian road grid has become
increasingly dysfunctional.

The grid has also taken control of West Bank water. Water is in
short supply throughout the region and is, for Israel, a major security
concern. Israeli water stations in the West Bank are surrounded by
barricades of barbed wire and are under military control; no outside
observer knows precisely how much they take, and the data is kept
secret as a matter of state security. It is known that Jewish settlers use
far more water than do Palestinians, famously maintaining swimming
pools and green lawns—striking extravagance in a very arid region.
Most of the West Bank aquifer is tapped for use inside Israel, inte-
grating the West Bank into Israel in a very physical sense (see chap.
3). Palestinian wells are actually going dry as Jewish use drains the
water table, and Palestinians are not allowed to drive deeper wells to
access dwindling supply.

The zoned A-B-C plan developed as part of the Oslo II Accord
(1995) supposedly clarified land arrangements for a staged withdrawal
from the settlements, but it in fact only more clearly demarcated the
Palestinian areas that the settlements had left still coherent (see map
6). Settlement construction actually accelerated during the Oslo era,
mostly through what Israel calls "natural growth" (additional resi-

Map 6.   Palestinian land left coherent by the Oslo II Accord of 1995. (Courtesy Palestinian Academic Society for the Study of International Affairs.)

dential units in existing settlements) rather than through new settlements. "Natural growth" is not haphazard; it follows a settlement master plan, which strategically expands the settlements along geographic contours and toward each other in ways that maximize their contiguity and their physical impact on Palestinian village land. Under the Sharon government, a new sprinkling of outposts has proliferated, and even lip service regarding any withdrawal is missing (except for minor adjustments to rationalize chunks of territory demarcated by the "security fence," or the Wall).

With the Jordan Valley turned over entirely to Israeli sovereignty and with great fjords of Israeli sovereignty plunging deep into the West Bank highlands (the Ma'ale Adumim bloc slices the West Bank entirely in half), the remaining chunks of the Palestinian "state" are small indeed. Once surrounded by Israel's twisting Wall (see map 9), the future Palestinian state is destined to be an archipelago of economically doomed and withering enclaves. Their certain inability to overcome this fragmentation and provide any basis for a healthy society has prompted their frequent comparisons to U.S. Native American reservations and South African Bantustans. The Wall is indeed deemed necessary by the Israeli government to partly contain the economic misery and simmering unrest certain to arise from this dismembered "state."[4]

Jewish settlements in the Gaza Strip configure very differently in Israeli politics. Far smaller in area, mostly arid, and with sandy soil, this coastal territory is grotesquely polarized between the massive impoverished Palestinian population of Gaza City, Khan Yunis, and Rafah and the tiny Jewish population anchored in a broad belt of settlements to the south (see map 7). The Palestinians here number over one million people and comprise one of the world's densest (and fastest growing) populations, much of it living in wretched poverty.[5] By contrast, the 7,500-odd Jewish settlers live in a broad belt of twenty settlements that, not incidentally, are located primarily over the arid Strip's scarce freshwater sources. Barricaded by military fortifications, guarded by hundreds of Israeli troops, and occasionally subjected to isolated attack, these settlements have been particularly inefficient and expensive for Israel to maintain.

The Gaza Strip settlements are certainly considered integral to

Eretz Israel (the land of Israel) by the settlers living there: Sharon's announcement in fall 2003 to give them up met these settlers' flaming denunciations. But the Strip's ideological and political value to Israel is actually more dubious for several reasons, First, the territory lacks the West Bank's biblical resonance, having fallen outside the major Jewish kingdoms or territories of antiquity.[6] Second, the Strip has very scant water resources; overuse of its overburdened aquifer is already causing desertification, severe salination, and dire problems with sewage treatment.[7] Most serious, as conditions worsen, the Strip's poverty-stricken and increasingly desperate Palestinian population is radicalizing steadily toward Islamic extremism. To political pragmatists like Sharon, the Gaza Strip therefore manifests as a growing burden rather than a precious and essential part of Eretz Israel. (It bears noting that Egypt, which held the territory between 1948 and 1967, also shows no enthusiasm for reabsorbing the Strip and its politicized Palestinian population.)

Hence, withdrawal from the Gaza Strip is both politically desirable and feasible for Israel. Sharon is indeed one of those keenly aware that withdrawing from Gaza will in several ways facilitate Israel's hold on the West Bank. First, aside from political capital gained by withdrawal, the sheer spectacle—settlers resisting, cries of state betrayal, traumatized children—will provide invaluable political theater to the Sharon government in demonstrating the far greater trauma of removing some thirty times that number from the Zionist heartland of the West Bank. Second, turning over the impoverished (and salinated) Gaza Strip to Palestinian sovereignty will allow Israel to divest itself of a desperately poor, rapidly growing, and politically radicalized Palestinian population. That this scenario will generate security problems—as desperate Palestinians seek jobs or vengeance in Israel—is foreseen by the security fence already in place around the Gaza Strip, which is designed to seal Israel off from that danger. But even advancing Palestinian misery might serve Israeli interests. A Palestinian population left to steep and fester in an overcrowded territory, sinking under the sociopolitical wreckage left by nearly forty years of occupation policy, could quickly provide wonderful fuel for Israeli propaganda and self-credibility in justifying sealing off the territory and rejecting its population's absorption into Israel. A spin-off

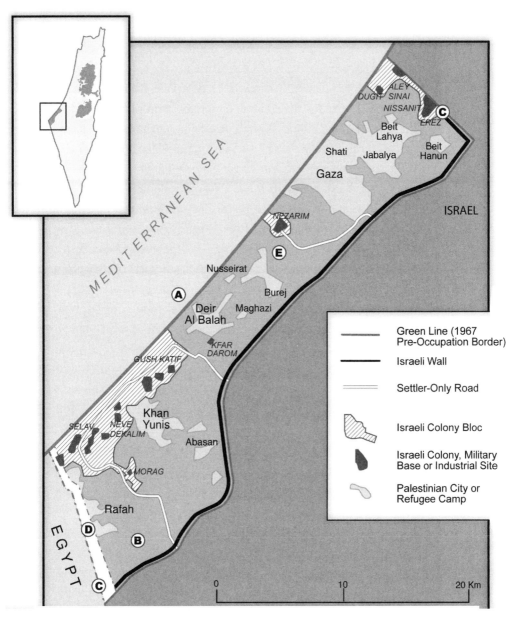

Map 7. The Gaza Strip. (Courtesy Palestine Liberation Organization, Negotiation Affairs Department.)

benefit is that a Palestinian government will then assume full blame for failing the impossible task of relieving poverty (and unrest) for one of the poorest and most densely populated populations on earth.

Palestinian visions for Gaza's future are not so pessimistic. After the Oslo II Accords, the Strip attracted a new Palestinian business class and new investments that might, under the right conditions, launch a major economic revival. With expanded independent port facilities, Gaza might find a role as an entrepôt for European trade to the Middle East and constitute a crucial outlet for West Bank exports. Much talk and some effort has also focused on developing its fishing fleet, building a tourist industry along its fine golden-sand beaches, and attracting some assembly industries. With its vast concentrated store of cheap labor, it is not impossible that the Strip could resurrect enough economic vitality to absorb significant parts of its workforce if granted the right political conditions.

But even supposing a full Israeli withdrawal and complete autonomy for Gaza, Palestinian nationalism cannot be transplanted to or satisfied in the Gaza Strip, as a few voices have suggested. Most obviously, a much larger Palestinian population (some two million people) resides in East Jerusalem and the West Bank, from which Palestinian businesses, industries, social networks, village life, and politics cannot imaginably be transferred to desiccated and overcrowded Gaza. Historically, Arab political and economic elites—and, crucially, Palestinian-nationalist elites and intelligentsia—have always been concentrated further north. Prior to 1948, they were concentrated mostly in Jerusalem and the northern port cities of Jaffa and Haifa. After 1948, they were concentrated in East Jerusalem and in cities of the West Bank highland corridor: Hebron, Bethlehem, Ramallah/El Bireh, Nablus, and Jenin. Since the 1970s, the major Palestinian universities have also been located in that corridor. The deep-historical (in some areas, ancient) archipelago of highland Palestinian peasant villages, with their famous olive and other fruit orchards and artisan industries, are still largely intact in the West Bank highlands (although under grave assault). The West Bank's village culture has indeed assumed an iconic centrality in Palestinian nationalism, which symbolically celebrates their emblematic cultural practices (music, dress, embroidery, and real or supposed values). Palestinian-nationalist affect and ambitions, as well as material logistics and essential planning toward a coherent national life, therefore focus heavily on gaining sovereignty in East Jerusalem and the West Bank.

For all these reasons, it is in the West Bank that Palestinian nationalists most anxiously seek to preserve the territorial integrity necessary to sustain a coherent Palestinian social and political structure. And it is Jewish settlements in the West Bank that therefore comprise the most crucial and stubborn danger to viable Palestinian statehood, as they continue to grow, to absorb more land, and to break apart and erode what remains of Palestinian society and national life. The East Jerusalem settlers will not be withdrawn, and the Gaza Strip settlers almost certainly will be. The rest of this book will therefore focus on the politics of Jewish settlement in the West Bank.

THE POLITICAL GRID

In some suspended realm of imagination, the West Bank settlements might be withdrawn. It might seem simple to move the people into Israel proper, turn the physical facilities over to Palestinian use (returning refugees would urgently need such housing), and integrate the settlement road grid into the Palestinian grid. Withdrawal would certainly entail some bitter and violent confrontations and would certainly be expensive (compensation costs to settlers alone could total US$2.5 to $5 billion), but the political payoff could seem well worth the upheaval and costs. It would relieve Israel of the miserably onerous military occupation, restore cohesion to the Palestinian economy and society, enable viable Palestinian governance and statehood, and, thus, defuse the Israeli-Palestinian conflict and permit normalization of Israel's existence in the entire region. Every peace proposal for the past two decades has therefore called (toothlessly) for removal of the settlers, on these assumptions. Chapter 3 examines various formulas in detail.

But regarding the West Bank, such plans are not appearing even in Israeli rhetoric, let alone practice. Now, as in the past (in the Camp David Accords in the 1970s, the Oslo Accords in the 1990s, President Bill Clinton's Camp David effort in 2000, and President George W.

Bush's "road map for peace" in 2002), serious discussion of a settlement withdrawal is always postponed to "final stage" or "permanent status" talks never reached. The motives driving this endless delay are less well recognized than they should be. Indeed, the delay is deliberate.

The actual politics driving construction of the settlement grid is too often occluded by some common myths. One such myth is that they reflect hard-line motives of particular politicians, like Ariel Sharon or Benjamin Netanyahu. But their growth actually accelerated to unprecedented speed under the liberal governments of Ehud Barak and Yitzhak Rabin, so the settlements clearly reflect something deeper and more durable in Israeli politics than simply a few hard-line personalities. A more common myth, held even by many Jewish Israelis, is that they are the creation and bastion of Zionist religious extremists, who through tiny swing-vote leverage and threats of violent resistance hold Israeli governments hostage to the detriment of a general peace. This belief is, of course, partly accurate. For religious and even many secular Zionists, the West Bank is indeed charged with special nationalist and/or religious-mythical significance. The Jewish realms of antiquity—the legendary kingdoms of David and Solomon, regions once known as Judea and Samaria—were located primarily in these highlands, and the West Bank settlements are promoted to potential Jewish immigrants on grounds of "redeeming" or "returning to" the long-lost Jewish homeland. The centrality of the West Bank settlements to the entire Jewish-national project is accordingly a vision held and promoted, with passionate intensity, by settler movements like Gush Emunim.

In truth, however, religious zealots are a distinct minority among the settler community (and are actually disliked by a majority of settlers). Most of the West Bank settlements are secular bedroom communities, to which the great majority of Jews are drawn by pragmatic incentives: affordable (heavily subsidized) housing within range of their jobs inside Israel and pleasant planned communities with good (also heavily subsidized) schools in which to raise their children. Certainly nationalist-nostalgia or even spiritual visions of "returning" to the Jewish homeland are part of their attraction even to these secular residents (the interplay of religious, ethnic, and nationalist motives in "secular" Zionist thought is complicated; see chap. 5). But many of these settlers would be willing to abandon these settlements if they believed it would gain Israel a genuine peace—although most would resist leaving the homes they care for and all would want financial compensation.[8] Consequently, the roughly two hundred thousand "secular" settlers comprise demographic ballast rather than direct support for the hard-core religious settlers who have promised to fight to the death rather than abandon "Judea and Samaria."

Indeed, in the event of a peace agreement, those few militant zealots could conceivably be removed by force. Their true political leverage lies not precisely in their militancy, however, but rather in the damage such a confrontation would cause to Jewish national unity (see chap. 3).[9] At this writing, anguished debates circulate in Israel about the uncertain moral authority of the Israeli Defense Forces to remove Jews from "redeemed" Jewish land and the ominous implications of open civil conflict for internal Jewish consensus about Israel's legitimacy as the Jewish state.

But the zealots' strident militancy has already been key to sustaining the settlement grid in a very different and more important sense: they have distracted domestic and international attention from the state's complicity in building the grid, while providing the government with plausible deniability. In fact, the entire settlement grid has been designed and subsidized by the state, in coordination with the settlement movements. Prime ministers such as Shamir, Rabin, Barak, and Sharon function (often enthusiastically) as facilitators for this policy, but they are not precisely its authors. That responsibility resides offstage, in a cluster of Jewish-national institutions: the Jewish Agency, World Zionist Organization, Jewish National Fund, and the Israel Lands Authority. None of these institutions can be described as captured by religious zealots; their authority and capacity regarding the settlements are rooted in the foundational law of the state and trace to the first decades of the Zionist project, prior to the state's founding. The World Zionist Organization (WZO) was established in 1897 and still pursues global Zionist outreach; it is famed in the United States for its mainstream international solidarity work (especially through such agencies as United Jewish Appeal), providing informational, educational, and cultural resources to Jewish communities and encouraging *aliyah* (Jewish immigration) to Israel. The Jewish Agency, its sister institution, was the effective government of the pre-1948 Yishuv, dominated by secular Zionists such as Ben-Gurion; after 1948, it was made the state agency responsible for Jewish-national interests (e.g., land) in Israel.

These institutions and especially their settlement departments, working in close coordination with the Israeli Housing Ministry, are responsible for planning, administering, and coordinating funding for the settlement grid. Designed by dedicated professionals working outside the direct sphere of government politics, their various "master plans" have steered a succession of Israeli governments in supporting the settlements while sheltering that support behind legal and political smoke screens. The statal character of these institutions and their role regarding Jewish-national interests are discussed later. Here, noting how they function in practice will illustrate their importance.

Consider, for example, the role of the Jewish Agency and WZO in building the Rehan settlement bloc, which today straddles the Green Line along the northwest shoulder of the West Bank (map 8). Israel's "security fence" now detours deeply into the West Bank, to place this bloc on Israel's side. Yet this maneuver is no recent development. A master plan by the WZO, published in 1978, laid out a basic strategy to build and expand this bloc as part of a larger strategy to absorb "Judea and Samaria," which was considered a "paramount national mission." "Settlement throughout the entire Land of Israel is for security and by right," affirmed author Matityahu Drobles in the plan's introduction. The settlements' geostrategic purpose was made plain.

> A strip of settlements at strategic sites enhances both internal and external security alike, as well as making concrete and realizing our right to Eretz-Israel.
> The Disposition of the proposed settlement will be implemented according to a settlement policy of blocks of settlements in homogeneous settlement areas which are mutually interrelated—this enabling, in time, the development of common services and means of production. . . . It must be borne in mind that it may be too late tomorrow to do what is not done today. . . .

There are today persons who are young or young in spirit who want to take up the challenge of national goals and who want to settle in J&S [*sic*]. We should enable them to do so, and sooner is better.

. . . Upon the approval of the plan proposed herein, the land settlement department will devote itself to drawing up a detailed plan for the development of settlement in J&S—including a timetable for the establishment of the proposed settlements—and the same applies for the thickening and development of the existing settlements and those now under construction.[10]

Yet the Rehan bloc's demographic weight was still small a decade later, when the Jewish Agency's Settlement Department proposed a five-year plan for its expansion. Published jointly by the Jewish Agency and the WZO in 1988, this plan further illuminates the bloc's explicit geostrategic function through ethnic engineering.[11] It also illuminates the strategic complementarity of these two institutions: because the project deliberately straddles the Green Line, the Jewish Agency would have to undertake the expansion within Israel, while the WZO would handle development in the West Bank.

The plan's opening summary refers to the Allon Plan, developed in the 1960s, which called for Jewish settlement in the Jordan Valley and along the Green Line as a security measure to consolidate Israeli state control. But in 1988, the Jewish Agency reported that the region known to Arabs as Wadi Ara and on Zionist maps as Nahal Eron "remains with a sparce Jewish population," noting that "an area of about 180 square kilometers is inhabited by less than 1,000 Jews amidst an Arab population of 160,000." Far from asserting that these Arabs were twentieth-century immigrants (a common Zionist claim), the WZO's Settlement Division entertained no illusions about Arab demographics and history.

The portion of the project area located inside the green line [i.e., inside Israel] currently has an Arab population of about 58,000 spread among 15 villages. Arab settlement in the region began some 400 years ago with the formation of three major villages: Umm El Fahm, Ar'ara and Kafr Qari, which eventually gave rise to most of the Nahal Eron (Wadi Ara) villages. . . . The rest of the project area—i.e. beyond the green line [i.e., in the West Bank], has an Arab population of 85,000 in 45 villages. Arab set-

Map 8.   The Rehan Settlement Bloc. (Excerpt from the Central Intelligence Agency map "West Bank and Vicinity" [July 1992], courtesy Perry-Castañeda Library Map Collection, University of Texas.)

tlement here began likewise four centuries ago, starting with the village Qabatiya, which proliferated in time into many of the existing settlements.

The major villages on either side of the green line—Umm El Fahm, Kafr Qari and Ar'ara—remain the largest foci of Arab population growth in the region. . . . The Arab population of the region has a typical growth rate of 3.2–3.5% per year. On the basis of this trend the Arab population can be expected to reach approximately 200,000 by 1998 and 280,000 by 2008.

The Jewish Agency offered a five-year plan designed to counter the growth of the Arab population: "the current deployment of rural settlements in the region has already achieved the primary objectives of state-owned land appropriation. What has to be done now is to increase the Jewish population." Development in the bloc had lamentably lagged.

Only a single cooperative settlement—May Ami—was established in the area during the first 20 years since the foundation of the state. Even afterwards, with the creation of another four settlements, the growth of the Jewish population proceeded at a sluggish pace, and so did the development of the region. This in contrast to the fast growth and territorial expansion of the local Arab population on either side of the green line.

The solution was to develop the settlement bloc further, to make it more attractive to potential Jewish settlers.

> . . . a cluster of rural settlements around an urban center with a population of about 12,000 as the focal point of the cluster. The urban center will provide the surrounding settlements with the necessary backing in terms of employment and services, thus allowing a proper and efficient functioning of the settlement system as a whole.

The plan laid out the project's needs in detail. Employment and facilities in Nahal Eron were inadequate to support a growing Jewish population; the entire social apparatus of a viable community would have to be created. Each of the four new settlements within the Green Line would be provided with basic services, including "day care, kindergarten, grocery store, club, secretariat, and clinic." New access roads for each settlement would be built (their precise length and width were specified), and the present road grid would be widened to provide "access to both the coastal plain and the Valleys." Securing necessary land would necessitate "transactions" that would be orchestrated by the Israel Lands Administration, and "the local land and water resources [then serving Arab towns and cities] should be located and placed under control in order to complete the allocation of farming land to the settlements." Job creation, to serve at least 50 percent of the new Jewish residents, would focus on industry, services, tourism, "and to a lesser extent agriculture." There would be construction of a "local industrial area for light industries and small businesses" and of a "roadside inn" for tourism to a neighboring forest—the latter developed in coordination with the Ministry of Tourism.

All this development was predicted to permit the present 178 Jewish families to expand at least to 2,840 families and ideally to 7,390 families. The plan's authors acknowledged that even if it succeeded in achieving the maximum growth target, demographic problems would still loom, but the chief goal would be realized.

> Even if this population goal is achieved, the existing numeric gap between the local Arab and Jewish populations will not decrease to any appreciable extent, in view of the fact that 20 years from

now the region will have an Arab population of about 180,000. Yet this population goal will enable the Jewish population of this problematic region *to gain land control and function in a proper manner.* (emphasis added)

Although it fell short of its population targets, the Nahal Eron five-year plan certainly succeeded in gaining "land control." In the past ten years of peace agreements (except in the Taba agreement of 2001), all proposed territorial divisions have carved the Rehan bloc out of Palestinian sovereignty (see chap. 3). Israel's "security fence" has already implemented that annexation by securing the Rehan bloc on Israel's side.

Pertinent to understanding the political clout wielded by the master plans of the WZO and the Jewish Agency is their funding web. The total projected cost of the Rehan bloc was US$7,982,000. The WZO alone, in charge of settlement construction on the West Bank side, was to supply $2,975,000 of this amount. But because the project straddled the Green Line, each component of the project had to be orchestrated through a strategic collaboration (see table 1). The Jewish Agency's legal setup confined its authority to Israel's side of the Green Line; the WZO would have to supervise settlements on the West Bank side. Other agencies, however, could operate on both sides. The Settlement Division's 1988 report summarized the interplay.

> Cooperation between agencies is essential, as is the need for establishing common priorities in the allocation of resources and regional development between the various participating organizations: the Jewish Agency, the World Zionist Organization, the Housing Ministry, the Defense Ministry, the Treasury, the Ministry of Industry and Commerce, the Transport Ministry, the Education Ministry, the Jewish National Fund, the Israel Land Authority, the regional councils, the Nature Reserves Authority, etc.

Such ministerial coordination with the Jewish Agency and WZO was—and remains—a central feature of settlement construction. In 2001, for example, settlement spending by state ministries was mostly by the Housing Ministry ($550 million) but with broad interminis-

TABLE 1. Funding Agencies of the Nahal-Rehan Bloc

Rehan C	"In all, the project will cost $1,900,000. The bulk of this amount $1,550,000 is to be provided *by the state of Israel through the [Jewish Agency] Settlement Division*, and the rest by the *Ministry of Housing*, the *Public Works Department*, the *Ministry of Industry and Commerce*, the *Jewish National Fund*, and the *regional [settler] council*, depending on the particular item."
Hinanit	"The acquisition of land for construction of about 80 housing units will cost about $2,500,000. It is proposed that the *Settlement Division* cover $100,000 of this amount, the rest to be obtained from the *Ministry of Housing*, the *Jewish National Fund*, etc."
Local Industrial Zone	"It is proposed that the *Settlement Division* provide one half of the land preparation costs, i.e. $300,000; the rest will be obtained from Industrial Buildings Company. The connection of utilities will be funded by the *Ministry of Industry and Commerce* and the *Ministry of Housing*. Another necessary measure is the construction of 1 kilometre of internal site roads at a cost of $125,000, to be funded by the *Settlement Division*. In all, the project will cost $825,000. It is proposed that the government cover $425,000 of this amount through the *Settlement Division* and that the rest be obtained from the *Ministry of Housing*, the *Ministry of Industry and Commerce*, and the *Industrial Buildings Company*."
Expansion of Regional School	"The whole project will cost $425,000 . . . It is proposed that the government participate with $150,000 in the above investment through the *Settlement Division*, the balance to be obtained from the regional settler council, the *Ministry of Housing*, and the *Ministry of Education*."
Development of the Umm Rehan Nature Reserve	[total cost, $207,500] "The following funding is proposed: $50,000 by the Settlement Division; the rest—by the *Nature Reserves Authority*, the *Jewish National Fund*, and the *Ministry of Tourism*. Once the public development is underway, private funding may be considered as an option."
Widening of Service Road	"Widening . . . will cost about $600,000, of which $200,000 would be obtained from the government through the *Settlement Division* and the rest from the *Ministry of Housing Public Works Department*, the *Ministry of Defence* and r*egional [settler] council*."
Paving New Road	"Paving . . . would cost about $1,500,000, $500,000 of which is to be funded by the *Settlement Division* and the rest by the *Ministry of Defence*, the [Ministry of Housing] *Public Works Department* and the *regional [settler] council*."

Source: Suggested Projects with the Participation of the Jewish Agency Settlement Department (1988)
(emphasis added)

terial coordination. A decade later, the pattern continued intact; B'Tselem reported settlement in 2003 as supported by

> the Ministry of Construction and Housing (generous loans for the purchase of apartments, part of which is converted to a grant); the Israel Lands Administration (significant price reductions in leasing land); the Ministry of Education (incentives for teachers, exemption from tuition fees in kindergartens, and free transportation to school); the Ministry of Industry and Trade (grants for investors, infrastructure for industrial zones, etc.); the Ministry of Labor and Social Affairs (incentives for social workers); and the Ministry of Finance (reductions in income tax for individuals and companies).[12]

Precise spending on settlements, however, remains a difficult subject to research. The 1978 WZO master plan for West Bank settlement construction understood the costs to be very major, predicting a cost of Israeli Lira (IL) 32 billion over five years, with an additional IL 22 billion to "thicken" existing settlements. Later independent assessments of actual spending have confirmed that the investment has been vast. In 2001, total spending on settlements by eight Israeli ministries was US$553.6 million, *not* counting defense spending, transportation, and funds transferred to the Settlement Division. Those missing pieces are very large. For instance, of the ILS 1.9 billion (roughly US$417 million) openly earmarked for settlements in the 2003 budget, the Religious Affairs Ministry spent ILS 50 million on synagogues and *mikves* (ritual baths). The Education Ministry (which provided US$35 million to settlement schools in 2001) gave a 90 percent tuition discount for settler children ages four and older to attend nurseries and free schooling—"as if they were all welfare cases," commented *Ha'aretz*.[13] In the 2001 budget, the Agriculture Ministry provided US$20 million to the settlements; in the 2004 budget, *all* of the Agriculture Ministry's budget was allocated for settlements.

Israeli government planners have indeed designated much of the West Bank and the Gaza Strip as Class A National Priority development zones, a status that allows special tax breaks and other incentives for settlers and industry. In this framework, the Housing Ministry funnels subsidies, grants, low-interest loans, personal benefits, and other incentives to settlers, specifically to help them buy or build homes in the West Bank and the Gaza Strip. Settlers looking for housing in Ariel, for example, can count on financing from the Housing Ministry and the Israeli Lands Administration up to 95 percent of the purchase price and an outright grant of US$5,700, supplemented by $300 per month from the private developer toward the first year of a special low-interest mortgage. In the Jordan Valley, the government was offering $22,800 to the first two hundred couples who applied to build a new home, with free university tuition for one spouse and a $2,700 grant if the couple found employment in the settlement itself. Free land, with 50 percent of building costs covered, is offered in some areas. With such incentives, buying or building a home in the settlements is significantly cheaper for a young Jewish family than buying or building in Israel itself.

Government support for private industry in the territories is also substantial, although it is even harder to quantify. It is provided through subsidies, direct grants, low-interest loans, and tax holidays. A major push was launched in the 1980s to attract industry. Figure 1 shows one promotional spread in a 1983 issue of the settlement magazine *Homecoming*.[14] A WZO brochure from 1984 hailed "Judea and Samaria" as Israel's promising new high-technology industrial zone.

> Special mention should be made of the effort underway to make Judea and Samaria the scientific and technological anchor of the entire nation. The newly formed Ministry of Science is pursuing a determined course of scientific development in the nation's heartland. A science-based park in Ariel, and a nuclear medicine facility in Ma'ale Efraim are but a few of the plans. . . . Software manufacturing, video production and metal working are but a few of the new enterprises. Judea, Samaria, and Gaza may well emerge within a decade as Israel's version of California's Silicon Valley, an ongoing base for dramatic research, design, experimentation and production breakthroughs.[15]

Ministry financing is only one portion of Israeli state spending in the territories. Funds are also channeled through political parties. From the 2004 budget, for example, the National Religious Party obtained ILS 125 million (about US$23 million) in state funds intended for settlements, and the National Union Party received ILS

LOOKING TO THE FUTURE: INDUSTRY IN JUDEA&SAMARIA

With central Israel full beyond capacity, it is becoming more and more economically feasible for investors to search for alternative areas for investment. With the highly-skilled population and the aid granted by the government, the region of Judea and Samaria is attracting many new industries to set up shop there.

Fig. 1. This 1983 advertisement promoting industry in the West Bank appeared in *Homecoming*, a promotional magazine for Jewish settlement and development in "Judea and Samaria."

6 million (US$1.3 million) for the same purpose.[16] Millions are also transferred to private Jewish cultural and religious organizations, which in turn transfer them to the settlements councils to help with building and maintaining facilities, parks, schools, services, and cultural life.

Of course, private Israelis have major economic interests in the territories—interests that the state has every reason to guard. The West Bank functions as a captive market: in 1999, for example, Israeli exports to the Palestinian West Bank totaled US$1.854 billion and comprised 71 percent of West Bank imports (about one-third of this number reflects trade with third parties transiting through Israel, with attached fees).[17] With its access to foreign markets (e.g., for olive oil) cut off by Israeli restrictions, the West Bank also provides cheap products and labor to Israel: in 1999, 97 percent of West Bank exports went to Israel. That statistic does not include private Israeli investment in Jewish settlements, which includes the shopping malls, cinemas, and industry. Losing all that investment to a comprehensive withdrawal would clearly strike a very heavy blow at Israel's already shaken economy. Israel's saturation of and interdependence with the West Bank economy is indeed one of the more formidable "facts on the ground" driving the one-state solution.

The real question is why, given all this state complicity in developing the settlement grid, anyone would credit the Israeli government with good faith in negotiating any major withdrawal from the West Bank. Palestinians certainly have ceased to do so, a disillusionment that partly explains the Palestinian political disarray at the end of the 1990s and, to some extent, even the rising rate of suicide bombers. Palestinians in the West Bank confront the expansion of the settlements not as a murky labyrinth of funding concerns but as a daily, dangerous, humiliating, and economically ruinous process in which land is lost, homes are bulldozed, impassible fences and walls are raised, roads are blocked, and olive orchards are razed. Over the past decade, Palestinians' growing inability to find work or subsistence— as their daily lives have become increasingly difficult and punctuated by frightening confrontations with Israeli soldiers and vigilante settlers—has recast international diplomacy as a mere cover for Israel's ongoing annexation and dismemberment of the Palestinian national territory. Israel's Wall, which will seal the Palestinians permanently within this amputee national existence, is seen as the capstone, rather than the substance, of this larger Israeli policy of expropriation and exclusion (see map 9). The effect among the Palestinians is rising desperation and the fresh legitimization of militancy—even, for the fringe few, the capacity to see suicidal terror as a righteous act of resistance.

Clearly, the extent of Israeli governmental complicity in building the settlements represents an immense political obstacle to their withdrawal, but even deeper ties concretize the state's commitment to the grid. Those ties transcend investments, security, and the role of any passing government or prime minister. Ariel Sharon, for example, has long been a key agent of the settlements, not only as prime minister, but also in his earlier role as Minister of Housing. However, it is not clear that, even given some unimaginable change of personality, Sharon himself could significantly change the policy if he wanted to, for the policy to settle all of Eretz Israel not only runs deeply through the fabric of Israeli politics but is embedded in the state's very design. Some of that design is evident in the conjoined Jewish Agency and WZO, which together orchestrated the Rehan bloc (discussed in the preceding section of this chapter). These institutions do not merely plan and administer the settlement grid. Strategically sheltered from the hurly-burly of Israeli electoral politics, their special charge as government agencies is to guard and nurture the Jewishness of the Jewish state. They are indeed the durable institutional expressions of Israel's foundational philosophy that Israel is truly the state of the Jewish people—a role that lends the political influence of these institutions a special fortitude. They therefore require a second look.

First, as noted earlier, the Jewish Agency and the WZO are designed to complement each other in orchestrating Jewish settlement in the occupied territories. Their separate existence, juridical and partly administrative, is largely a legal fiction. The two organizations share board members, staff, planning, and authority; once within their coffers, funds gained from their respective Jewish solidarity networks abroad are almost entirely fungible. Both organizations have settlement departments, but this is a legalistic (rather than programmatic) distinction; the two departments were originally one agency (split in 1971) and still coordinate so closely on settlement policy that (as we have seen earlier in this chapter) master plans are cosigned between them. Only their jurisdiction differs: the WZO operates in the territories; the Jewish Agency, inside Israel. This division is a great political and legal convenience when orchestrating settlement across the Green Line, as the institutions' respective mandates and funding sources can be insulated from the political implications of settlement in occupied territory.

Most important, the Jewish Agency and the WZO are not really, as they are sometimes called, "parastatal" (i.e., outside the state but working in concord with it); they are actually state agencies. Prior to Israel's independence in 1948, the Jewish Agency functioned as the government for the Zionist settlement project in Palestine, coordinating Jewish immigration, settlement, development, diplomacy, and politics. After independence, the Jewish Agency and the WZO were legally reconceived as the "authorized agencies" of the state for Jewish immigration, absorption, and settlement in Israel and for all matters regarding Jewish-national interests.[18] As "Jewish" is the only national identity recognized by Israeli law to have collective privileges, and much of the state's resources are consigned to Jewish-national use, this role of the Jewish Agency and the WZO actually makes them administrators of major portions of Israel's assets, such as land.

The special standing of Jewish identity under Israeli law is not well understood by most but is fundamental to the Israeli-Palestinian conflict and requires a short explanation here. A cluster of laws defines Israel as the "Jewish state" and establishes Israel's two-tiered system of citizenship, which privileges "Jewish" nationality.[19] The Law of Return (1950) grants any Jew the right to immigrate to Israel (unless the person is deemed unsuitable, for security or other reasons, by the Minister of Immigration). The Citizenship Law (1952)—often mistranslated as the "Nationality Law"—grants anyone arriving in Israel under the Law of Return (i.e., Jews) Israeli citizenship without further procedures, immediately upon entering the country. The Population Registry Law (1965) then provides that such citizens are classified as having "Jewish nationality" (not "Israeli nationality," which is prohibited under Israeli law). The World Zionist Organization–Jewish Agency (Status) Law (1952) authorizes the Jewish Agency and its various arms to administer most of the state's land and properties and a plethora of other resources in the interests of that Jewish nationality. The Jewish Agency's administrative authority reaches far through Israeli society, including

> [t]he organizing of immigration abroad and the transfer of immigrants and their property to Israel; co-operation in the absorption of immigrants in Israel; youth immigration; agricultural settlement in Israel; the acquisition and amelioration of land in Israel by the institutions of the Zionist Organization [later the WZO], the Keren Kayemeth Leisrael [Jewish National Fund] and the Keren Hayesod [United Israel Appeal]; participation in the establishment and the expansion of development enterprises in Israel; the encouragement of private capital investments in Israel; assistance to cultural enterprises and institutions of higher learning in Israel; the mobilization of resources for financing these activities; the co-ordination of the activities in Israel of Jewish institutions and organizations acting within the limits of these functions by means of public funds.[20]

The interplay of the Jewish-national organizations and civil-state institutions regarding land is strategically internecine. For example, the Jewish Agency has authority over the Jewish National Fund (JNF), which holds Jewish-national lands (some 13 percent of Israel's territory) in trust for "the Jewish people." JNF lands are administered by the Israel Lands Authority (ILA), a state institution which also administers "state lands, totaling some 80 percent of the country."[21] JNF lands administered by the ILA must be administered in the interests of the Jewish people. But as the *nation* represented by the state is actually Jewish, the Basic Law also makes *state* land inalienable from the "Jewish people," not from the "Israeli people" (again, no "Israeli people"—or Israeli nation—exists under Israeli law). Hence, when the ILA itself—a state agency—provides resources to Jewish settlement in the occupied territories, it is operating as a state agent acting officially not for *Israeli* public interests but for *Jewish-national* interests.

In effect, this means that Palestinians, as non-Jews, may have no legal standing to challenge the expropriation of their land. Palestinian village land might be seized initially for military purposes, rendered uncultivated (which may be accomplished by bulldozing its orchards or by banning Palestinians from access to it), declared "empty" and therefore "state land," and then administered by the ILA to serve the Jewish people—that is, the settlements. No Palestinian appeal is likely to avail, because appeals must be addressed to these same authorities. In this way, some 60 percent of the West Bank has already been alienated from Palestinian use.

Hence, it is not as private or rogue institutions but as *central state authorities* that, in their vision and their policy, the Jewish Agency, WZO, and JNF have already annexed the West Bank and the Gaza Strip. All these organizations' resources (e.g., the WZO's lucrative revenue networks in the United States) are channeled into implementing their single vision of an Israel united between the Mediterranean and the Jordan River, as the 1978 WZO "Master Plan for the Development of Settlement in Judea and Samaria" (cited earlier in this chapter) made plain. Indeed, until the Oslo Accords, no public map issued by any Israeli government agency, including the Israeli Defense Forces (IDF), showed the West Bank or Gaza Strip as distinct territories; even on a recent IDF map of the "security barrier," the land of Israel stretches unhindered to the Jordan River. (This practice casts as disingenuous the strident Zionist denunciations of some Arab and Palestinian maps of "Palestine" that also omit the Green Line.) Only political and security obstacles—Palestinian and international protest and Jewish unwillingness to move into the territories—have slowed implementation of that vision, forcing painstaking political care, erection of obfuscating funding networks, and incremental expansion disguised under fig-leaf formulas such as "natural growth." Completing the grid has taken time.

Successions of Israeli government administrations have worked hard to provide that time. In the international spotlight, one arm of the state, prime ministers leading Israeli parliamentary politics, have sometimes offered grand statements about territorial compromise, absorbing international attention for months or years. But they have always insisted on postponing serious debate or decision about the settlements, offering one excuse or another—for example, waiting for an election; a new international summit; the signing of an agreement; or some condition, such as the evaporation of Arafat or the cessation of Palestinian violence (which is caused partly by the settlements themselves). Each delay seemed short-term but did so by design. Precisely through successive chunks of time—six months here, two years there—the settlements' status was always consigned to "permanent status" talks that never came. Meanwhile, out of the spotlight and actually sheltered by the distractions of international diplomacy, the other arm of the state, the Jewish-national institutions, worked steadily with the settler movements to annex territory they already consider an integral part of Israel. And now it is too late.

3. Passionate
Intensities
or Why No Other
Plan Will Work

All diplomacy and debate about the Jewish settlements in the West
Bank and the Gaza Strip mention their withdrawal or "dismantling"
as a necessary measure for peace. But "dismantling" the West Bank
settlements is a far more daunting prospect than most people realize.
As described in chapter 2, the settlement grid is no bundle of temporary housing that can be taken down and carried off on trucks; it is a
huge and deliberately sprawling network of modern cities and sub-
urbs built of stone and concrete. Its economic weight is equally monumental; just evacuating the settlers, while leaving the settlements
intact, would cost billions of dollars in lost private and business
investments and in relocation and compensation costs. The grid's
political weight is even more tenacious, being embedded in the programs and even the design of state institutions, including the ministries, some parties, and the Jewish-national state agencies (the Jewish Agency, the World Zionist Organization, the Israel Lands
Authority, and the Jewish National Fund).

To effect any meaningful withdrawal, then, very hard political decisions would have to be made and vast resources would have to be

dedicated. Only a political will of iron—of some Israeli prime minister with an unassailable political base, able to muster the necessary resources and navigate the storms of controversy—could reverse the present trajectory toward annexation. Yet that will is conspicuously missing, for a very good reason: there is no sufficient political pressure, internal or external, to create it.

To some hopeful observers, the necessary political will seemed to manifest briefly in Yitzhak Rabin, who negotiated the 1993 Oslo Accord. The 1995 Oslo II Accord laid the basis for the Palestinian Interim Self-Government Authority (PA) and seemed to signal that a staged withdrawal of Israeli military forces, withdrawal of the settlements, a viable Palestinian state, and a stable peace might finally be in the offing. But that impression was an illusion. Nothing in Oslo II called for withdrawing any settlements; the entire question was postponed (as always) to never-reached "permanent status" talks. Indeed, behind the scenes, the settlement grid grew rapidly during Rabin's tenure and continued to expand under Labor Prime Ministers Shimon Peres and Ehud Barak as well as Likud's Benjamin Netanyahu, more than doubling its population in the 1990s. Indeed, for political reasons explored in this chapter, no meaningful settlement withdrawal was in Rabin's political sights. While he gestured with one hand (internationally) about their withdrawal, he signaled with the other (domestically) for their growth.

Despite his skilled diplomatic maneuvering, however, Rabin's posturing about a meaningful withdrawal from the occupied territories engaged Israel's political minefield, leading to his assassination in 1995. The religious-nationalist youth who killed him hardly defines Israeli public opinion, of course. Jewish-Israeli opinion is deeply divided about the settlements; the grid's most eloquent critics include leftist Israelis and Israeli-Jewish human rights groups. Some people denounce the settlements because their ruinous impact on Palestinian society so starkly violates Israel's proclaimed liberal-democratic values; others denounce the settlements simply because they so clearly ruin any peace plans. Centrist and even some right-wing voices now call for withdrawing the settlements because of their ominous implications for a binational state (as explained later in this chapter). But all these opponents of the settlements lack sufficient political cohesion to affect state policy seriously, especially in the fearful context of Palestinian terror attacks and the country's climate of security emergency. Israeli state policy is instead steered by currents of Zionist thought, which hold that withdrawing from the West Bank would make no political or moral sense or would even defy the will of God. This segment is no microminority of zealots. In the last decade, it has become a well-organized and growing coalition of right-wing religious and ultranationalist groups who have gained central state influence and for whom the settlements have a symbolic value beyond material calculation. Any serious attempt at a major settlement withdrawal is precluded by this camp, not so much by direct electoral clout as by its capacity to threaten the very fabric of Israeli national unity. If, under some compelling circumstances, an Israeli government made a withdrawal attempt, abiding fissures within Israeli politics would split apart, rupturing Zionism's "national pact" (discussed later in this chapter) regarding the mission and legitimacy of the Jewish state. Long before that, bullets would fly.

This symbolic ideological weight of the Jewish settlements ultimately cements their physical, economic, and institutional weight and wrecks any prospects for the proposals commonly floated, formally and informally, for their evacuation. Such proposals can be grouped roughly into three categories: (1) full Palestinian sovereignty in the West Bank, with all settlers evacuated and settlements turned over to Palestinian use; (2) full Israeli sovereignty, with Palestinian cities and villages under some form of local Palestinian autonomy; or (3) partitioned sovereignty, with the states of Palestine and Israel holding proximate chunks of territory, with either (a) complete ethnic separation (with all settlers evacuated from Palestinian territory) or (b) partial ethnic separation (with Jewish settlers in Palestinian territory either retaining Israeli citizenship and some package of extraterritorial autonomy or accepting citizenship in the "State of Palestine"). Any of these formulas might seem reasonable and feasible to their advocates. But given the convergence of ideologies and physical realities on the ground, none will work.

In a fantasy theory involving nonexistent conditions, the Israeli-Palestinian conflict would be rapidly and well resolved by full Palestinian sovereignty over the West Bank, which is why most of the international community has long endorsed it. Certainly the Palestinians themselves are primed for this solution. The Palestine Liberation Organization (PLO) formally abandoned all territorial claims within Israel in 1988, the PA has sustained this position, and all but a few extremist factions are in accord. At the same time, having suffered through various unviable partition negotiations during the failed Oslo negotiations (begun in the 1990s), the PA has also rejected any option other than full sovereignty in the West Bank and the Gaza Strip. Politically, the institutional basis for statehood is also laid; the Oslo process confirmed the PLO principle of free elections and a parliamentary system long insisted upon by the majority of the Palestinian population. Indeed, in the late 1990s, during a few relatively rosy years of partial Israeli withdrawal and optimistic international donations, hard work by reinvigorated Palestinian professionals brought forth a whole new apparatus of ministries to rebuild the health and schools systems, civil record-keeping procedures, and all the essential services of a modern state. (Almost all this new infrastructure was demolished by Israeli Defense Forces during raids in 2002.)

Even in its birth throes, such a Palestinian state could present no conceivable threat to Israel. It should in fact be a far safer formula for Israel. Palestinian statehood would defuse most of the militancy now inspired by the occupation; for all its totalizing rhetoric, even Hamas has agreed to accept a state in the West Bank and the Gaza Strip.[1] The Palestinian government would also be most anxious to contain any trouble that would sabotage relations with its immensely powerful former occupier and primary trading partner. (The current PA is indeed dominated by Palestinian business interests who have always hungered for such relations, hoping to profit.) But Palestinian sovereignty in all of the West Bank has always been necessary to state capacity in that effort, because only with full national reintegration can a Palestinian government administer state institutions and services (in health, education, agriculture, labor, trade, justice, planning, industry, etc., as well as security) with the effectiveness necessary to stabilizing, rebuilding, and policing Palestinian-national society.

Stabilizing such a state would, of course, be a tough project. Old bitterness and divisions would linger, and political volatility would persist for some years. (South Africa's conflicted experience of inter-factional trouble, discussed in chapter 5, is illustrative here.) Some early struggle would be necessary to eject or marginalize the PA's ossified crony leadership and to undercut recent gains by nondemo-cratic forces, such as Hamas. Containing wildcat violence by Palestini-ans and settler militants would initially be difficult and would tax the fortitude of both sides. But the great majority of the Palestinian pop-ulation is exhausted by the occupation and shares a burning desire for peace, which, if enabled through effective government, should be sufficient to allay or contain the worst Palestinian extremists so that a process of economic recovery and social healing might begin.

There is only one difficulty with this scenario: it is not going to happen, because the Israeli government will not—and indeed can-not—let it happen. Two obstacles (not to exclude others) are sufficiently crippling to preclude it. First and most obvious are those Zionists who consider withdrawal from "Judea and Samaria" unthinkable and would turn on any government that attempted it. Their logics, passion, and formidable political leverage constrain all possible solutions to the conflict—although not in ways commonly thought—and can be explained here, for they are highlighted in a dilemma that arises particularly in this scenario: disposition of the set-tlement grid.

Given that the settlements cannot be "dismantled" or otherwise carried away, it might seem obvious that they must fall under Pales-tinian sovereignty in the event of full Palestinian governance in all of the West Bank. Assuming that most or all Jewish settlers would reset-tle in Israel, the empty facilities would then be turned over to Pales-tinian use. The grid would provide invaluable new housing and com-munity facilities for the growing Palestinian population, including returning Palestinian refugees. With some investment to reintegrate the Arab road grid, the new Palestinian state would also quickly gain a much-needed network of fine highways. (The Geneva Accord, a maverick and much-publicized peace initiative issued in 2003 by left-ist Israelis and some Palestinian professionals, made precisely these assumptions.) But this vision—an easy and obvious answer for secular-liberal thinkers—too lightly dismisses the West Bank settlements' symbolic value for Israel's nationalist and religious right wing. It therefore also underappreciates the dangers of this plan for Jewish-Zionist unity, which no Israeli government has any motive to risk.

The symbolic value of the Jewish settlements varies greatly with differing schools of Zionist thought, but a broad brush can delineate the mechanisms at work here. As explained in chapter 2, financial support for the settlements is orchestrated not only by the state but also by religious political parties, settler movements, and Jewish cultural and religious groups, who view the entire grid not simply as towns and neighborhoods but as the material expression of Jewish "redemption" and "return." For these supporters and architects, Jewish resettlement of long-lost biblical territory is both a nationalist and a spiritual quest, reflecting the Jewish people's special relationship with God and with the land that biblical myth maintains was given to the Hebrews by God. Exile from this land by nefarious alien rulers (the Babylonians in 587 BCE, the Romans in 70 and 132 CE) has been the archetypal motif for two millennia of Jewish diaspora tradition. Therefore, to the settler movements, the settlements in "Judea and Samaria" are not simply homes and buildings but "the fulfillment of an ancient dream."[2] That most settlements are officially secular in their ethos and internal codes of behavior is no obstacle to this vision, for it embraces them all, as an early guiding light, Rabbi Abraham Isaac Kook, proposed: "The spirit of Israel is so closely linked to the spirit of God that the Jewish nationalist, no matter how secularist his intention may be, is, despite himself, imbued with the divine spirit even against his own will."[3] Indeed, although otherwise mutually suspicious, religious and secular-nationalist settler factions converge on this question: for both, it is unimaginable that these precious religious and/or nationalist expressions of redemption and return to the land of the ancient kingdoms be turned over to Palestinian Arabs—who, they further imagine, would use them only to plot more Jewish destruction.

This sense of an essential Jewish-national or Jewish-spiritual quality manifesting in the physical West Bank settlements is not confined
to the ultra-Orthodox or right-wing nationalists. In more subtle
forms, it threads through more secular Zionist currents as well, such
as right-wing tendencies in labor Zionism (which glorified Jewish
manual labor on the land), for which the settlements also manifest as
unique carriers of ethnonationalist sentiment and mission and whose
possession by non-Jews would therefore strike a deep note of pain
and offense. Some history is illustrative here: when Israel withdrew
from the Sinai to its present boundaries in 1982, implementing its
peace with Egypt, the Jewish settlement of Yamit (on the Egyptian
side) was not simply abandoned but dynamited by then defense minister Ariel Sharon, to prevent exactly such an offensive transfer of
Jewish work to Arab hands. Sharon has openly suggested the same
fate for the Gaza settlements. Yet dynamiting the entire West Bank
grid (which, in any case, would leave the delicate highland landscape
horribly scarred) would result in vast piles of ruined Jewish towns in
the biblical territory and would therefore be no better psychologically. (It may be worth noting that blowing up the settlement grid
would also manifest as a ghastly racist crime to the international community. But as global opprobrium would certainly amount only to
diplomatic hand-wringing and some finger wagging, it is unlikely to
have any independent impact.) For right-wing and especially reli-
gious-Zionist supporters of the settlements, either scenario would
resonate with the deepest Jewish ethnic traditions regarding dispossession, expulsion, exile, suffering, and loss. It would be an unacceptable crime and would delegitimize any Israeli government that
attempted it, whatever that government's democratic backing, as former Knesset member Elyakim Haetzni, of the Kiryat Arba settlement, warned in 2003:

One cannot decide to carry out a pogrom, and this is a pogrom:
We are taking our soldiers and policemen to carry out a pogrom,
to destroy houses, to drag people out of their homes, to remove
the bones of the dead from the cemeteries. Democracy cannot
do such things according to the rules of democracy itself. A local
newspaperman came to me and asked me, "And what if there's a
majority?" I told him: "We are five in a boat and there's no food.

We're going to die of starvation, and decide by a referendum, four against one, to eat you. Does that obligate you? Will you still say 'democracy'?"[4]

This ideological problem also draws Jewish diaspora politics significantly into the political equation. As noted in chapter 2, the World Zionist Organization solicits funds for the settlements from a myriad of Jewish institutions, grassroots Jewish cultural groups, and Jewish congregations in other countries, especially Western Europe and the United States. Accordingly, tens of millions of dollars in Jewish diaspora donations are sunk into the stones and palm-lined avenues, day-care centers and kindergartens, health clinics and art centers, and greenhouses and sprinklers of the settlements.[5] Through these donations, Western Jews vicariously participate in the Zionist dream of Jewish cultural, spiritual, and national fulfillment. These donors would therefore be equally repelled by the specter of Arabs taking over the Jewish homes so lovingly built with heartfelt donations from afar.[6] Indeed, the WZO solicits such funds partly to cultivate precisely that sense of connection and to energize Zionist lobbying of the U.S. government (see chap. 4).

The political trouble portended by transferring the Jewish settlements to Palestinian ownership is not precisely universal Jewish outrage. As noted, in both Israel and the United States, Jewish opinion about the settlements is actually deeply divided; most favor "some" withdrawal, and a good 20 percent favor complete unconditional withdrawal. Division itself is the problem. For instance, a 2003 survey by the Jewish Agency found that 32 percent of U.S. Jews agreed that the settlements are obstacles to peace, but 27 percent disagreed; 34 percent agreed that the settlements are vital strategic assets, while 24 percent disagreed. As comparable minorities had no opinion or were not sure, these figures signal a significant moderate (or muddled) center and a solid progressive camp. But they also signal a growing polarization: on one end of the spectrum is a freshly articulate liberal secular-democratic camp, both Zionist and "post-Zionist," who finds the ethnocentrism and zealotry of the religious settlers morally repugnant; on the other end is the growing coalition of religious-nationalist Jews, sometimes called "neo-Zionists," who urge the settlements' expansion toward a theocratic, territorially maximalist, and ethnically exclusive vision of Israel's future (a split discussed in chap. 5).[7] If the Israeli government announced its intention to withdraw the settlements from the Jewish biblical heartland, this neo-Zionist camp would certainly mobilize all its forces to denounce and change that government, as well as lobby the U.S. government to abandon it.[8] Jewish political polarization would then greatly intensify, both in Israel and in the Western diaspora, threatening an open rupture in Jewish unity and in the polite veil normally drawn over deep divisions among European and U.S. Jews about support for Israel and its policies toward the Palestinians.

Precluding such an open schism within world Jewry is far more important to any Israeli government than appeasing angry Palestinians or an uneasy international community. No narrow party interest—for example, electoral gain to some political party that commanded a withdrawal—would be worth the internal civil turmoil that would challenge the government's very legitimacy. Given that external pressure by the international community is so lax, the Israeli government has no motive to trigger such a crisis by turning over to Palestinian use territory and projects that some consider essential nationalist emblems. Jewish national unity has been sustained by avoiding precisely such showdowns. In sum, full Palestinian sovereignty within the West Bank is politically possible only in some imaginary world in which the settlements' symbolic value carries no such internally divisive force for Israel.

If the settlements can be neither destroyed nor abandoned and left for Palestinian use, only one alternative remains—keep them where they are, with the settlers in them. The dilemma here is the settlers' political status. Some feeble suggestions have been raised that settlers unwilling to leave could simply live under Palestinian sovereignty, and a very few—so religious or apolitical as to value life on the land above all—might be willing to do so. But as a grand strategy, this proposal is a fantasy. To the vast majority of neo-Zionists especially, abandoning Israeli sovereignty over the biblical heartland would manifest as a direct betrayal of Zionism itself, triggering the hard-line political mobilization previously described. Mere Jewish presence on the land has never been Zionism's goal, for Jews lived in the region before Zionism arrived.⁹ True Jewish *statehood*, to enable Jewish national revival and "redemption," has been the central imperative. In this view, having Jews live in the biblical territory under Palestinian (alien) rule would only return the settlers to the condition of Jewish life under the Romans, the Babylonians, or any of the unreliable, oppressive, and sometimes lethally dangerous alien rulers in Jewish collective memory through two millennia. Such a prospect is viewed with fear and anathema.

Of course, fear of these particular rulers would not be only symbolic. The immediate future would be fraught with tensions. A Palestinian state with Jewish settler communities in its territorial bosom would require a careful constitution, a transition period, perhaps a truth commission, definitely land and water redistribution, and other difficult labor toward coexistence. The new Palestinian government would doubtless work hard toward building a workable system, given the stakes (minimally, its own survival); but its early capacity to contain all dissenting splits would be fragile. Jewish fears of extrajudicial troubles in the immediate future—harassment by still-resentful young militants, a nervous and cold local Arab community, Jewish-targeted robberies and other crime, sluggish protection from local police and town authorities—would hardly be unfounded.

Worse fears—for example, of mass expulsion of the Jewish population—are greatly overdrawn. Even for purely pragmatic reasons, no such official measure by Palestinian authorities is imaginable, as expelling Jewish settlers whose presence is secured by treaty would spell the vulnerable Palestinian state's prompt demise or economic strangling by Israel. But also, with Israeli occupation gone, the very motive for anti-Jewish violence—which Zionism has always recast as anti-Semitic in origin—would evaporate. Hence, a kind of racial terror, of vengeful Arab natives seeking Jewish extermination, is more a classic settler-colonial paranoia than the likely outcome of a democratized Palestinian state (a matter discussed further in chap. 5). Indeed, Jewish language about bloody Arab revenge echoes strongly of identical Afrikaner forebodings about ethnic cleansing and mass murder by blacks upon any end to apartheid. Based on the same precedent, lingering violence on the part of the Jewish settlers is at least as likely.

Even a few bad incidents, however, would have major symbolic effect in reinforcing deeply held fears about Jewish vulnerability and victimization. Indeed, the two hundred thousand Jewish settlers now living in the well-funded bubble existence provided by Israeli rule in the West Bank would have every reason to abjure rule by a fraught young Palestinian government, which, for all its democratic impulses, would surely be grappling for years to come with ugly internecine feuds, battles over corruption, funding shortages, and security crises. (Partly for this same reason, Arabs in Israel have also indicated their unwillingness to live in the new state.) A great majority of settlers would move back to Israel rather than accept such conditions, but some 20 to 40 percent would strongly resist the loss of their homes, some 37 percent have said they would rely on rabbinical authority to make them move, and some 10 percent have vowed to resist violently.[10] This threat of violence by the zealous few (with various numbers following, depending on circumstances) is why liberal Israelis tend to believe that the settlement problem traces to a small fanatical minority holding the entire country hostage to their extremist views.

Hence, much more important than rings of armed zealots defending the settlement barricades are the implications of that spectacle for Israel itself. The religious zealots indeed signal, rather than comprise, the leverage implicit in their political position: for this reason, the two largest parties in Israeli politics, Likud and Labor, support the zealots in all but name, and we have seen the state's deep institutional backing for the settlements. The settlers' leverage actually derives from a brooding fault line within Israel's ideological substratum. Zionist unity in supporting Israel has always relied on an uneasy compromise between secular, liberal, Conservative, Orthodox, and ultra-Orthodox currents, all of which have very different understandings of what a Jewish state must be like—democratic or theocratic, ethnonationalist or civil-nationalist. Establishing the Jewish state initially required a kind of national pact among these mutually antipathetic Zionist camps. Lurking in Israel's body politic, this pact has worked so far largely because all have agreed to avoid any serious showdown. But cold coexistence, through power sharing, has substituted for true reconciliation, and no agreement was ever reached on such crucial questions as whether the land of the biblical kingdoms is essential to the Jewish state. An open breach on that question could delegitimize the Jewish state for one faction or the other. No Israeli government wishes to provoke such a schism by participating in a shooting standoff with the religious right. Indeed, given the parliamentary system, no government would survive the effort.

Because the notion of getting the Jewish settlers to accept Palestinian rule is a political nonstarter on several counts, strategists have alternatively suggested that the settlers could preserve autonomous authority over their own affairs and perhaps keep their Israeli citizenship. In effect, this approach would extend extraterritorial Israeli sovereignty to the settlements.[11] But as the settlements have been built in blocs, with additional "outposts" establishing a honeycomb of contiguous lands, that solution translates into some kind of partition plan (discussed later in this chapter) and therefore does not equal full Palestinian sovereignty.

Water, the second problem crippling a full Israeli withdrawal, is an even more intractable factor and is considered by some analysts to be the deal breaker. Water is scarce throughout most of the Middle East; competition for riverine and watershed control entails regular international negotiation and triggers occasional clashes. Israel uses much higher amounts per capita than its neighbors, both to sustain the Western lifestyle demanded by its population (unlimited showers, pools, green lawns) and for its famous agriculture ("making the desert green"). This urgent need for water is not simply material. Israel's very raison d'être is the "ingathering of the exiles": Israel is supposed to comprise the true homeland of the Jewish people. Its legitimacy in that role therefore has always relied on its ability to attract and retain Jewish citizens in residence (which has resulted in very elaborate and well-funded state mechanisms and WZO global outreach for orchestrating *aliyah*—the immigration, or "ascension," of world Jewry to Israel). More pragmatically, given Israel's democratic system, secure Jewish dominion over the state requires maintaining a Jewish majority. But Western-oriented Jewish citizens would be much less likely to come to or stay in a country lacking basic Western comforts or presenting a landscape rolling back to the dustier conditions of more sustainable seasonal agriculture. Not only could any serious decrease in the already inadequate water supply cause serious trouble to Israeli agriculture and city management, but it could trigger a stream of Jewish emigration back to Western Europe and the United States.

For all these reasons, the West Bank aquifers are indispensable to Israel. Much of Israel's freshwater comes from the Sea of Galilee (also called Lake Tiberius or Lake Kinneret), which is fed largely by watersheds draining from southern Lebanon and the Golan Heights. A coastal aquifer has also been important. But a good third of Israel's supply comes from the rain-fed West Bank aquifers (see map 10): the western Yarkon-Tanninim Aquifer provides some 340 million cubic meters annually to the Tel Aviv, Jerusalem, and Beer Sheba districts; the Nablus-Gilboa Aquifer in the northern West Bank supplies Israeli agriculture in the Galilee with some 115 million cubic meters annually. The highland West Bank aquifers are even more essential to Israel because overuse has dangerously lowered the water tables elsewhere. The coastal aquifer is seriously depleted, drawing seawater into the system. In Gaza, where wells are pumping at twice the replacement rate, salination is rendering the water undrinkable. The Sea of Galilee is now at its lowest level in recorded history, also risking salination. The Jordan River, which feeds from it, is reduced to a trickle, contributing to a precipitous drying of the famous Dead Sea, which has dropped some 260 feet over the past forty years and is officially deemed to be "dying."

Israel has expanded its water sources by developing major recycling systems and elaborate runoff collection systems. But to sustain its water overuse, Israel must also rely on limiting Palestinian use. Compared to the Palestinians, Israelis use some three times as much water per capita and some ten times as much for agriculture. To maintain this consumption, Israel uses some 93 percent of the West Bank aquifers' annual rainwater recharge (Palestinians use the rest). Overtapping has drained the water table, drying up a number of Palestinian village wells. Other Israeli diversions and bans on any new or deeper Palestinian wells have widely damaged Palestinian agriculture; whole villages have lost their orchards with the cutoff of their traditional water sources. Any sovereign Palestinian government in the West Bank would seek to restore these sources and repair that agriculture. But to do so, it would have to bite deeply into Israel's already inadequate quota.[12]

Therefore, for Israel, it is the scarcity of water that most objectively precludes full Palestinian sovereignty in the West Bank. Indeed, more than any other factor, water graphically demonstrates the indivisibility of this delicately balanced, ecologically sensitive territory. Neither side can rely on the other to sacrifice its basic needs for water (however differently each side understands the notion "basic"), and no peace negotiation has made any progress on the topic. No "security fence" can provide water security for Israel either. The most wildly gerrymandered partition cannot do that. Hence, water is also the silent factor driving Israel's full annexation strategy (discussed next) and, ultimately, the one-state solution.

FULL ISRAELI SOVEREIGNTY

Complete annexation of the entire West Bank is the present trajectory of Israeli government policy, despite the Sharon government's lip service about a Palestinian state. That full annexation has been the plan since the 1970s is reflected in adamant statements by Israeli prime ministers from Begin through Sharon, all Israeli peace proposals (including the Oslo Accords), government maps of Eretz Israel that show one country between the Mediterranean and the Jordan River (with no Green Line or any border for the West Bank), doctrines and programs of the Jewish-national state agencies orchestrating the settlement grid, the extension of Israeli civil law into the settlements, and policies of the Israeli civil administration that supervises the military occupation itself. It is also embedded in the thinking not only of the neo-Zionists previously mentioned but of a broad spectrum of Israel's Jewish-Zionist and Christian-Zionist supporters, for whom a synthesis of security concerns, mytho-history, cultural-ethnic-religious mission, and Christian millennialism have gelled as a geographical imaginary that naturalizes the West Bank as an intrinsic part of Eretz Israel and grants its "retention" the moral authority of a fundamental nationalist—or even divine— imperative.

But, Israeli annexation has always confronted the problem of a massive indigenous Palestinian population, and this obstacle has complicated its public rhetoric and internal rationalizations. For its more hard-line proponents, the simplest (and manifestly only) solution is to transfer the Arab population out of the country; in a 2003 survey, 46 percent of Israelis favored this solution.[13] But as countervailing democratic and humanitarian sectors reject such measures as inhumane (or simply as terrible publicity for Israel), mainstream (or public) planners have instead proposed an archipelago of autonomous enclaves surrounding Palestinian towns and village clusters. This model is largely identical to the two-state solution vaguely endorsed by the Sharon government: from his perspective, it is of little significance if a politically debilitated Palestinian sector in noncontiguous territory is called a "state." Nominal Palestinian statehood in the archipelago would indeed resolve some serious long-term political trouble portended by full Israeli annexation (as discussed later).

For the Palestinians, the dire portents of this plan are obvious. The Palestinian population of 1.3 million in the West Bank and eight hundred thousand in East Jerusalem cannot sustain any viable economy or politics in the patchwork of enclaves already delineated by Israel on maps generated in the Oslo negotiations begun in the 1990s (see map 6). Palestinian "autonomy" in such an archipelago would amount to little more than basic town services (garbage collecting, civil registry, limited policing) and limited civil law. Even if rationalized into somewhat larger chunks, as suggested by the route of Israel's "security fence" and Sharon's own map (map 12, proposed in 2001), the noncontiguous territory still could not sustain any integrated strategy toward efficient transportation, electricity and communication grids,

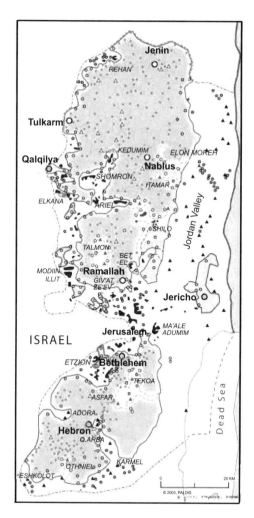

Map 9. Actual and Projected Route of Israel's "Security" Wall in the West Bank. (Reproduced from "Israel's Final Push: The Fence Map is the Road Map" in *The Wall in Palestine: Facts, Testimonies, Analysis, and Call to Action.* © 2003 Palestine Land Development Information System.)

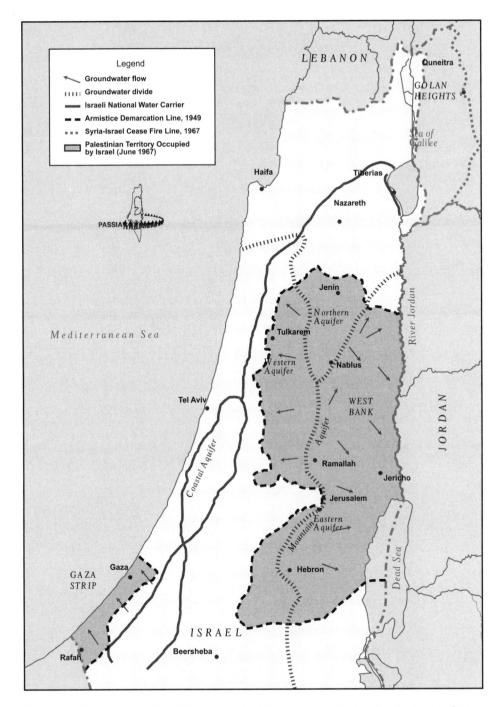

Map 10.   West Bank Aquifers. (Courtesy Palestinian Academic Society for the Study of International Affairs.)

integrated markets, labor mobility, or export-oriented production. Especially, Palestinians could not gain access to the water sources necessary to restoring Palestinian agriculture (as discussed in the preceding section of this chapter) or manage water distribution among villages cut off from each other by Israeli territory. Defense would be entirely impossible and would depend entirely on Israel—the historical enemy.

National cohesion for an "autonomous" Palestinian sector is also rendered impossible in this formula—which, of course, is its point. Road closures, military checkpoints, the "security fence," and other travel obstacles raised by the Israeli military occupation have already ruined the PA's administrative capacity and are fostering serious factional splits. Reifying that fragmentation by establishing permanent ethnic enclaves would ensure continuing Palestinian national dissolution. Moreover, as growing poverty and withering life chances impel emigration of the more educated and professional classes, Palestinian society will gradually be drained of the skilled business and political leadership always essential to nation- and state-building. Soon the West Bank enclaves would replicate the model described earlier regarding the Gaza Strip: the Palestinian people would be left to dwindle into a subordinated ethnoracial subclass, whose poverty and misery can be blamed on the incompetent and nepotistic local Arab authorities certain to be favored by such circumstances.

These outcomes are indeed highly desired by such architects as Sharon, whose whole goal is the destruction of Palestinian national life. For this reason, development assistance to moderate these outcomes, which some suggest and expect, cannot be expected from Israel. Indeed, Sharon himself has compared the Palestinians' future "state" to North American Indian reservations and South African Bantustans, fully aware of their corrosive impact on whole peoples: assisting the Palestinians to flourish in their "Bantustan" is not on his agenda. Instead, Bantustanization is designed to doom the Palestinians to mounting poverty and social disintegration—a fate ensured especially as their confined population is expected to double by 2010.

So clearly disastrous are such conditions for the Palestinian people that it requires a special twist to imagine the Palestinians bringing it on themselves. Still, one common Zionist rejoinder is that the long-exiled Jewish nation so clearly needs the land and has such a clear right to it that the "Arabs" are clearly irrational, obdurate, and bloody-minded in clinging to the biblical highlands—especially when they have "so many other places to go." In this view, the Palestinians carved their own plight by refusing any fair land partition, and their insistence on retaining the land is driven solely by a hatred for Jews and the Jewish state. But Palestinian political thought about the land reduces to anti-Semitism no more than Palestinian nationalism reduces to the leadership of the PLO elite. Chapters 4 and 5 offer short discussions of Palestinian-national ideology and politics, but, again, a broad brush can clarify the immediate constraints here. For, despite all Palestinian political weakness, division, and errors, it is the Palestinian's passionate attachment to the land that most stubbornly cripples the option of one Jewish state.

To make sense of the dynamics at work, any discussion of Palestinian politics today is burdened with some initial recasting of regional history. The trivialization and even erasure of the Palestinians' connection to the land is a major Zionist accomplishment, helped also by Christian biases. Like the Christian narrative, the Zionist narrative knows this land through a metahistory (traced from Abraham through four millennia) that imagines the Hebrew/Jewish experience as the sole consistent thread—even though, for much of that time, Jews were a small minority or even a microminority in a region seized by great events and civilizations centered on other ethnic or cultural identities. Further Zionist obfuscations—that Palestinians did not "exist," arrived as immigrants, and imagined themselves as a nation only to attack Jews—have complicated Westerners' ability to grasp the fundamental Palestinian claim as an indigenous population struggling to repel a far more erudite and well-funded European settler invader.[14]

As a population and culture, the Palestinians today reflect a very complicated history. Palestine sits at the crossroads of Europe, Asia, and Africa; armies, empires, migrations, and trade routes have flowed through the territory for millennia, and its importance to the Abrahamic faiths has made it (unfortunately for its inhabitants) a destination for uncounted pilgrims and crusaders. Empires and kingdoms, including the Jewish kingdoms, have come and gone, each contributing offspring, linguistic shreds, and waves of new architecture. Thirteen centuries of Muslim rule, aside from establishing Islam and the language of Arabic, also consolidated Palestine within the Muslim-Arab civilization, linked through Muslim trade networks to West, Central, and South Asia, under a succession of rulers. Today's Palestinians reflect this *longue durée* in their phenotypical spectrum (which runs the gamut from Irish red to sub-Saharan African black), in the literature and history that frame their cultural references, and in the myriad of local Arabic place-names for rocks, paths, stands of trees, or mountain passes, drawn from ancient legends, traditions, myths, and syncretic oral histories assembled through the millennia.[15]

The Arabic place-names also reflect a very intimate connection between the local people and the land—a connection established through many centuries, in the panoply of villages whose great age and organic blending with the rocky terrain make the Palestinian landscape so lovely to visitors. Like most entrenched agricultural and pastoral cultures, Palestinian village life is culturally and spiritually interlaced with the landscape to the point of perceived fusion. The land is the mother, the source of life; a local field, orchard, spring, or hill is perceived by the family who works and lives near it as being imbued with a living character; olive trees are famously cared for as children or friends. This worldview is often poorly appreciated by Westerners, for whom land has become a mere commodity—especially as the Arabic place-names that suggested it were systematically expunged by Zionist mapmakers in the 1920s and 1930s. It is much better appreciated by Arabs and other societies closer (in memory at least) to a pastoral cultural base. This syncretic pastoral Muslim-Arab culture was deeply embedded in Palestine when Zionist settlements began to buy up land in the 1880s.

Pastoral and agricultural peasant life does not, of course, define Palestinian society. In the nineteenth century, Jerusalem was a major Ottoman administrative center, and expanding agricultural exports were enriching a rising merchant class centered also in the port cities of Jaffa and Haifa. Palestinian society was indeed deeply class-stratified and was fragmented between its urban and peasant sectors, although such divisions were crosscut by clan relations and patronage politics centered on dynastic notable families. (In a famous example, absentee landlords in the early twentieth century sold major tracts of land to Zionists, displacing thousands of peasants.) By the early twentieth century, the new Palestinian-nationalist movement was led by the usual convocation of urban merchants, educators, journalists, and professionals, who sought to deflect European colonial ambitions and build a more classically bourgeois-national independent state (much as Latin American nationalists had done a century earlier). But the movement was also a mass phenomenon, in which the peasantry mobilized to resist Zionist land expropriations. As the Palestinian-national effort coalesced in midcentury in pitched confrontation with the vastly better-organized Zionist movement, its proponents in villages and towns had to bridge their social gulfs to achieve vital national unity. Mass Palestinian flight in 1948 especially fused peasant and urban experiences of exile and loss. Hence, the pastoral mystique of land that filtered into Palestinian bourgeois-nationalist thought helped to compose, with unusual power, a coherent territorial frame and nostalgia for modern Palestinian-nationalist identity. In this trajectory, Palestinian nationalism is the mirror image of Zionism: Zionism used a nation-building ideology to settle the land; Palestinian settlement in the land generated a nation-building ideology.[16]

It is therefore not merely symbolic or co-optive that Palestinian-nationalist iconography incorporates folklore (embroidery, dress, dance, music) drawn from Palestinian village life: agriculture is the society's economic base and nostalgic origin, rooting the national project and imaginary in the orange and olive groves and in the ancient terraces and wells that sustain them. Nor is it simply Muslim religious fixation that focuses so intently on Jerusalem, historically the administrative, economic, and political, as well as spiritual, center of the region. The fabric of meanings that today comprises Palestinian-Arab culture and nationalist thought builds from a cultural and political matrix of villages and cities that rotates around Jerusalem. The Palestinian society (and cultivation) still in place in the West

Bank highlands is therefore collectively experienced and conceptualized by Palestinians as the last breath of genuine Palestinian social and
national existence. Holding that territory together and sustaining its
Jerusalem nexus are understood as the essential (and imperiled) conditions for Palestinian cultural and national survival. This identification with land cannot be unilaterally reconfigured by any PLO or
PA elite, whatever pressures are applied by an uncomprehending U.S.
interlocutor. Hence, one of Arafat's negotiators at the Camp David
summit in 2000 gave a notoriously unhelpful (and classically Arab)
response to President Clinton's demand that he produce some coun-
terproposal for territorial division: "How can I cut off my hand?"

Like the Jewish settlement grid, therefore, Palestinian society is
anchored in the land by economic, demographic, sociological, and
ideological weight. Palestinian (and pan-Arab) hostility toward Zionism was inspired by Zionism's effort to rupture this intimate relationship to the land, first by purchasing large tracts from absentee landlords and expelling thousands of Arab cultivators in the name of
"Jewish labor" and later by conquest and mass expulsions (in 1948
and 1967). From family experience, Palestinians have always known
what the "new historians" have recently confirmed: these expulsions—some 750,000 people in 1948 (with five hundred Arab villages
within Israel razed to prevent their return) and another 400,000 people in 1967—were deliberate campaigns by Israeli leaderships to
"cleanse" the land (Ben-Gurion's term) of the Arab presence.[17]

The settlements are perceived by Palestinians as continuations of
Israel's "cleansing" policy. Every addition of a housing unit to a Jewish settlement is seen as seizing incrementally, by force, another frag-
ment of the last material foundation for Palestinian culture and
national life. Horribly, this crawling expropriation also converts otherwise innocent Jewish families, including those just looking for a
good life and perhaps some spiritual fulfillment, into geostrategic
instruments of conquest—human missiles of Palestinian national
destruction. Hence, Palestinians who attack civilian settlers do so on
the understanding that civilians are not precisely "civilians" in this
case: growing Jewish settlement is here seen as a strategic aggressive
act—a perception confirmed by the settlers' weaponry, by the army's

enforcement of laws that expropriate Palestinian land, and by government support for religious-nationalist claims of supreme Jewish rights to the land. The terrible Palestinian suicide bombings, inexcusable in their destruction of innocents, reflect this confusion: in this conflict, implanting ordinary daily Jewish life in the land is the state's political instrument for establishing and naturalizing Jewish dominion over the land.

In light of Palestinian attachment to the land, the risks for Israel in annexing the West Bank with some Palestinian enclave embedded in its midst are obvious. The progressive ravaging of the Palestinians' landscape, loss of their economic subsistence, and generally decaying conditions for Palestinian national survival will result neither in Palestinians' passive acquiescence to national demise nor in their sullen mass exit from the territory. Desperation, despair, and hatred for the force that so unrelentingly wrecks their society will instead trigger more suicide bombers and other desperate acts. Officially, Israel's infamous Wall is intended to contain precisely that looming danger, by sealing off what is left of Palestinian society within a walled Bantustan or reservation. That plan might seem ill-conceived, for the Wall's long-term capacity to thwart all creative efforts by Palestinian terrorists to get around, over, or under it is dubious. Certainly, the plan would require Israel to station soldiers permanently in the guard towers built every few hundred meters along the Wall's colossal bulk.

The Wall will better contain a more serious "risk" arising from the enclave plan. Even under stifling conditions, Palestinian society will not evaporate within its Bantustan; it will remain rooted in its nonviable territory. The vast majority of Palestinians are indeed not militants but simply people trying to feed families and maintain homes, whose core resistance strategy has always been simply to hunker down, get by, and retain what they can. Moreover, in crushing Palestinian agriculture, industry, and services, Israeli occupation policy long ago established patterns of ethnic interdependence by forcing hundreds of thousands of Palestinians from the West Bank and the Gaza Strip to seek day labor in the Israeli economic sector (including in settlement construction). This employment has plummeted in recent years with Israeli security and trade barriers (Israel has actually imported some foreign labor to replace Palestinian labor).[18] But with full Israeli annexation and without a physical barrier dividing them, Israeli settlements and Palestinian enclaves would be juxtaposed in such close quarters that these long-established labor patterns would insert hundreds of thousands of Palestinian workers regularly into Jewish settlements and into Israel itself, and ethnic intermixture would greatly increase. Within a decade or two, juridical separation would become socially meaningless, and Israel would have some 2.5 million Palestinians filtering into its political body—and its gene pool.

In this event, Israel would face a political crisis. Two million disenfranchised (mostly poor) Palestinians embedded in Israeli society would ruin any lingering pretense Israel might make to being a true democracy, and the disenfranchised Palestinian population would be unlikely to tolerate its own exclusion forever. As its own national base disintegrated, it would agitate for political representation, challenging Israeli democracy on its own principles. If the Palestinians did eventually gain the vote, they would combine with 1.5 million Israeli Arabs to compose an ethnic majority—wrecking the Jewishness of the Jewish state. Whether or not they would then impose an authoritarian regime and take revenge on the Jews (a nightmare prediction commonly made by Zionists), that majority would certainly not support the Jewish-national domination of state resources, such as land, loans, and other privileges that today are selectively steered to Jewish citizens alone. The Jewish *state*—at least, in its present form—would cease to be (a prospect discussed in chap. 6). Primarily to avert this future, increasing numbers of Jewish Israelis support withdrawing from the settlements and granting Palestinians a state of their own.[19]

Hence, Israel's Wall, ostensibly intended to contain Palestinian attack, primarily guards against the specter of a binational state, the fear of which runs openly in Israeli debates. For instance, in a draft statement, Conservative rabbis meeting in Jerusalem in February 2004 stated frankly that the Wall is "a legitimate tool for self defense" and is also essential to "protect the Jewish and democratic character of the state of Israel."[20] Hence, by calling the Palestinian enclaves a "state," Sharon is protecting the strategy of full annexation: within their own walled ghetto-"state," the Palestinian nation will fester and wither but cannot demand political rights from Israel.

Erecting a barricade resembling the Great Wall of China in order to enclose the "barbarian hordes" (i.e., to ward off Palestinian social integration and miscegenation) promises such trouble, however, that it dooms this plan. The walled-off Palestinian ghetto now in the making generates such ruinous conditions for the Palestinian people that no stable peace can ensue. Facing personal misery and national extinction, the Palestinians will continue to resist, cling to their failing national institutions, publicize their plight, suffer Israeli sanctions, and appeal for help. The Arab world, at least, will continue to see suffering Palestinians on their media and know their situation to be abominable. This "solution" to Israel's demographic-security dilemma must therefore be unacceptable to an international community now desperate to defuse the reactions of Islamic terrorists—who, not entirely unreasonably, see the wretched Palestinian situation as a hallmark of the West's neoimperial callousness and anti-Arab/anti-Muslim bias. Even domestic Israeli politics may not stand the strain: aside from any humanitarian concern about the Palestinians themselves, a walled ghetto is so clearly a bastion of racial defense that liberal-leftist Israeli groups are already appalled by what it signifies for Jewish nationalism and are mobilizing against it. As Palestinian conditions worsen, the spectacle may ultimately tear Israeli politics apart.

In the longer run, such a gruesome apartheid system must fail even to secure its own objectives. Israel's own Arab minority now comprises some 20 percent of the population. Given that minority's higher birthrate, the Jewish state will no longer be comprised of a Jewish majority in forty or fifty years. Barring the horror of the Arab citizens' forced expulsion, this demographic change will require shifts in Israeli public policy to adjust to a more egalitarian, ethnically mixed democratic ethos and legal system. At that point, a walled Arab ghetto in the heart of the country will lose its political sense, while its insult to Israeli democracy will become more intolerable to liberal Israelis themselves. Although Zionism's ethnocentric and exclusivist currents seem now to be gaining ground, its democratic ethos also runs deep and strong. At some point in the future, after much unnecessary suffering by the Palestinian people and security risks to Israel and the world, the Wall's gates will be left open, and Israel will join the ranks of those Western democracies grappling with the usual package of ethnoracial dilemmas—class, political access, hiring biases, affirmative action, and the rest of it.

In summary, full Israeli sovereignty will not work in two senses. Certainly, it will not bring Israel or anyone else a stable peace, and it is likely to make regional security problems much worse in the near future. Over a longer period, neither can it forever preserve Israel as a Jewish state.

SHARED SOVEREIGNTY AND PARTITION

Because full Palestinian sovereignty in the West Bank is blocked by the Jewish settlement grid and Israel's water needs and because full Israeli sovereignty so clearly savages Palestinian political aspirations and faces its own trouble down the road (a binational state), finding some way to share sovereignty within a divided West Bank was the Sisyphean effort of the Oslo Accords process, begun in the 1990s. The supposed mutual goal of the parties was to find some stable arrangement that would allow a partial Israeli territorial withdrawal sufficient to provide for a viable Palestinian state. (The same goal was mouthed in President George W. Bush's pointless "road map for peace" in 2002.) Throughout the Oslo process, both Israel and the PA negotiated on the assumption that a two-state solution, with some gerrymandered division of land in the West Bank, was the only basis for peace.

But Israel's actual agenda did not reflect the spirit of mutual recognition suggested (insubstantially) by Rabin in 1993 and hailed then as earthshaking by a credulous Israeli and international community. Rabin's diplomatic acceptance of a two-state solution indeed represented only a tactical shift in the long-term strategy to consolidate Evetz Israel within all of the territory of Palestine as defined by the British Mandate. The Oslo process was enlisted to that end. It never entailed a freeze on settlement construction, which should have been its first gesture and proof of faith. Nor did any Oslo discussion broach the crucial question of Israeli-state complicity—through the veiled role of the Jewish-national state institutions—in planning and funding the grid. Instead, the Israeli government was free to expand the grid with renewed vigor throughout the decade, while the various Oslo agreements served primarily to co-opt Palestinian assistance in maintaining the necessary security to do so. In this context, when Prime Minister Sharon shocked his right-wing supporters by endorsing a Palestinian "state," it could not have signified the capitulation to Palestinian national aspirations that some might have thought. What, then, did it signify?

The actual purpose of the Oslo process and the character of Israel's present "two-state solution" can be illuminated by reviewing Israel's past diplomatic reversals on the question. Before Israel's independence in 1948, the Zionist movement lobbied Britain and the United Nations hard for a two-state solution, based on the "two peoples in one land" paradigm (eliding the conflict's settler-colonial quality as experienced by the Palestinians, which would have delegitimized partition). Britain and Europe obliged: in the 1940s, various commissions tried, through territorial gerrymandering, to resolve the accelerating dispute between, on the one hand, the Jewish proto-nation, comprised mostly of European immigrants, and, on the other, the much larger, indigenous Palestinian proto-nation. The UN partition plan of 1947 (see map 11), the most famous of these plans, was embraced by the Zionist movement but famously rejected by the Arabs.

Zionists and their sympathizers often cite Arab rejection of the UN plan as evidence of recalcitrant and irrational Arab hostility to a fair solution. But the difference in views is unsurprising: the UN plan granted six hundred thousand Jewish settlers (then 43 percent of the population) dominion over 57 percent of Palestine—including 95 percent of its best agricultural land; half of Galilee, including Lake Tiberias; and the entire central coastal region, including Palestine's two major port cities of Jaffa/Tel Aviv and Haifa (then 61 and 65 percent Arab, respectively). Overall, the proposed Jewish state was still 40 percent Arab and embraced hundreds of Arab villages. The Arabs

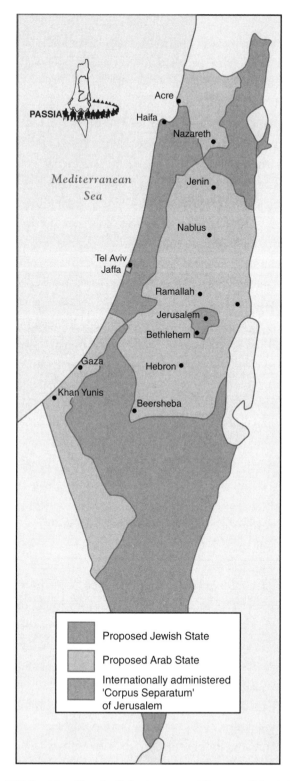

Map 11.   UN Partition Plan for Palestine, 1947. (Courtesy Palestinian
Academic Society for the Study of International Affairs.)

instead declared war. But after six months of fighting, the badly supplied and badly led Arab coalition army faded before better-organized Zionist forces. A secret deal between the Zionist movement and Jordan's King Abdullah also undercut Arab military efforts.[21] A year after the UN partition resolution, the Zionist forces had absorbed half the area of the proposed Arab state, and Israel became independent in 78 percent of Mandate Palestine.

Less well remembered today is the Zionist strategy behind the early seeming spirit of compromise. In the 1930s and 1940s, Zionist debates and major conferences considered the wisdom of endorsing British and UN proposals for partition. Some adamantly rejected the idea, insisting on all the territory. But Israel's founding father, David Ben-Gurion, the leader and architect of Israel's independence push, was among those who argued successfully for its acceptance—as a diplomatic maneuver to gain leverage with the British and UN for later efforts toward Israel's real goal. "Erect a Jewish State at once, even if it is not in the whole land," Ben-Gurion wrote in 1937. He concluded: "The rest will come in the course of time. It must come."[22]

And of course, it did come, in 1967, when Israel seized the rest of Mandate Palestine and promptly consigned the principle of partition to the trash heap of history. Throughout the 1970s and 1980s, both Israeli and PLO political platforms held firmly to one-state solutions—respectively, to a Jewish state and an Arab or Palestinian (secular-democratic) state, each claiming all the territory of Mandate Palestine. But in 1988, facing reality (and losing its leadership role to the first intifada in the territories), the PLO finally accepted a two-state solution, recognizing Israel and endorsing a Palestinian state in the West Bank and the Gaza Strip.[23]

Israel's first response, however, was absolute rejection. Through the 1980s, Israeli leaderships held that a Palestinian state would only comprise a platform for attacking Israel; in any case, they claimed, the Palestinians were mostly immigrants and not a true nation, lacked any legitimate claim to the land, and so did not deserve a state. A prodigious mythical historiography—concocted by Zionist academics specifically to support this claim—had long since embedded in popular Jewish-Zionist consciousness and now came to dominate and bog down all debate (see chap. 5). For Israel's supporters, a Palestinian state was illegitimate and unthinkable; for Palestinians and their supporters, it was the only just solution, and the two-state solution became a banner goal.

But by 1990, Israel's diplomatic position again reversed, for the settlements had expanded to the point where some solution to the Palestinian presence had to be found. One reason was simple security. As Palestinian land and resources dwindled, wedged ever more tightly between settlement roads and blocs, popular Palestinian desperation was cresting and escaping Israel's control. The first intifada, launched in December 1987, generated hundreds of Palestinian deaths, thousands of injuries, tens of thousands of arrests, and a miserable crisis of security and international image for Israel, as well as bitter domestic division. To contain an increasingly unmanageable security situation, Israel now needed more effective Palestinian leadership and, hence, began the Oslo Accords and rapprochement with Arafat, who was brought back into the territory on the condition that his political machine restore control. But the other (more serious) reason was demographic. As settlement construction crawled across the landscape and divided Palestinian society into a patchwork, the dreaded binational state loomed. Suddenly, the two-state solution was *Israel's* need—now that a Palestinian "state" could be formed according to Israel's terms, in debilitating conditions within noncontiguous territory. In 1995, Yitzhak Rabin explained: "We had to choose between the Greater Land of Israel, which means a binational state whose populations would comprise, as of today, 4.5 million Jews and more than 3 million Palestinians . . . and a state smaller in area, but which would be a Jewish state. We chose to be a Jewish state."[24]

This diplomatic shift was not easy. Large segments of Israeli and diaspora Jews were so steeped in the one-state solution that they had to be coaxed into considering that a Palestinian state might actually resolve Israel's difficulties rather than simply install a "terrorist state" on Israel's doorstep. By the late 1990s, however, a few observers were suspecting that the settlement grid had extended too far and began to call for debate on a very different one-state solution—a unified secular-democratic state, and the end of permanent Jewish dominion over its governance. In alarmed reaction, by late 2003, Israeli spokespeople were increasingly adamant that a two-state solution must be the basis for peace. Recognizing the binational threat, many of Israel's supporters now also made the conceptual jump: territorial partition, endorsed and authorized by the international community since the early twentieth century, was again the moral and enlightened solution. It could not be dismissed now, they claimed, only to serve nefarious Arabs who sought to destroy the Jewish state from within. Any just peace must therefore rightly be based on partition—but now only of the West Bank and the Gaza Strip.

The two-state solution has always entailed a myriad of difficulties. UN Resolution 181 of 1947, which presented the previously discussed partition plan and map, was a detailed list of provisions for managing not only security but access to holy places, religious and minority rights, customs and tariffs, shared access to Jerusalem, economic union between the two states, freedom of transit, and so forth. Similarly, the Oslo II Accord (1995) detailed plans for communications, border crossings, trade and finance, mutual access to holy sites, and dispute resolution. Always postponed in these formulas were the problems of water, access to Jerusalem, and the Palestinian right of return. The last concern is especially sensitive because it is basic both to Palestinian politics and international law yet so directly threatens Israel's Jewishness (and raises the specter of later remunerations to Palestinians for lost property in Israel itself, now worth billions of dollars). But all these issues require an agreement about territorial borders. Negotiators in the Oslo process therefore spent years absorbed in microdisputes about exactly where those borders should be drawn. As U.S. President Clinton began to push for an agreement at the Camp David summit in 2000, negotiations generated multiple maps.

The question in the Oslo talks was not whether to evacuate or "dismantle" all the settlements; given the size of some of them and the politics involved, that was deemed out of the question. But flexibility seemed to lie in whether smaller or outlying settlements might be evacuated and whether Israel's annexed areas could be reduced accordingly. Israel's first "final status" proposal, made in May 2000, preserved most of the settlement grid, dividing Palestinian land into

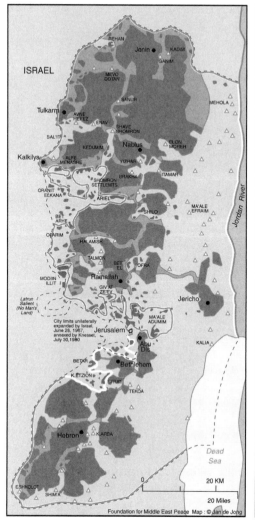

Map 12. Palestinian Sovereign Areas according
to the Barak/Sharon Proposals, 2001. (Courtesy
Foundation for Middle East Peace.)

Map 13. Projection of Final Status Agreement
proposed by Israel, Camp David, May 2000.
(Courtesy Foundation for Middle East Peace.)

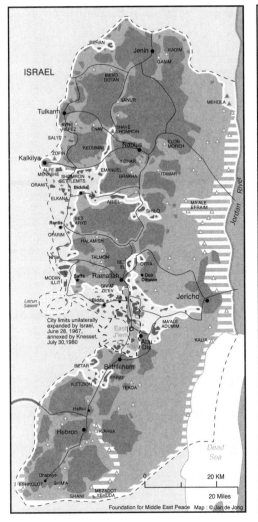

Map 14. Israeli Proposal for Final Status Map, December 2000. (Courtesy Foundation for Middle East Peace.)

Map 15. Taba Agreement, January 2001. (Courtesy Foundation for Middle East Peace.)

four isolated blocs and transferring 25 percent of the West Bank to permanent Israeli sovereignty (see map 13). This plan was rejected as entirely unacceptable by Arafat's team at the Camp David meetings in July, but discussions labored on. In December, a new Israeli proposal sustained roughly the same plan but reduced Israeli land, especially in the central region, so that only 10 percent would be under Israeli sovereignty (see map 14). It still divided Palestinian territory into enclaves, however, and Israel's continuing insistence on control of the Jordan Valley meant that the Palestinian state would be entirely surrounded by Israeli territory and would depend on Israeli prerogative for all access to the outside world. The last map associated with the Oslo process was drawn up at subsequent secret talks between Israeli and Palestinian negotiators, who negotiated intensively for three months in the Sinai city of Taba. Issued in late January 2001, this plan reduced Israeli annexation to 6 percent, confirmed future Palestinian sovereignty over most land along the Green Line, and provided, for the first time, a narrow but solid belt of territorial contiguity between the Palestinian state's northern and central blocs, reconnecting the crucial north-south transportation corridor between the main Palestinian highland cities (see map 15).

To some, the whole Taba compromise seemed an extraordinary breakthrough, and a last wave of optimism passed through leftist-Israeli and Palestinian circles. But this optimism was ill-founded. Israel's proposed territorial accommodation at Taba did greatly exceed previous ones; superficially, a mere 6 percent of West Bank land "transferred" to Israel might seem so close to full Israeli withdrawal as not to matter. That the 6 percent still cut deep troughs through Palestinian territory, sustaining its partition into three enclaves, was the darker fact obscured by this superficially small figure. And of course, the crippling problems of refugees, Jerusalem, and especially water were still unresolved. The role of the Jewish Agency, the WZO, and the JNF in orchestrating the still-expanding settlement grid also remained undiscussed, and their steering authority remained unchecked. The same fatal pitfalls that had plagued previous proposals still lay ahead.[25]

In any case, upon taking power in February 2001, the Sharon government promptly rejected—and even retroactively erased—the Taba agreement. Indeed, in order to blame the collapse of the Oslo process entirely on Arafat (who rejected Israel's first proposal at the July 2000 Camp David talks), Sharon's government has pretended—mostly successfully—that the later six months of talks never took place. A few critics have dug behind the story of Arafat's rejection and blamed Barak's government for presenting impossible conditions at Camp David and Sharon's government for jettisoning a process that actually seemed to be going somewhere.[26] But Sharon's consignment of the Taba agreement to oblivion as clearly signals a different reality: that an increasingly lame-duck process, pursued by liberal and pragmatic Israelis and newly enthusiastic Palestinian professionals working in rare isolation at Taba, generated a plan that was unworkable for real-life Israeli politics and would never have flown. In other words, it failed and was forgotten because it was never politically viable in the first place.

In the end, the entire Oslo decade amounted only to more "facts on the ground": the Jewish settler population had doubled to 230,000 strong. By 2003, the Oslo process consisted only of postmortems. With the Bush regime supporting Israel even more unilaterally than usual, the power balance was so clearly on Israel's side that in the fall of 2003, Sharon simply announced a policy of "unilateral disengage-ment"—a "permanent status" on Israel's terms. Withdrawal from the Gaza Strip was part of that status. But as Israel's astonishing Wall snaked among settlements and villages in the West Bank countryside, its route quickly indicated that "unilateral disengagement" in the West Bank meant full Israeli sovereignty, with angry natives confined to a walled enclave—to which "statehood" would be conceded as insurance against the Palestinians' eventual ethnic miscegenation into the Jewish state and to which the millions of Palestinians in diaspora could not conceivably return. The Wall's route indeed reflects plans that Sharon has nursed since the 1970s. Its exact course is not set, having changed several times—as far-flung settlements insisted on inclusion and, occasionally, as rare international objection to the more glaring ruin of Palestinian lands and property suggested a minor tactical adjustment.[27] But it is already a unique construction. Not since the Cold War has the world seen so massive a barricade, and never has the modern world seen such a breathtaking monument to ethnoracial defense.

FACING A DIFFERENT FUTURE

Sharon's two-state solution—anchored by the Wall and by "facts on the ground" that he himself has worked a lifetime to help build—is meant to remove the Palestinian problem forever from Israel's landscape and national soul. Here, as everywhere in the world, a calculated program of civilian population transfer has had its uniquely powerful political effect: de facto presence has led inexorably to de jure possession of the entire territory. Israel's new sovereign border only waits to be recognized by a world community that lacks all conviction.

Yet the two-state formula is already unworkable. If Israeli governments had yielded twenty years ago to creation of a Palestinian state in the West Bank and the Gaza Strip, the Jewish state might have been stabilized—for a few more decades. But now the Palestinian population is too large and politicized, and the land remaining to Palestinian national culture is too fragmented and claustrophobic, to sustain the two-state solution as Israeli policy has framed it. Bounded by the wall in such grotesque fashion, the crippled Palestinian "state" will foster bitter Palestinian resistance, endangering not only Israel but also—as pan-Arab and Muslim outrage transduces into expanding global terror networks—the entire international community. If the Palestinian state were not so bounded, ethnic intercourse (of every kind) in so gerrymandered a territory would ensure a binational state within decades. Ironically, Sharon's lifelong mission to consolidate "Greater Israel" has only hastened the one-state solution he utterly rejects, by seizing Palestinian land to the point where their encasement and his own plan are equally unviable.

But the preceding portrait grants too much influence to Sharon and his ilk. Ultimately, Israel-Palestine itself was always far too small and sensitive a region to sustain two states. The Jewish state now faces the last act of its own Greek tragedy—the Zionist project to reconstitute a Jewish nation-state in an ancient land already holding an indigenous national society. Still too democratic in character to tolerate expelling the Palestinians en masse a third time, yet too ethnocentric to absorb them, Israel wavers on the knife edge of its own self-identity, as a putatively civil democracy formally premised on ethnic hierarchy, a "light unto nations" that relied for its formation— and still relies for its preservation—on ethnic cleansing. For the Jewish state is inherently unstable as long as non-Jews live within it; only by ethnic cleansing in each succeeding generation can it ensure continuing Jewish dominion. Neither the Wall nor a crippled Palestinian state will permit that formula to endure. Israel will only suffer needlessly, politically and physically, from the apartheid formula it has invented in its own unenlightened self-interest—until, inevitably, someday Jews cease to be a majority.

Hence, the one-state solution is not an option to be argued. It is an inevitability to be faced.

4. Lacking
   All
   Conviction
The Key External Actors

Israel's annexation of the West Bank has an inexorable momentum. In the policy and practice of the Jewish-national institutions, Israel has indeed already annexed both East Jerusalem and the West Bank, holding the biblical territory (and its water) in an unshakable grip. And yet, as chapter 3 repeatedly indicated, one necessary condition has always enabled Israel's latitude in pursuing this track: no external pressure. That condition requires explanation, for the Israeli-Palestinian conflict has never lacked anxious international efforts to resolve it.

Indeed, no other international conflict has received so much international attention. The UN Security Council passed over two hundred resolutions on related issues between 1948 and 2003 (more resolutions than have been passed on any other topic), and no year in the past four decades has lacked some version of the "Middle East peace process."[1] Causes for this concern are myriad. On a purely pragmatic level, the conflict fatally undermines economic development in the region, by crippling cooperation on every regional concern: trade, oil pipelines, water management, labor migration, and, not least, the general investment climate. Moreover, in both Europe and the Arab world, no one has failed to grasp that the Israeli-Palestinian conflict is the principal issue "poisoning" East-West relations: it has aggravated anti-Western sentiment, fed into pan-Arab nationalism, fueled Cold War polarizations, radicalized popular opposition, and fostered grass-roots resistance movements—which are now spinning into terrorist networks of frightening capacity.[2] It has also translated into a succession of open wars and other crises (e.g., Israel's invasion of Lebanon in 1982) that have rippled out globally to inspire Islamic and other kinds of regional radicalism. All parties share a burning need to lay it to rest.

But decades of peace talks, declarations, envoys, mediators, plans, and summits have failed to resolve the conflict. Why has international involvement remained so unproductive?

Since World War II, international collective security has supposedly been guarded by the United Nations and especially by the Security Council. But in practice, the international system still relies on great-power politics, as the Security Council's own design indicates (with five major powers holding permanent seats and veto authority). Altering the political equation in the Middle East has therefore always required some determined great power actor to lead and leverage serious collective action. By universal consensus, that actor has always been the United States, the principal Western power in the Middle East since World War II. Hence, international diplomacy has counted on U.S. leadership to steer the "Middle East peace process,"and each U.S. president since Eisenhower has eventually "engaged" with the conflict, sent emissaries, and launched some new round of multilateral negotiations, under one label or another.

Given Israel's dependency on U.S. aid and patronage, it would seem that U.S. efforts should have generated some return. Although Israel is far from a client state (its initiatives sometimes inspire tail-wagging-the-dog analogies), Israeli policy has indeed changed promptly on the rare occasions that serious U.S. pressure has been deployed—for example, when Eisenhower rejected Israel's 1956 occupation of the Sinai Peninsula and when the administration of the first President Bush insisted that Israel freeze settlement construction. The puzzle, then, is why the United States has been so feckless and unproductive in resolving a conflict that so seriously impacts its own interests.

But that puzzle itself assumes a myth—that the U.S. government has the political will or even the capacity to arbitrate fairly (a fantasy impressive for its durability in the face of overwhelming contradictory evidence). Fully grasping the inevitability of a one-state solution requires understanding why, under current conditions, no U.S. president (of either party) can or will even try to force the withdrawal of settlements necessary for a stable two-state solution. It also requires grasping why, absent a major international emergency, no one else can bring the United States to do so. Certainly none of the Arab states, either singly or collectively, can have any serious impact on U.S. accommodation of Israeli government policy. The Palestinians cannot have such impact either, even through any foreseeable change of leadership. The only wild card so far overlooked in the international game is Europe. Whether the European Union can coordinate with some new constellation of international actors to meet the coming crisis with a more effective policy toward Israel and can alter the international political climate sufficiently to change the all-important U.S. role are the burning questions of our time.

THE GEOSTRATEGIC "SPECIAL RELATIONSHIP"

U.S. support for Israel is a venerable tradition, taking its early impetus from the Truman administration, which cooperated with Zionist lobbyists on the postwar dilemma of settling Jewish refugees and recognized Israel within minutes of its declaration of independence. The alliance with Israel gained force over succeeding administrations, especially in the hands of Henry Kissinger (secretary of state under the Nixon administration), who, in his largely autonomous shuttle diplomacy, adopted Israel's security within its post-1967 borders as a pillar for U.S. regional peacemaking. Even by the 1970s, the U.S. connection to Israel was described by U.S. politicians as a "special relationship." In the 1980s, under President Reagan, that relationship blossomed into a full-fledged strategic alliance, targeting communism and the Soviet "evil empire." By the 1990s, it was politically sacrosanct, the given condition from which all other policy must build. After the millennium, under the administration of George W. Bush, the "special relationship" reached its apex: Israeli foreign policy itself was fully internalized as U.S. policy, in ways even dangerous to U.S. interests (as discussed later in this chapter).

Throughout all these decades, friendship to Israel was defended by U.S. governments in moral terms: as fulfilling a historical obligation to protect the Jewish people, standing by a "Western" partner struggling for survival in a hostile Muslim "Orient," and supporting "the only democracy in the Middle East." Although sometimes deployed cynically, these moral arguments carried genuine importance for many policymakers in the U.S. government—some (e.g., Kissinger) because they were active Zionists themselves, others for general ethical reasons, reflecting their adoption of the Zionist argument that Israel was the Jewish national home and the crucial bastion defending Jews from anti-Semitism. These ideas became especially forceful in the U.S. Congress, whose understanding of the Israeli-Palestinian conflict by the 1980s was steered almost exclusively by the powerful Zionist lobbying of the American-Israeli Political Action Committee (AIPAC, discussed later in this chapter).

But the U.S. "special relationship" with Israel was not welded solely—or, in its early decades, even mostly—by morality or idealism; it always took its pragmatic force from colder geostrategic logics. Narratives of Jewish tragedy and survival fleshed out and rationalized U.S. support through the years, but to gain full U.S. commitment, those arguments were necessarily congruent with U.S. security interests as interpreted by harder-nosed foreign-policy architects, such as George Shultz, Zbigniew Brzezinski, and James Baker.[3] That interpretation has sometimes been challenged, for U.S. security has demonstrably suffered for its posture of unilateral support for Israel. Still, for those who view international affairs through a realist lens (or as a kind of power game among state governments),[4] the close U.S. alliance with Israel makes full sense.

The reasons supporting the alliance are clear. Most obviously, Israel is a pro-Western, "first world" state in an ideal geostrategic position for monitoring politics in the world's prime oil fields. One dimension of this role is sheer military power (as used in 1981 when Israel bombed Iraq's new nuclear reactor), but more subtle influence is even more important. With possibly the best intelligence services in the world, Israel can track Arab and Muslim politics with insight that the U.S. Foreign Service and Central Intelligence Agency (CIA) have always conspicuously lacked. Enjoying this key advantage, Israel has certainly pursued its own interests in the Middle East in ways sometimes damaging to U.S. interests, but its larger foreign-policy orientation has always been firmly in the U.S. camp. During the Cold War, for example, Israel's much-vaunted claim to be "the only democracy in the Middle East" was less a normative than a geostrategic formula, deployed to the Reagan administration by AIPAC publicists who argued that, as a democracy, Israel was the only reliable ally countering Soviet ambitions in the region.

Ironically, since the Cold War ended, Israel's strategic value has been reconfigured in U.S. policy as a committed ally in the "war on terrorism." Occluded in this familial claim is the fact that Israeli policy itself has greatly fostered Islamic terrorism. For example, Hezbollah, in southern Lebanon (now commonly cited by Israeli and pro-Zionist analysts in the United States as possibly the most dangerous terrorist group in the world), sprang directly from Israel's ravaging occupation of southern Lebanon from 1982 to 2000.[5] Similarly, al-Qaida takes one of its primary justifications for attacking U.S. targets from tacit U.S. support for Israel's occupation of Jerusalem and Palestinian land. Since the attacks on the World Trade Center in New York on 11 September 2001, however, the common threat of Islamic terror facing both countries, although itself partly born of the U.S.-Israeli alliance, is cementing that alliance rather than corroding it. In this new "war on terrorism," Israel's brilliant intelligence services and geographic access seem to provide even more invaluable assets to lagging U.S. skills and experience.

The U.S. alliance with Israel is also sometimes criticized for its sheer cost, but these complaints miss important dimensions of the U.S. aid involved. Less of the military aid rebounds to U.S. military industry than is suggested on paper, but the usual strategic benefits nevertheless accrue. As everywhere, shared military technology solidifies Israel's strategic cooperation with the United States by ensuring ongoing contact and information sharing.[6] Moreover, some of the U.S. aid apparently conveyed to Israel is actually funneled elsewhere, in the form of arms sales, advising, and training to friendly regimes in developing regions. Israel is particularly valuable to the United States in this surrogate role, partly because its sophisticated intelligence and banking institutions make such transfers efficient and reliable, but especially because it is not commonly seen in the developing world as an imperialist agent. The intelligence-gathering facilitated also by Israel's international development aid programs, coupled with its unmatched high-tech expertise in surveillance, has greatly assisted the United States on such foreign-policy goals as subverting the Nicaraguan Sandinista revolution and the Guatemalan leftist-guerrilla movements in the 1980s.[7] Hence, the United States has many reasons to consider its relationship with Israel "special" and to prioritize this alliance over any other.

Difficulties with the alliance have always been apparent, however, leading Middle East experts in the State Department and top private think tanks to urge U.S. presidents to resolve the Israeli-Arab conflict as a matter of urgency. Most obviously, U.S. efforts to stabilize its hegemony in the oil-rich region have been repeatedly damaged by crises involving Israel: especially Israel's 1956 attack (with Britain and France) on Egypt, in which Israel seized all of Egypt's Sinai Peninsula for nearly a year; the 1967 Six-Day War, in which Israel seized Syria's Golan Heights, the Jordanian-controlled West Bank, the Gaza Strip, and, again, the Sinai (see map 16); and the 1973 Yom Kippur War, a surprise attack on Israel by Egypt and Syria to regain those territories, which initially rocked Israel and required emergency U.S. military assistance. Spin-off effects from these conflicts were possibly worse for U.S. interests: the 1967 war, for example, revitalized the PLO under Arafat's more militant leadership and radicalized leftist Palestinian factions toward a series of frightening international terrorist attacks (e.g., the Munich Olympics massacre in 1972, the Achille Lauro affair in 1985, and the Pan Am airline hijacking in 1986). Responding to U.S. military assistance to Israel in 1973, the Arab members of OPEC (the Organization of Petroleum Exporting Countries) orchestrated a brief punitive oil embargo that triggered the first "oil shock" and sent the world economy into a tailspin.

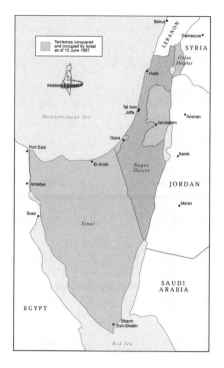

Map 16. Territories occupied by Israel after the 1967 War. (Courtesy Palestinian Academic Society for the Study of International Affairs.)

The conflict that blew back on the United States most directly was Israel's 1982 invasion of Lebanon to crush the PLO, which generated hundreds of thousands of internal Lebanese refugees, some ten thousand Lebanese casualties, and ultimately the ruin of the Lebanese capital, Beirut—then one of the Middle East's finest cities. Lebanon's anarchic misery backlashed directly on the United States in 1983, when a Shi'ite Lebanese suicide bomber killed 241 U.S. Marines based near Beirut. Initially welcomed by the southern Shi'a for ridding them of PLO abuses, Israel's subsequent occupation of southern Lebanon until 2000 entailed so much local brutality—razed homes, arbitrary arrests, torture—that it created, from what had been a tiny fringe group, the Shi'a guerrilla movement Hezbollah. Although never directly relevant to U.S. security, Hezbollah would become an important node in transnational Islamic militancy, linking to the terrorist efforts threatening U.S. interests everywhere.

Indeed, every major international conflict in the Middle East for the last half century—except the Iraq-Iran war in the 1980s, Saddam Hussein's subsequent invasion of Kuwait in 1990, and the U.S. wars on Iraq in 1991 and 2003—has involved Israel. Keeping Israel out of conflicts has also been a U.S. task (e.g., in the First Gulf War, excluding Israel became a concerted project for the United States, to enable the Arab alliance against Iraq). U.S. support for Israel through all these upheavals has brought serious costs: alienating Arab governments, forcing them, at least, to posture their objections to placate angry domestic constituencies; conveying extra political capital to openly anti-U.S. stands by Syrian, Iraqi, Libyan, and Iranian regimes; granting the Soviet alliance extra allure during the Cold War; and generally impeding consolidation of the *Pax Americana* so longed for by American and European oil companies.

Still, through the 1980s, all this trouble from the "special relationship" with Israel was calculated by U.S. foreign-policy strategists as more than compensated by its geostrategic advantages. In fact, U.S. hegemony largely held sway in the region. The vast majority of Arabs and Muslims, although clear about U.S. oil interests and its Israeli alliance, remained receptive to U.S. influence—and even welcomed it—on the belief that U.S. hegemony might bring them more development, democracy, and freedoms. Arab regimes waved the Palestinian flag periodically to legitimize themselves, but most of them secretly or openly collaborated with U.S. interests. The Arab League occasionally issued communiqués of outrage about Palestinian dispossession and suffering in refugee camps, but in direct action, it managed only a trade boycott (progressively weakened by cheating). Palestinian terror attacks manifested only as ugly stings by extremists, which seemed to call only for yet closer coordination between U.S. and Israeli intelligence. Even by the early 1990s, "a few stirred-up Muslims"[8] did not seem to merit serious U.S. concern when compared to the mighty missions assisted by Israel, such as containing Soviet influence in the region and, ultimately, reducing the Soviet Union to political rubble.

The fatal flaw of the United States' purblind vision was demonstrated in 2001, when the contribution of the Palestinian problem to radicalizing Islamic movements was given terrible expression in al-

Qaida's devastating attack on U.S. soil. Certainly, that attack did not arise solely from the Israeli-Palestinian conflict. A confluence of U.S. errors had fostered the disaster, particularly U.S. support for Muslim-guerrilla resistance to the Soviet occupation of Afghanistan and for the madrassas, or Islamic religious schools, fostered originally by the U.S. (with Saudi help) as crucibles for anti-Soviet Islamic indoctrination.[9] But with the Soviet defeat in 1989, Osama bin Laden shifted to target the United States itself, for he saw U.S. hegemony as equally dangerous to Muslim values. Three specific U.S. crimes especially were cited in his pronouncements: U.S.-led sanctions on Iraq, which were causing terrible human suffering (especially malnutrition, poor medical care, and consequent deaths of a half-million children); U.S. military presence on Islamic holy land in Saudi Arabia, especially after the First Gulf War; and the Palestinian problem. Of the three, the first was most universally scandalous at the time. But the last was best understood and most broadly detested among the Arab and Muslim worlds as a whole.

The Palestinian problem had indeed remained a burning grievance and symbol in Arab popular consciousness since the original Palestinian *nakba* (catastrophe), in 1948. Over the decades, PLO corruption and abuses dampened regional Arab support for the Palestinian cause, and high-handed PLO actions in Jordan and Lebanon alienated both local populations and their governments. But the first intifada, in 1987, restored the Palestinians (in Arab popular perception) as icons of righteous resistance to Israeli oppression. The second intifada, which erupted in 2000 (triggered by Ariel Sharon's incursion with hundreds of riot policemen onto the Temple Mount), was fully televised.[10] Arab populations are not insulated by Israeli censorship (as are U.S. viewers) from video coverage of Israeli army violence in the territories, and scandalizing scenes of shootings, beatings, and house demolitions appeared nightly on Arab news media. For the religious, footage of Israeli teargas and bullets targeting protesting Muslims in Jerusalem, on or around the Haram al-Sharif ("Noble Sanctuary," or Temple Mount), also manifested as a sacrilege.

For millions of Arabs and Muslims who would otherwise have remained skeptical, these images added fresh legitimacy to al-Qaida's anti-Western propaganda. The festering Palestinian situation was now contributing heavily to a problem that had not previously existed for the United States—a transnational Islamic terrorist threat enjoying a geographically vast and sympathetic mass base, congealing ideologically around the Palestinian problem as a central symbol of Western imperialism. This threat was uncontainable by the military *über*-technology on which U.S. hegemony has come to rely.

Hence, in many ways, the "special relationship" with Israel could be argued to be damaging U.S. hegemony in a region that might otherwise slip tidily into the U.S. pocket. A purely realist lens might therefore suggest that U.S. interests could be much better served by a more balanced policy—for example, orchestrating the viable two-state solution so anxiously sought by Arab states and the international community. In 2003–4, as al-Qaida metastasized into a splintered array of global threats and as Palestinian politics radicalized toward Islamic extremism under increasing Israeli pressure, sheer self-preservation might have been expected to inspire the United States to launch much more serious efforts toward that end.

Apparently for these very reasons, the administration of George W. Bush formally endorsed a Palestinian state in June 2002, lauding the stable peace to be generated by "two states, living side by side, in peace and security."[11] Presidential language endorsing Palestinian statehood was unprecedented in U.S. diplomacy, and Arab and European governments joined the new round of meetings, in anxious hope that the initiative would indeed provide for the Palestinian self-determination long considered the *sine qua non* of a stable peace. But the U.S. shift was illusory. The Bush plan did note perfunctorily that "settlement activity in the occupied territories must stop" (citing recommendations from a 2001 report by U.S. Senator George Mitchell)[12] but called for no substantive withdrawal of the settlements themselves, mentioning vaguely only Israel's withdrawal to "secure and recognized borders." Any substantive Israeli action was indeed still predicated on the Palestinian government's successful termination of all terror attacks and violence. Worse, the Bush plan indicated that the "provisional state of Palestine" must consolidate security for Israel—and Egypt and Jordan—*before* the vital questions of its own borders and capital would be negotiated: "The final borders, the capital and other aspects of this state's sovereignty will be negotiated between the parties as part of a final settlement."[13]

Far from adopting a more pragmatic approach to the Middle East crisis, the Bush administration was throwing its weight behind Israel's Bantustan policy—and enlisting the Palestinians themselves to realize it. Given its futility (for a Bantustan state could not possibly generate a stable peace), the new plan actually promised further to injure U.S. interests in the region. But U.S. interests were not precisely the plan's concern, as its fatal weaknesses signaled. Instead, the Bush administration had exaggerated the established pro-Israeli bias in U.S. foreign policy beyond all precedence. Understanding the character of that change requires a brief look at the political and ideological dimensions of the "special relationship" between the United States and Israel.

THE POLITICAL "SPECIAL RELATIONSHIP"

Prior to the administration of George W. Bush, through thirty years of uneven involvement in the Middle East, U.S. diplomacy held fast to certain principles: for example, that the settlements were obstacles to peace and that both a territorial agreement and Palestinian return to lands and property in Israel must be negotiated by both partners to the conflict. This diplomatic respect for the Palestinian position, articulated also through U.S. endorsement of UN Security Council Resolutions 242 and 338, enabled the collective myth of "honest broker" that shakily supported the U.S. mediator role. Yet in April 2004, President Bush ditched the UN framework by publicly stamping approval on the "larger" Jewish settlement blocs while unilaterally removing from negotiations the Palestinians' right of return within Israel. The international community was aghast at both the abrupt shift and its timing. The United States, it seemed, had fused its interests with Israel to the point of abandoning the very pillars for diplomacy, just as Arab politics were arching toward dangerous sensitivity. Urgent international interest therefore focused on the coming 2004 U.S. presidential elections, which had the potential to bring in a new president who could restore to U.S. foreign policy some measure of detachment and revive some "peace process" on which the international community could again pin its collective hopes.

Yet the hope vested in a potentially new administration was misguided. A new president might have indeed reconfigured U.S. foreign policy in the Middle East by adopting a more multilateral approach and might perhaps have resurrected from the wreckage of the Iraq occupation some more pacific basis for cooperation among U.S. and Arab governments. But under prevailing political conditions, no Democratic president would have had the political capacity to bring the slightest substantive change regarding U.S. policy toward Israel or Israel's policy toward the Palestinians. The problem was not simply Zionist sympathies or a failure of imagination; U.S. politics precluded such change.

Foreign and even many domestic observers often fail to grasp the character of the pro-Israel bias in U.S. politics, not least because its constructive analysis—or even its mention—is instantly attacked, by a vocal cadre of Zionists, as anti-Semitic. The accusation is clearly invoked instrumentally to protect Israel from criticism, but it cannot be dismissed entirely on those grounds; throughout history, to serve virulently racist agendas, anti-Semites have invented charges of Zionist/Jewish conspiracy, and they sometimes exploit the subject of U.S. policy on Israel to further them. Hence, even Jewish criticism of Israel—which is, in fact, lively—is mostly confined to internal Jewish forums. Criticism is slower to arise in the mostly Christian U.S. polity, because sympathy for Israel has naturalized in U.S. popular culture through a combination of influences. Western-Christian assumptions about the Holy Land, stereotypical images of the "Orient," and principled moral tenets about Judaism and anti-Semitism (matters discussed in more detail in chap. 5) are all in play.

It was no historical accident, however, that these biases assembled to steer U.S. popular views and foreign policy toward unilateral support for Israel. A skilled lobbying effort by a complex of pro-Israel actors has drawn on these biases syncretically to instill a romanticized, Israeli mytho-history into American popular consciousness and cement pro-Israeli views into U.S. political discourse. A quick sketch of that network here, drawn from the few serious studies of it, will illustrate how the pro-Israel camp holds such exclusive influence in U.S. foreign policy regarding the Middle East.[14]

The most obvious political actor is AIPAC (the American-Israeli Political Action Committee, mentioned previously in this chapter), the official lobby group that has brilliantly promoted Israel's interests in the U.S. government since the 1960s. Since the early 1980s, AIPAC has enjoyed almost exclusive influence over congressional attitudes and policy-making regarding Israel and has become by far the most skilled lobbying organization serving a foreign interest (and one of the best in any category). Its leverage is certainly material, although not—as sometimes thought—primarily financial. Though millions of dollars of campaign donations, channeled through direct action campaigns by AIPAC's sixty thousand members, do significantly enhance AIPAC's influence in Congress, AIPAC's leverage derives mostly from its ability to coordinate much larger, well-organized Zionist electorates. For the Democratic Party, this is the traditionally liberal-leftist Jewish vote, long a mainstay constituency. For the Republican Party, it is the traditionally conservative right-wing Christian-Zionist vote, which has become, over the past two decades, a highly organized and crucial electoral bastion (and which, as a populist constituency, was almost exclusively responsible for the Bush victory in the 2000 presidential race).

AIPAC's true influence in Congress has also been gained through genuine persuasion. Given relatively feeble Arab lobbying and particularly incompetent Palestinian lobbying, most U.S. congresspeople glean their understanding of the Middle East primarily or even solely from AIPAC's professional and expertly tooled pamphlets and briefings. (Galloping ignorance of world affairs aggravates this dependency; some 70 percent of U.S. congresspeople do not even hold a U.S. passport, and over 90 percent have never traveled outside the United States. The vast majority of congressional trips to the Middle East have been guided tours of Israel sponsored by the Israeli state.) Hence, AIPAC's financial and electoral incentives are glossed in the Congress by naive but genuine beliefs in a peace-loving Israel, in irrational and anti-Semitic Palestinian terror, in a terrorist and deceitful Palestinian leadership, and in intransigent hostility to Israel among the Arab states.

But AIPAC is only one key voice in an impressive network of pro-Israeli influence built painstakingly over the past decades and that has come to hold substantial influence inside the Beltway, in Washington, D.C., in the 1990s. This network is not, as both its detractors and its defenders claim, precisely a "Jewish lobby"; it represents only select political positions and is indeed most strongly opposed by other Jewish voices. Yet it obtains the impression of a Jewish lobby through its own aggregate claim to represent Jewish interests and through the influence of the Jewish-American organizations that are key to its political clout—for example, the Anti-Defamation League (ADL), the American Jewish Congress, the American Jewish Committee, B'nai B'rith, the Jewish Institute for National Security Affairs (JINSA), and such complementary media "monitors" as the Committee for Accuracy in Middle East Reporting in America (CAMERA). By the end of the 1990s, a more powerful conclave promoting neoconservative and Zionist agendas rose to special political eminence, composed especially of the Washington Institute for Near East Policy (WINEP, founded by a former AIPAC research director), the American Enterprise Institute (where, at this writing, Richard Perle is resident scholar), the Institute for Advanced Strategic and Political Studies (IASPS, whose home office is in Jerusalem), the Center for Security Policy (which claims Perle, Douglas Feith, and Elliott Abrahms among its members), and the Project for a New American Century. When members of these organizations took central posts in George W. Bush's government, their doctrines slipped directly into U.S. foreign policy. They also helped to usher through a packet of complementary domestic initiatives, such as House Resolution 3077, which sought influence over the U.S. intellectual community by making federal funding for university language programs contingent on sympathetic curricula regarding foreign affairs.[15]

These high-octane institutes do not operate solely on high-level hobnobbing. They take their political clout from a very broad constituency, including millions of U.S. Jewish- and Christian-Zionist communities whose wholehearted emotional attachment to Zionism and spiritual investment in Israel are routinely mobilized to support pro-Israeli legislation and political candidates. Much of this network is not overtly political. Such organizations as the United Jewish Appeal and Israel Fund engage well-meaning local people all over the country in sympathetic support of Israel based on highly filtered contact with the Zionist narrative of "return" and "making the desert green." Christian-Zionist groups understand their support for Israel in dreamy millennialist terms, springing from a deeply felt commitment to biblical prophecy. Yet both constituencies have also been steeped in a totalizing package of pro-Israeli and anti-Arab propaganda, so they mobilize readily, on blazing principle, to defend any challenge to Israel or to Zionist versions of Middle East events. For Christian Zionists, this local activism reflects a spiritual commitment to Israel's existence, which portends the end times and the return of Christ. For Jewish Zionists, as one U.S.-Jewish newspaper observed, "rooting out perceived anti-Israel bias in the media has become . . . the most direct and emotional outlet for connecting with the conflict 6,000 miles away."[16]

On a scale that is the envy of lobbying groups everywhere, this pro-Israel constituency carries impressive weight in congressional voting—for example, prompting rapid bipartisan passage of the highly criticized HR 3077. But being nationwide and genuinely grassroots in character, it can also launch direct action in almost any city or local public setting. Jewish-Zionist communities and right-wing Christian associations, such as the television empire of Christian Evangelical Pat Robertson, are regularly recruited to send torrents of negative mail in response to any local news coverage deemed critical of Israel, to participate in blacklists of film stars or academics deemed unfriendly to Israel, or to block—by canceling subscriptions and advertising—the showing of critical film documentaries or the distribution of unfavorable books.[17] Even Jewish- and Christian-Zionist individuals not politically active on a regular basis are still morally primed to use their veto on hiring committees, boards of trustees, and editorial boards of schools, universities, publishing houses, newspapers, and radio and television stations. Local intellectuals regularly contribute to editorial pages of local newspapers, providing the ill-informed American readership with regular infusions of Israeli-Zionist mytho-history and with steady impressions of Arab terror and Israeli innocence.

This network is far from defining domestic U.S. popular views on

Israel, which have become increasingly critical. It does not define Jewish-American views either—which, again, are deeply split. But with Zionist organizations so effectively targeting the media, strikingly little debate on Israel reaches national forums. And because any countervailing voice is notably missing in the Congress, the pro-Israel network wields formidable leverage in steering presidential foreign policy. Regardless of a president's genuine sympathy for Israel or lack of it, the mechanisms are purely political. All U.S. presidents must rely on their party for political efficacy in the position. As already noted, both the Democratic and the Republican Parties have become secured, by their respective electoral constituencies, for pro-Israel policy-making. Hence, by the 1990s, no U.S. presidential candidate could gain a party's endorsement in the first place without confirming ironclad support for Israel or could subsequently take action counter to the Israeli government's interests in any substantive way without losing that party's support. If a president overrode or ignored the party by pursing a genuine peace process, in the greater interest of the nation, both presidential capacity and the party's electoral future might be shattered—a risk no president has been reckless (or high-minded) enough to take.

In theory, a U.S. president's support for Israel might take many principled forms. Liberal and leftist Jews and Jewish Israelis often have quite different desires about U.S. policy, and a U.S. president might well pursue a range of strategies deemed helpful to Israel that run counter to a particular Israeli government's immediate wishes. But as AIPAC lobbies the Congress on behalf of the Israeli government, presidential policy-making has been steered to support the policies of whatever Israeli government is in power (e.g., by quietly tolerating the expansion of Jewish settlements in the West Bank). Even advisors who would argue for a different policy, in the interest of a stable peace, are conspicuously missing from high-level U.S. government positions. Hence, the best-intended U.S. efforts—such as President Clinton's hard work on the Oslo Accords—never seriously challenged Israeli government policy in any way that would trigger AIPAC retaliation (e.g., by cutting the annual U.S. aid package to compel the all-important settlement freeze). As already noted, the administration of the first President Bush did briefly make $10 billion in loan guarantees for Israel contingent on a settlement freeze. But the delay was short, the guarantees were soon extended, and the massive loans (for settling a million supposedly Jewish immigrants from Russia) freed Israeli funds for further settlement construction in the territories.

This understanding of U.S. foreign policy in the Middle East casts the Bush declaration in April 2004 in a different light, as merely the continuation of a long-standing and increasingly uncritical pro-Israeli policy. Bush did jettison long-standing diplomatic positions in openly endorsing Israel's settlement strategy in the West Bank and unilaterally dismissing the Palestinians' possibility of return to Israeli territory. Still, the gesture was more rhetorical than substantive, for even through the Clinton administration, the United States had long supported Israel's settlement policy in all but name. When the diplomatic fig leaf was roughly removed, a scandalized reaction rippled through the international community, as the most basic terms of the "peace process" were unilaterally declared dead letters. But a certain hollowness echoed in the international protest at what amounted to clumsy abandonment of a diplomatic fiction: for the United States had never intended to prevent the Jewish settlements' expansion or force their withdrawal, everyone knew it, and George W. Bush was now simply admitting it.

In one respect, however, the Bush administration did alter the political equation in Israel-Palestine—by taking the "special relationship" with Israel to the point of radically reconceiving the U.S. role in the Middle East. The shift was immediately visible in a newly bellicose U.S. role there, particularly in the invasion of Iraq. But the rationale driving that shift was not immediately obvious to most observers, as it was confused—deliberately—with the "war on terror." Overthrowing Saddam Hussein was initially publicized as necessary to U.S. security, to eliminate Saddam Hussein's weapons of mass destruction and his support for al-Qaida. As both excuses progressively failed, Iraq's occupation was recast as a moral mission to liberate Iraqis from tyranny and to democratize Iraq and, ultimately, the entire Middle East—a grandiose vision appealing to a hearty portion of the naive American electorate (if alarming to a better-informed international community). But sheltered under the U.S.

vice president and secretary of defense was a cadre of advisors who had long planned the invasion on a very different agenda: to reconfigure the Middle East in ways favorable to Israeli security. Put into action, that policy sealed the final doom of the two-state solution by eliminating the last possibility for any meaningful Israeli withdrawal from the West Bank, while greatly increasing regional tensions about the Israeli-Palestinian conflict. It accordingly warrants brief explanation here.

THE "NEOCONS" IN PERSPECTIVE

The actual nature of the neoconservative takeover of the Bush White House was not immediately apparent to most observers. The administration initially appeared merely hawkish—if to an unusually reckless degree. But as the war on Iraq took shape, observers soon realized that a more fundamental shift in policy was afoot. The very structure of U.S. power in the Middle East had altered, as the U.S. role underwent a basic change.

Every president before Bush recognized that although Israel and the United States are fast allies, their interests in the Middle East are very different. Israel is a local contender for regional influence; the United States is a global superpower exerting hegemonic influence over multiple regions and seeking alliances with numerous states. These different roles generate quite different strategic goals for the two states regarding the region as a whole. From the perspective of U.S. pragmatists (e.g., advisors to the Reagan, Bush *père*, and Clinton administrations), the best scenario for the United States in the Middle East is clearly a strong state system, in which friendly Arab regimes can contain domestic dissent and help secure a stable oil supply. In this light, any opponent to U.S. interests must be firmly contained, but any friendly player can be cultivated. Saddam's terrible regime therefore manifested to Reagan-era strategists as a valuable (if covert) ally in containing Iran's Islamic revolution and was accordingly supplied with weaponry and intelligence in the 1980s. Saddam's invasion of Kuwait in 1990 did not alter this realist calculation, for Iraq remained an important oil producer and regional power whose foreign policy should clearly be recaptured to serve U.S. interests. The Clinton administration therefore sought regime change not through democratization but simply through a Baathist coup, hoping that the same clique of generals—still wielding a powerful Iraqi state—could continue to serve U.S. interests by containing worrisome Kurdish and Shi'a politics while balancing Iran's influence in the Persian Gulf.

Israel's interests are arguably better met by a completely different scenario, featuring weak Arab governments incapable of posing any coherent threat to Israel or its regional influence. Israel's interests are therefore arguably best met by fostering weak states that it can control by manipulating client factions, such as the Maronite Christians of northern Lebanon (whom Israel supported in the country's ruinous civil war in the 1970s and 1980s, which for some years destroyed the Lebanese central government). One Israeli analyst, Oded Yinon, spelled out this logic in a much-cited essay, "Strategy for Israel in the 1980s," published in 1982 by the World Zionist Organization.[18] Yinon explicitly endorsed Arab-state fragmentation or "dissolution" as Israel's modus operandi.

> Lebanon's total dissolution into five provinces serves as a precedent for the entire Arab world, including Egypt, Syria, Iraq and the Arabian Peninsula, and is already following that track. The dissolution of Syria and Iraq later on into ethnically or religiously unique areas, such as in Lebanon, is Israel's primary target on the Eastern front in the long run, while the dissolution of the military power of those states serves as the primary short term target. Syria will fall apart, in accordance with its ethnic and religious structure, into several states such as in present-day Lebanon. . . . This state of affairs will be the guarantee for peace and security in the area in the long run, and that aim is already within our reach today.
>
> . . . The entire Arabian Peninsula is a natural candidate for dissolution due to internal and external pressures, and the matter is inevitable especially in Saudi Arabia. Regardless of whether its economic might based on oil remains intact or whether it is diminished in the long run, the internal rifts and breakdowns are a clear and natural development in light of the present political structure.

From this perspective, under Saddam, Iraq was too strong a state, as his army threatened Israel's capacity to act unilaterally in the Middle East. The best solution for Israel was therefore not a Baathist coup but a weak regime—or even "dissolution" of Iraq altogether into its component ethnic or clan factions, as Yinon indeed urged.

> Iraq, rich in oil on the one hand and internally torn on the other, is guaranteed as a candidate for Israel's targets. Its dissolution is even more important for us than that of Syria. Iraq is stronger than Syria. In the short run it is Iraqi power which constitutes the greatest threat to Israel. Every kind of inter-Arab confrontation will assist us in the short run and will shorten the way to the more important aim of breaking up Iraq into denominations as in Syria and in Lebanon. In Iraq, a division into provinces along ethnic/religious lines as in Syria during Ottoman times is possible. So, three (or more) states will exist around the three major cities: Basra, Baghdad and Mosul, and Shiite areas in the south will separate from the Sunni and Kurdish north.[19]

As noted earlier, this vision of "dissolving" Iraq and Syria is antithetical to U.S. strategic interests, as it would generate entirely new and unpredictable local governments prone to unexpected policy changes. Nevertheless, it was wholly endorsed by a cohort of neoconservative ideologues, who later gained control of U.S. foreign policy in the administration of the second President Bush and fused Israeli policy into U.S. strategy. Their thinking was illuminated in a now-famous 1996 policy brief they composed for Israeli Prime Minister Netanyahu, titled *A Clean Break: A New Strategy for Securing the Realm*. The brief was prepared by a working group that included later Bush administration officials Richard Perle, Douglas Feith, and David Wurmser.[20]

Although it illuminates the deepening U.S. alliance with Israel, *A Clean Break* is less meaningful today as a literal plan (for its details have necessarily adapted over the years) than for exposing the strategic thinking of people who later became pivotal to crafting U.S. foreign policy. Richard Perle, leader of the working group that prepared it, became chairman of the Pentagon's Defense Policy Board, which was set up to advise Secretary of Defense Rumsfeld and quickly usurped the State Department's role as principal strategizing authority regarding the Middle East. Rumsfeld himself set up the Office of Special Plans, also in the Pentagon, which hired Perle and Douglas Feith to launder intelligence toward supporting a war on Iraq and became the primary organ arguing that Iraq had terrorist connections and weapons of mass destruction. Feith himself later became undersecretary of defense for policy, the third highest civilian position at the Pentagon, working closely with Deputy Secretary of Defense Paul Wolfowitz (described at a National Christian Leadership Conference for Israel as a "tireless champion of close political and defense ties between Israel and the United States"). In October 2003, David Wurmser, a much-published writer on Israeli strategic planning (who had argued that the Middle East should be broken down into "tribal, familial and clan unions under limited governments"), became Middle East advisor to Vice President Cheney, who comprised a second center of power within which all these architects of policy were sheltered.[21]

All these men worked closely with the neoconservative and Zionist think tanks mentioned earlier, which orchestrated a supportive media campaign by ensuring a steady supply of sympathetic pundits to news programs and editorial forums. Moreover, several held seats on major law firms and corporations involved in Middle East oil, security, and construction contracts worth billions of dollars.[22] Neoconservative, Zionist, and business agendas thus entangled within the administration of the second President Bush in a web of influence largely invisible to the U.S. public: "World Domination, Inc.," one impressed Arab intellectual called it.[23]

Under President Bush, that web operated with unique autonomy, as the president was entirely unequipped to filter their information but was readily persuaded to translate it into action they prescribed. Insulated by his screen of neoconservative advisors from political complexities, Bush was also intellectually insulated by his own open disdain for "the elite" (intellectuals and some journalists) and further by his Evangelical certainty that his advisors' analysis provided insight into the will of "the Almighty," which he was committed to serve.[24] With the Christian-Zionist lobby also fully enlisted, a sacred and Manichaean aura now radiated from the White House as a U.S. policy of regional aggression.

These new architects of U.S. foreign policy took their grand under-standing of world affairs from long-established neoconservative doc-trines, which emphasize narrowly realist interests and the bold unilat-eral use of U.S. power. Their antecedents traced to the 1970s and Cold War organizations, such as the Committee on the Present Dan-ger and the Department of Defense's Office of Net Assessment, which, through the Cold War, urged major increases in U.S. military spending to counter the Soviet nuclear threat. Richard Cheney reflected this school, for example, as he operated from no clear ideo-logical motives (aside from much-rumored continued service to his old corporate connections). Through the 1990s, these archrealists had progressively shifted the seat of foreign policy from the State Depart-ment (and its career foreign-service professionals) to the Pentagon and, within the Pentagon, from established regional experts to their own desks—especially within what became the inner sanctum for intelligence laundering toward the invasion of Iraq, the Office of Spe-cial Plans.

But as *A Clean Break* illustrated, players like Wolfowitz, Perle, Feith, Wurmser, and their associate Harold Rhodes (also holding Pentagon leverage) also brought a hard-line Zionist worldview to Middle East policy. In this light, U.S. policy in the Middle East should enhance Israel's security by eliminating any potential threat. The Arab world itself was seen as a collection of venal regimes ruling over populations culturally predisposed to obdurate hostility toward Jews and toward Western and democratic values. Only by co-opting those leaders or making clear their lack of options—or even replacing those leaders where necessary—could the United States and Israel secure their cooperation.

In other words, the cadre now grouped under Cheney and Rums-feld had internalized the "iron wall" doctrine of early Zionist hard-liner Ze'ev Jabotinsky (1880–1940), the same view shared by Netanyahu and Ariel Sharon: that Arab leaderships, understandably unwilling to accept U.S. (or Israel's) presence and influence, can be leveraged into compliance only if brought to admit the unquestioned power of U.S. (or Israeli) military might.[25] This view excludes ideas of territorial compromise, norm building, incremental reform, or devel-opment-driven democratization, which might otherwise seem obvious methods for gaining U.S. hegemony and warming relations with such old foes as Libya, Syria, and Iran. Instead, it relies on shows of strength backed by willingness to inflict devastating harm. Coupled with the giddy post–Cold War hubris that seized other neoconservative U.S. strategists, it called for replacing any Arab regime that presented any threat to Israel (e.g., in Iraq, Syria, and Iran), and the goal of such regime change was not strong Arab states but weak and compliant ones.

Enabled by an equally compliant president, this worldview quickly translated into a posture of unprecedented U.S. bellicosity and threats of military aggression against the famous "axis of evil"— beginning with Iraq. Invading Iraq to effect regime change violated international law, however, and seriously alarmed the international community; in its debates, the UN Security Council faced its most serious crisis since the Cold War, and long-standing U.S. allies were alienated. Nevertheless, in March 2003, on flimsy evidence (manufactured mostly by the Office of Special Plans in the Pentagon), yet with British support, U.S. troops for the first time invaded and occupied an Arab state. Initial gains were dramatic; the Iraqi army was instantly defeated. U.S. realist interests would then normally have called for rebuilding Iraq as a strong state with a strong military, as a powerful new ally in the Persian Gulf. But in accordance with Israeli goals, the Iraqi forces were instead quickly disbanded—throwing two hundred thousand Iraqi soldiers out of work, against the urgent advice of the U.S. State Department. Ahmad Chalabi was flown in and prepared to assume power, on the strength of his promises to Perle and others that he would secure Iraq's friendly relations to Israel.[26]

That the entire plan would very poorly serve U.S. interests was predictable. The occupation quickly spun into Iraqi nationalist reaction against the U.S. occupation and greatly damaged U.S. credibility in the Arab world. Rather than behaving like a regional hegemon with multilateral interests, the United States was now an occupying power in brash, nineteenth-century "civilizing" mode, exponentially inflating every postcolonial sensitivity and fear in the Arab world. Worse, the inevitable U.S. abuses of military occupation—torture in the prisons, ill-managed checkpoints with regular civilian casualties, violent and terrifying searches of homes, mounting civilian casualties—began strikingly to mimic Israeli occupation practices. Rumors of direct Israeli advising in the prisons and in military tactics also stoked Arab resentments.

Moreover, rumblings of more invasions cast the United States as an unpredictable aggressor. Especially, the world community was startled when, days after Baghdad fell, U.S. threats began to suggest that the second domino would be Syria. Quick international reaction forced U.S. officials to retract these hints, but ominous warnings continued to emerge. *A Clean Break* had indeed emphasized overthrowing the Iraqi government largely in order to destabilize Syria. Still insisting on the return of the Golan Heights, Syria was the last impediment to the *Pax Israeli* that would secure Israel's long-sought regional influence. Israel also held Syria complicit in the operations of Hezbollah (the Shi'a guerrilla movement in southern Lebanon), which, through determined guerrilla tactics in the 1980s and 1990s, had wrecked Israel's efforts to consolidate its authority in Lebanon. *A Clean Break* spelled out this reasoning.

> Syria challenges Israel on Lebanese soil. . . . Given the nature of the regime in Damascus, it is both natural and moral that Israel abandon the slogan "comprehensive peace" and move to *contain* Syria, drawing attention to its weapons of mass destruction program, and rejecting "land for peace" deals on the Golan Heights. . . . Israel can shape its strategic environment, in cooperation with Turkey and Jordan, by weakening, containing, and even rolling back Syria. *This effort can focus on removing Saddam Hussein from power in Iraq*—an important Israeli strategic objective in its own right—*as a means of foiling Syria's regional ambitions.*[27] (emphasis added)

On 20 November 2003, a compliant Congress passed the Syria Accountability Act (S 982) which instructed the U.S. president to impose sanctions on Syria in order to "halt Syrian support for terrorism, end its occupation of Lebanon, stop its development of weapons of mass destruction, cease its illegal importation of Iraqi oil, and hold Syria accountable for its role in the Middle East, and for other purposes." In May 2004, the Bush administration declared trade sanctions.

U.S. threats then floated ominously toward Iran. Through a U.S.

realist lens, Iran was a former linchpin ally: it had been lost to Islamic revolution in 1979 but was still potentially invaluable regarding mutual interests in stabilizing Central Asia, and it was now leaning toward some dignified rapprochement with the West. But through the lens of *A Clean Break*, Iran was simply a prime supporter of Hezbollah and perhaps Hamas, with hints of becoming a nuclear power; again, the brief's authors had called for hard-line treatment and possibly regime change.[28] This view was rapidly incorporated into U.S. policy: in President Bush's first State of the Union address, he roughly discarded the Clinton administration's delicate gestures toward more friendly relations with Iran and denounced Iran as part of the "axis of evil." The move promptly frightened the Iranian theocracy into renewed rejectionism and discredited the burgeoning Iranian reform movement as a tool of U.S. pressure.

None of these U.S. moves seemed to reflect a realist or even hawkish understanding of U.S. interests and therefore baffled many foreign-policy analysts. The Bush administration's grandiose claims of intent to "democratize" the Arab world actually imperiled U.S. leverage in the region and, in the view of many specialists, damaged U.S. security rather than enhanced it. But as knowledge of *A Clean Break* filtered among the international community and as a spy scandal involving AIPAC and Perle's Pentagon Office of Special Plans began to bloom in the mainstream media in the fall of 2004,[29] the reasoning behind the Iraq effort became clear. U.S. policy did reflect Israel's interests. The invasion of Iraq was steered toward eliminating Saddam Hussein's regime (also a goal of realist thinkers like Cheney), but on terms more favorable to Israel than to the United States—that is, generating a weak and factionally divided Iraq, whose debility and dependency would facilitate the longer-term goal of undermining the neighboring Syrian government and Iran's support to Islamic militancy.

Of course, the original plan emanating from the Office of Special Plans had included installing a compliant government led by Chalabi, based on his promises to secure Iraq's majority Shi'ite community as Israeli allies. But even Chalabi's failure and Iraq's floundering transitional government quickly suited Israel's long experience in manipulating factional politics. By late 2004, once Israel recognized the U.S.

occupation to be crumbling, Israeli agents were working in the north to cultivate new leverage with the Kurds.[30]

Unfortunately, a fragmented Iraq also rapidly fostered terrorism, and—as U.S. hegemony eroded in the region—the United States was decreasingly able to contain it. The "special relationship" was now making U.S. interests more magnetic targets for outraged Islamic and Arab opposition groups, on one hand, while freshly implicating Israel in U.S. aggression, on the other. The policy therefore seemed to portend incalculable new dangers for the entire international community. When the Bush administration openly endorsed Sharon's plan to partition and annex the West Bank in April 2004, the package cohered as promising serious trouble, in the shape of fearful and defensive Arab and Iranian reaction, proliferating resistance and terrorist strikes, and growing militant anti-Americanism.[31]

In sum, by the time of the U.S. presidential elections in 2004, the Bush doctrine of "democratization" and the "war on terrorism" expressed in the invasion of Iraq had damaged the U.S. image as "honest broker" beyond the capacity of any potential new president quickly to repair it. The "war on terrorism" was now embedded in U.S. national discourse; any "soft" stand on that "war"—for example, greater emphasis on negotiation and compromise rather than belligerence—was now difficult to argue domestically. As all local terrorist groups were now conflated into a single amorphous global foe called "terrorism," Israel's own war on Palestinian terrorists had been redefined as a common cause rather than a causal factor. In other words, Israel was now positioned as an indispensable ally in a "war" against Islamic militancy heavily inspired by outrage at Israel's own policies.

Under these political and security conditions, a dramatic U.S. switch to bring any kind of serious political pressure on Israel was precluded. Only a true international crisis, coupled with serious diplomatic pressure by U.S. allies, might have granted a new president at least the temporary political authority to buck his own party and take emergency action toward a stable Israeli-Palestinian peace—if such an idea could even be aired in Washington. But no one held the necessary political leverage to sway U.S. policy. At least, neither the Arab states nor the Palestinian Authority held any such influence. Less clear was the enduring inefficacy of Europe.

THE ARABS

One of the major successes of the Zionist lobby in the United States has been to instill a sweeping stereotype of the Arab world as a mighty and hostile anti-Semitic bloc, a balustrade of threat against tiny Israel hunkered on the edge of the Mediterranean. Certainly, geography and demographics superficially support this view. But from the Arab perspective, in terms of power, the reverse is true. Actual Arab weakness is indeed a key factor forcing the one-state solution.

Contrary to the central stereotype, the Arab world is in fact desperately anxious for a negotiated peace with Israel. Their incentives are burning. Especially the frontline states—Egypt, Jordan, Syria, and Lebanon—suffer regularly from border security problems (Palestinian guerrilla incursions, retaliatory Israeli actions, and, in Lebanon, regular Israeli air strikes) and have faced major wars or destabilizing insurrections almost every decade. Their trade remains hampered, business investment is deterred, their own populations are radicalized, and Palestinian refugees create political factionalism and trouble. (About 2.5 million Palestinian refugees live in these four states.)[32] But these effects are not local; the entire Arab world has been injured. Regional trade, water management, and business investments have all been hamstrung. Each war shakes the entire region, generating more refugee flows, staggering costs, capital flight, and fresh moral outrage that rattles the legitimacy of unpopular Arab regimes.

Indeed, by 2004, the gravest danger arising for Arab governments from the Palestinian problem was growing anger and a revolutionary mood arising from their own radicalizing populations. Most Arab citizenries have long resented, disliked, and distrusted their own governments—which, as a body, reflect the always-sordid legacy of European colonialism in their corruption and nepotism. The Gulf and Hashemite monarchies, originally installed by the British, cling on with fragile success based on flagrant welfare patronage, while social-ist dictatorships or "authoritarian democracy" (as in Egypt) hang on by shreds of frayed revolutionary legacies buttressed by repression. Indeed, the Arab world mirrors many of the difficulties faced by decolonized Africa: unrepresentative elites struggle for domestic legitimacy and national unity among fragmented polities thrown together within boundaries drawn originally by Europeans.

As noted earlier, these governments have long managed to glean some domestic legitimacy by mouthing support for Palestinians and claiming some genuine consideration by the United States in its pol-icy-making. But by the late 1990s, the "peace process" was manifest-ing as a master deception. U.S. policies in Iraq further cast coopera-tive Arab governments as incapable quislings actually facilitating U.S.-Zionist plots against helpless Muslim, Palestinian, and Arab brethren. Popular Arab and Muslim willingness to cooperate with these governments was rapidly withering, and otherwise unpopular radical alternatives—for example, strikes by al-Qaida—were gaining grudging popular sympathy for offering at least some gesture toward protest. This rising threat of grassroots trouble preoccupied such leaders as Egypt's Hosni Mubarak, who spoke anxiously in the spring of 2004 of the Palestinian problem fostering "regional instability."

Yet the Arab governments were unable to act effectively even while their political landscapes heaved with unrest. The Bush administra-tion's blanket assumption that Arab governments could contain their own fragmenting polities was indeed one of the neoconservatives' most dangerous gambles. Despite all the high-flown language in Arab forums about Arab unity and despite the region's vast oil wealth, which might seem to suggest political power as well, the Arab world remains as politically weak as any developing region, for reasons often poorly understood in the West.

First, since Israeli lobbyists make so much of Israel's military vul-nerability, it is worth clarifying that, for the Arab world, military action against Israel has long been out of the question. The last effort was thirty years ago: a brief alliance between Syria and Egypt in 1973 that gained no ground but made a political point sufficient to trigger the Camp David Accords.[33] Today, the conditions for any such effort are long gone. For one thing, all the Arab states except Syria are—

politically and economically—deep in the U.S. pocket. Egypt is a staunch U.S. ally, as is Saudi Arabia and Jordan. No general Arab attack on Israel is imaginable in these conditions. Moreover, Israel has always been the strongest military power in the region, and its supremacy is now overwhelming. Its nuclear weaponry is its trump card, but its superb air force and high-tech electronics—and the looming shadow of its U.S. protector—make it invincible. As a consequence, Israel can and has freely struck Arab targets at great distances, not only in its invasions of surrounding states (it ransacked Lebanon in 1982 with near impunity), but with its long-range bombing of the (French-built) Iraqi nuclear reactor in 1981 and its bombing of PLO offices in Tunisia in 1985. Certainly, no Arab ground campaign against Israel could even begin to assemble without preemptive Israeli attack, even in the impossible conditions of U.S. evaporation. The most that any hostile Arab government might manage would be secretive isolated gestures, like Iraq's Scud missile attacks during the First Gulf War. Israel is indeed vulnerable only to terrorism—which, with the failed Palestinian peace talks, is quickly rising into a much greater threat.

Military action against Israel is not even a glint in the eye of Arab states for other reasons as well. First, the Arab world as a whole remains highly dependent on Western markets and expertise. Indeed, many Arab governments rely on western patronage to prop themselves up, because they are failing politically and economically. Contrary to stereotype, most Arab countries have no oil and very modest gross domestic products. As is typical of postcolonial countries, they also suffer from highly unequal domestic incomes and robust poverty rates. Egypt's economy is seriously faltering, with the extreme-poverty rate mounting over 25 percent. Jordan and Yemen both lack anything close to sufficient resources for their populations and are major labor exporters. But even the oil exporters, including the Persian Gulf emirates, remain dependent on Western expertise and corporate linkages to sustain their own oil industries. Arab elites in these countries also have strong social ties to the West, with family homes and major investments in Europe and North America. (Only Baathist Iraq, with its socialist party and major oil reserves, managed to develop more equality in national development—at the cost of brutal repression.) The Arab world as a whole is in fact hooked into the globalized economy with as much dependency as Latin America, relying entirely on the core "first world" countries to consume its primary products and to supply finished goods.

Popular protest and incipient revolt have always brooded in this unhappy setting. Labor unrest plagues even the oil exporters, for if their large and vulnerable guest workforces are taken into account, the fabulously wealthy Gulf emirates have the most grossly unequal incomes in the world. The Saudi government particularly is under pressure from an excluded and irate migrant-labor sector. But all classes and sectors have taken offense at these inequities, and stormy internal politics in every Arab state reflects a climate of burning dissatisfaction, emerging occasionally in democratic, communist, or Islamic challenges that have been met with sometimes brutal state repression. (Failure to recognize or remember the many courageous efforts toward greater democracy raised by Arab opposition parties is one of the West's more hurtful insults.) As these pressures grow, Arab governments must lean yet more heavily on Western patronage for loans and special trade deals to help them buy off or suppress domestic dissent.

Second, any coordinated Arab policy regarding Israel has been derailed because, despite its purported unity, the Arab world remains divided and internally contentious. Pan-Arab nationalism (which casts the Palestinians as "brother Arabs") has always been far grander in rhetoric than in reality. An identity discourse developed especially in the 1950s and 1960s, Arab nationalism was promoted especially by Gamal Nasser of Egypt to enhance strategic cooperation among states in the Middle East and North Africa. The idea then was to cultivate solidarity toward gaining some regional independence from former colonizers, while managing the economic and political stresses of decolonization. In its early years, the discourse gained some appeal and generated the Arab League. But Arab national unity has always suffered from deep regional cultural differences, political rivalries, distrust among rival elites, and ideological splits. The Arab League has suffered accordingly (collapsing entirely at its crucial May 2004 meeting in the midst of the Iraq war, riven impossibly by political fissures).

Moreover, during the Cold War, the region was polarized, like all developing regions, by the U.S.-Soviet rivalry. For example, in the 1970s, the Iraqi Baathists chose a Soviet affiliation, which was one reason for the U.S. ban on arms sales to the country (which then had to be circumvented secretly in the 1980s to support Iraq in its war against Iran). U.S. support for Israel also fostered Soviet leanings among some frontline states: Syria, too, cultivated an Eastern alliance, as did Egypt under Nasser. None of these countries were ever simply client regimes, but the East-West and socialist-capitalist polarity—with Morocco, Tunisia, Algeria, Lebanon, and Jordan (among others) firmly oriented toward the West—rendered pan-Arab unity ineffectual. After the Cold War, all the Arab governments recrafted their alliances toward friendship or at least fence-mending with the United States, a process facilitated by the Clinton administration's multilateral foreign policy. But new divisions emerged, especially the First Gulf War (begun in 1990), which again split the Arab League, and the U.S. invasion of Iraq in 2003, which so forcefully recalled old colonial conquests. Some states, impressed by the specter of a United States breaking all normal bounds, scrambled for favor; others tried to balance their public positions to contain furious domestic protest.

Hence, it is not surprising that no coordinated or forceful Arab posture has emerged regarding the U.S. role in the Israeli-Palestinian conflict. But in fact, no Arab regime is overly fond of the Palestinians, and not only because, in the past, the PLO proved itself a dangerous rival to state governments (especially in Jordan and Lebanon). Wherever they go, Palestinians import a genuinely democratic ethos, a political philosophy cultivated (if distorted) by the old Palestine National Congress system in the PLO. Struggling to retain their power through patronage, exclusion, and repression, Arab states tend to view the highly educated and democratically minded Palestinian diaspora as a most unwelcome import. Arab states have therefore resisted absorbing Palestinian refugees and migrants not simply on principle (to support Palestinian efforts to return to Palestine) but primarily out of concern for their own self-preservation. Kuwait's Sabah ruling family, for example, relied almost entirely on a Palestinian professional class to manage the country's governmental and financial sectors but, over three generations, never granted Palestinians citizenship.

The only event that could galvanize serious collective action by Arab states to confront Israel would be Israel's forcible transfer of the Palestinian people from the territory of Eretz Israel, urged by some right-wing and religious Zionists. To the Arab and Muslim worlds, that expulsion would manifest as so outrageous that Arab leaders would have to act forcefully or face mass rebellions and their own overthrow. The long-disabled Arab political fist would then find sudden solidity. For precisely that reason, even Israel is self-constrained from that action, and the Palestinians are left stranded in the territories, the pressures building toward explosion.

THE PALESTINIANS

The other influence that might be expected to sway U.S. policy is, of course, the Palestinians themselves. Their failure to do so stems from several sources. As discussed earlier, Palestinian influence or even dissemination of the Palestinian experience—for example, news coverage of abuses under Israeli occupation—has been blocked or greatly diluted in the U.S. context by the Zionist lobby, which has skillfully cast Palestinians as irrational, their arguments as illegitimate, and their plight as self-inflicted or a collective Arab plot. Palestinian terrorism has played into those stereotypes, as the terrible actions of a radical few breathe validity into sweeping Zionist stereotypes of Arabs and Muslims—and Palestinians in particular—as murderous anti-Semites. But Palestinian political incapacity in the United States cannot be blamed entirely on skilled Zionist lobbying or Western orientalism.

The obvious actor is infamously incapable. The Palestinian Authority carries the political and moral authority to represent what should—on its face, but also for its import for regional instability—be a compelling case. The present PA, however, is still dominated by the former PLO crony leadership, centered until recently on Arafat, which over four decades of diaspora existence became largely a self-serving patronage machine. This "leadership" has done little to help and much to ruin the Palestinian cause in international politics. Arafat had mafioso notions of leadership; he always controlled Palestinian politics through patronage and payoffs. Surrounded by sycophants and fully convinced of his own mythos, he had no talent suitable to state- and nation-building. With good cause, Israeli leaderships denounced Arafat for various rejectionist postures and blunders; increasing numbers of Palestinians came to share this disdain.[34]

Worse, that patronage culture passed long ago to the crucial PLO embassy in Washington, D.C., where, at the dawn of the Oslo process, the PLO representative was known primarily for his skill in cultivating crony social relations among the U.S. Palestinian-Arab elite. No coherent lobbying or networking, like that cultivated by the PLO's London office, ever emerged at the global imperial seat; the Washington PLO office could not have been less effective if it had been bought long ago by Israeli intelligence.

Yet Arafat's crippling influence also traces to Israeli intervention more than is commonly recognized. Indeed, despite strident Israeli denunciations of Arafat's failure to stop terrorism, and while he was loathed by Israel's leaders (and particularly by Ariel Sharon), he remained a key asset for Israel precisely because a truly effective PLO has never been in Israel's interests. In fact, since the 1970s, Israel's policy has been to prevent any more effective leadership from aris-ing—even, some suspect, to preserve Arafat's life during Israel's own military attacks. For while in exile, Arafat fulfilled one vital function for Israel: he was able—for the most part—to control and limit Pales-tinian guerrilla or terrorist action to ineffective symbolic acts, while subverting any genuinely democratic Palestinian process that might cohere into more effective Palestinian political or diplomatic action. Israeli occupation policy was therefore consistently to eliminate, by assassination or expulsion, any rival to Arafat who might more effec-tively represent Palestinian-national interests either domestically or to Western audiences.

The Oslo process reflected this long-standing policy. By recogniz-ing Arafat's role and reaffirming his crony leadership as head of the PLO, the "sole legitimate representative of the Palestinian people," Israel and the United States helped Arafat reclaim leadership from genuinely effective internal Palestinian local leaders, who were then conducting a mostly nonviolent insurrection that was shaking Israeli politics and garnering considerable international sympathy. Reinstalling Arafat into the Palestinian territories in 1993 was therefore a desperation measure intended to bring the intifada back under control. The immediate effect was positive for Israel; with direct access to the Palestinians in the territories, Arafat and Fatah (the Palestinian faction founded by Arafat) were able to repurchase the intifada's grassroots networks for top-down direction and to sabotage the mass solidarity that had given the intifada its early high spirit and ideals. Oslo did, however, also have early positive effects for Palestinian nationalism, as a genuinely effective Palestinian bureaucracy began to form despite Arafat's nepotistic vision, building from international funds and revitalized Palestinian talent. For a few giddy years, the institutional makings of a true Palestinian state briefly flowered.

But the effort was short-lived, collapsing in a crucial confluence of events. First, once Arafat was back in the territories and wielding a new influx of foreign-aid funds, his nepotism and corrupt crony cadre were more fully exposed to domestic Palestinian scrutiny, and his mystique rapidly broke down for widening circles.[35] Second, his failure to stem ongoing settlement construction and brutalities by the ongoing Israeli occupation brought Palestinian disillusionment and bitterness. The second intifada, which broke out in 2000 and launched terrible new rounds of violence, reflected growing mass Palestinian frustration. Finally, Israel's subsequent rejection of Arafat's headman role capped his marginality. Disgusted with Arafat's inability to play his assigned role, Ariel Sharon and the Israeli Defense Forces argued that the intifada actually traced to a cunning plot by Arafat to deploy terror to force a peace agreement. The argument was a ploy: Israel's own intelligence service, the Shin Bet, had determined that the second intifada was actually a spontaneous popular eruption, tipped by Ariel Sharon's famous incursion onto the Temple Mount (with hundreds of policemen as escort). Arafat had been forced to accommodate that popular explosion, following rather than leading his outraged people.[36] But Israeli government rhetoric prevailed, and with Arafat's role discredited, Israel was able to claim a complete absence of Palestinian leadership and to justify abandoning Oslo. The new PA offices of health, education, and development—their computers, archives, and furniture—were physically smashed by Israeli forces in raids in 2002, and Arafat's patronage networks were savaged. Israeli roadblocks, arrests, and restrictions further ruined Arafat's capacity to control events, facilitating accusations that he was doing nothing to stop loose-cannon Palestinian violence and particularly the rise of Hamas.

The measures employed to crush the PA also preempted any coherent Palestinian political effort either to replace Arafat or reform the PA. With their cities and towns increasingly cut off by Israeli settlements and roadblocks, the Palestinian population, suffering periodic raids and closures, was hard-pressed to manage even basic daily needs. A plethora of intelligent, articulate Palestinian intellectuals and journalists issued independent statements and articles, but these manifested as scattered expressions rather than a coherent position. In any case, none carried the charisma or popularity to replace Arafat; they could only suggest a new foundation for forming a truly democratic cabinet. But under conditions of occupation, any effective governance and democracy was impossible.

One maverick effort was made to circumvent the stalemate: in October 2003, a few Palestinian politicians joined liberal Jewish Israelis in crafting a new formula for a two-state solution soon known as the Geneva Accords. The accords graphically illustrated a Palestinian will toward peace so scathingly denied by Sharon and AIPAC; many people, on all sides, greeted them with excitement. But the accords remained hamstrung by lack of mass legitimacy and by their own programmatic weaknesses; in the end, the accords amounted to only a sidebar in the useless peace process.[37]

Hence, by 14 April 2004, when President Bush authorized permanent Israeli settlements in the West Bank at his joint press conference with Ariel Sharon, Arafat's PA could do nothing. Little more than a symbolic relic (trapped in partly ruined Ramallah offices), the figurehead for a demoralized Palestinian-national movement, Arafat could only strike a posture of tragic dignity for Arab and Muslim audiences appalled by television coverage of growing Palestinian national misery. Certainly Arafat's PA could do nothing to further the settlement withdrawal necessary to creating a viable Palestinian state.

Arafat's death (in November 2004) seemed to provide a historic opening for reforming the PA and breaking the impasse. But the window was painfully narrow. In the presidential elections of January 2005, a liberal coalition headed by Mustapha Barghouthi sought to sweep out the PA with a new democratic and professional leadership. The Sharon and Bush administrations, however, endorsed Mahmoud Abbas, a close associate of Arafat, whose entrenched position in the old guards of the PLO, the PA, and Fatah ensured his continuity of connections with Israeli and U.S. interests. From the Israeli and U.S. perspectives, the new Palestinian president's proper role was the same as the old: to enhance Israeli security by containing Palestinian violence. And indeed, Abbas affirmed with new energy that the Palestinian movement must abandon armed struggle, to fulfill the conditions presented by Israel for any concessions. An exhausted Palestinian population agreed, worn down by the futility of the intifada and the crushing Israeli repression it had generated. They were also ready to endorse almost any candidate favored by Israel and the United States, believing he would bring long-promised relief from Israeli occupation. Abbas won the election handily.

Yet no Israeli or U.S. statements during the elections mentioned any specific Israeli promise or obligation to reciprocate Palestinian efforts at reform. Especially, no one mentioned withdrawal of the settlement grid—where construction proceeded apace. The Palestinian elections did trigger newly hopeful international diplomacy, and journalistic language flowed lushly about "historic opportunity" and "new opening for peace." New rounds of the "peace process" were clearly portended, promising to recapture and absorb international attention for months or years. The mood was not entirely futile; some suspension of attacks for Israel and minor relief to the Palestinians from Israeli occupation brutality might be achieved—barring new rounds of violence triggered by Israeli assassination strikes or by disenchanted Palestinian militants. But given Israeli prerogatives, unfettered by a slavish U.S. administration, no conceivable reform by the PA could halt or even slow construction of Israel's advancing settlement grid in the West Bank. Regarding Zionist "return" to "Judea and Samaria"—a mission now guarded by a prime minister whose bullish adherence to the grid's construction was unparalleled in

Israeli history—a reformed PA, under Mahmoud Abbas or anyone else, would have no more political leverage than the old one.

"NEW EUROPE"

The only remaining actor capable of bringing serious pressure on the United States, although widely dismissed in this capacity by analysts, is Europe. "Europe" is, of course, a complicated entity, constantly reimagined through the centuries and, as a union, still in the making. In 2004, as the U.S. occupation of Iraq faced disaster and President Bush unilaterally redefined Israeli-Palestinian diplomacy, the European Union was grappling to absorb ten new members, compose a constitution, and reconcile its deep internal economic disparities. A foreign-policy split was also imported with this expansion, for the new members were Central European states who still viewed the United States gratefully for its Cold War support. Scraping Soviet socialism off their feet, these states were also predisposed to hunger for U.S. corporate investments and development assistance—already provided by the United States deliberately to consolidate U.S. influence in "New Europe."

The Bush administration was particularly crude in affirming that U.S. interests were therefore securely inserted into this coalition. In its rhetoric, "Old Europe" (a reference primarily to the old U.S. political counterweights France and Germany) was an obsolete relic, out of tune with the new age promised by U.S. hegemony. "New Europe," if only through some countries' vetoes, promised to consolidate the EU for U.S. neoliberalism and foreign policy. Struggling toward the consensus necessary for a new constitution, the EU therefore seemed to face years of negotiations before any independent foreign policy might even begin to gel. Regarding Israel, such a coherent policy remained especially hampered. Germany, for example, remained so vulnerable to Israel's strategic charges of anti-Semitism that any open criticism of Israeli policy was charily avoided, as a political third rail.

Yet, rapidly worsening world conditions suggested the possibility of more rapid change. As U.S. policy destabilized the Middle East, a common threat of instability and terror attacks affected the entire world community. In March 2004, a series of major train bombings in Madrid brought what had been an abstract threat to terrible reality; close calls in London and Paris further suggested a rapidly spreading danger. New doubts about the U.S. alliance and a mood of nervous solidarity were rising even in Central Europe, which was reacting to perceptions that the U.S. hegemon had become dangerously unpredictable and reckless. A major insurrection in Iraq, another U.S. invasion, related upheaval in another Middle East state, or some convulsion in the Palestinian territories (e.g., forced transfer of the Palestinian population) might rapidly alter the political calculations of "New Europe" and stimulate a much faster reorientation of its members toward internal unity and a coherent foreign policy than had been anticipated.

In this case, Europe could immediately wield one serious weapon: a trade boycott. In 2001, Israel's exports to the EU totaled US$7.7 billion, almost one-third of its total exports, while Israeli imports from the EU totaled $13.9 billion, 41 percent of its imports. An EU trade boycott of Israel would therefore demolish Israel's economy. Recognizing the potential of this weapon, the European Parliament called for precisely that measure, in resolutions in 2002 and 2003. The proposals were only rhetorical flourishes, given the lack of EU consensus on the question (and countervailing business and financial interests); the promise of severe U.S. opprobrium was also a clear deterrent. But in light of disintegrating international security, sheer self-preservation could force Europe to seize the initiative. The same concern might inspire action from others who hold sufficient international standing—for example, Australia, New Zealand, and South Africa, as well as networks in developing regions—to pressure both U.S. policy and the conflict itself.

The political obstacles remain clearly monumental. The EU has every reason to abjure a showdown with the United States over Israel. Cold War habits of passing off Europe's security to the U.S. military behemoth also die hard. But the EU is no passive recipient of U.S. wishes; it has already deployed its economic leverage in a successful trade dispute with the United States, defeating U.S. tariff barriers to European steel imports. U.S. capitulation to that boycott reflected the United States' need to validate World Trade Organization mechanisms on which it, too, relies, but it also reflected growing EU capacity and willingness to use its collective economic hand. In rising emergency conditions—with terrorism portending disasters feared by all—the EU might be brought rapidly to cohere as a security community and might turn its economic clout, for the first time, toward changing the terrible equation in the Middle East.

The question, then, would be what kind of peace that effort should seek—or what can still be achieved.

CONCLUSION: THE IMPENDING DEBATE

European statesmen and analysts have been prominent among the voices critical of U.S. policy in the Middle East. Yet their very ire toward U.S. behavior has reflected their continuing failure to grasp that the United States has become internally incapable of acting seriously to resolve the conflict—and that no new president in the foreseeable future is likely to make any substantive difference to that condition. U.S. geostrategic interests, coupled with the Zionist tilt of its domestic politics, has long confined its diplomacy on the Israeli-Palestinian conflict to vaporous pronouncements and diplomatic pantomimes. In practice, rather than "honest broker," the U.S. diplomatic team has accommodated whatever position the Israeli government wished it to take. Decades have accordingly been wasted while various stages of the ineffectual U.S.-led "peace process" consumed earnest international diplomatic attention, obedient media fascination, and the scarce resources of desperately concerned human rights networks. This stage show has been so insubstantial and pointless that, even by the 1980s, Noam Chomsky interpreted the term *peace process* as diplomacy-speak for "anything the United States is doing at the moment."

For three decades, the only material result of the U.S. "peace process" was actually to preclude effective international action on the most crucial Israeli-Palestinian matter, steady expansion of the settlement grid—by always promising but never reaching its serious discussion. In the 1990s, the Oslo process actually enlisted the PLO's help in consolidating the grid's security. Following Oslo's failure, the Bush team duly presented a "road map for peace," which made brief reference to a settlement withdrawal but ultimately provided only another catchphrase to absorb (and waste) international attention. Never backed by any U.S. action, the "road map" had a true hollowness that was formalized in April 2004, when Bush publicly endorsed the settlement grid and authorized Israel's annexation of the West Bank. In composing the president's formal letter to this effect, the Bush team's only gesture toward Arab and international concerns was slightly more tepid rhetoric than the Sharon government had sought, to placate "Arab and international sensitivities."

Still, in one dimension of his startling remarks at a press conference on 14 April, endorsing Sharon's settlement strategy, President Bush was perfectly correct: "the realities on the ground and in the region have changed greatly over the last several decades and any final settlement must take into account those realities and be agreeable to the parties."[38] This phrase rang absurd in light of the larger context: the Palestinians certainly did not and will not agree to a Palestinian "state" that can be no more than an unviable ghetto and to which no mass Palestinian return would be possible. But the "realities on the ground" were, indeed, realities: the settlements sprawled across the West Bank landscape, and no power existed to force their removal. Even an EU boycott could not force Israel to do that, because the political strain would tear the Jewish nation asunder.

But if the two-state option is permanently crippled by the settlement grid, how can the conflict be resolved and the Middle East stabilized? The solution lies elsewhere, in democratization, as was pursued in South Africa and Northern Ireland. And the central obstacle to pursuing a united democratic multiethnic state in Israel-Palestine is obvious. In his landmark speech of 14 April, Bush rushed inattentively over one line that, read differently, would have conveyed its writers' obvious emphasis: "The United States is strongly committed and I am strongly committed to the security of Israel as a vibrant *Jewish* state" (emphasis mine). That phrasing reflected the writers' better understanding that it is precisely the Jewishness of the Jewish state that is now on the table. For if Jewish settlement in the West Bank has already expanded too far, then a Palestinian state is no longer viable, and the two-state solution promises only gathering crisis and possible explosion. And if the only alternative to that explosion is the one-state solution, then Zionism itself is approaching a crisis.

5. Tracing the Inner Threads of Zionism

The crisis looming in the occupied territories obviously comprises a ruinous formula for Palestinians. But it also bodes very ill for Israelis, for the Bantustan plan will consign Israel's Jewish population to a permanent state of threat. Withering in their walled enclave, the Palestinian people will continue to resist conditions of daily misery and political destruction. And as their population grows rapidly within its sealed territorial vessel, the demographic, economic, and political pressures will build to critical mass. Juxtaposed in the highlands, pressed together cheek-by-jowl in gerrymandered borders, Jewish and Palestinian sectors cannot endure such pressures indefinitely. The formula is explosive, promising increasingly desperate acts of violence and possibly even mass insurrection by the Palestinians. If such unrest triggers more intense Israeli repression or, in the worst case, even an attempt to expel the Palestinians en masse from the territory—an action advocated by extremists already gaining influence in the Israeli government—a specter of regional conflagration would face Israel and the international community as a whole.

With the U.S. occupation of Iraq in 2003 raising regional tensions still further, forestalling that worst-case scenario became a matter of collective urgency. The Palestinian *nakba* (catastrophe) is now a banner grievance not simply for compromised Arab governments and their disgruntled populations but for terrorist networks with far greater ambition and capacity than the region has seen previously. No longer simply oil and business interests but international collective security itself is imperiled. If the obstacle to peace has been lack of sufficient political will and a compromised U.S. role, could more forceful collective efforts leverage these "two peoples in one land" to negotiation, compromise, reconciliation, and peaceful coexistence? Such was the suggestion of chapter 4, in observing the potential for a Europe-led initiative.

Yet some new collective effort can avail nothing as long as the basic character of the conflict and its resolution remain misconceived. Even if the moribund two-state solution were somehow temporarily resuscitated through desperate effort by a (still-missing) international coalition, it would remain unworkable, because it was flawed from the start, resting on the discredited idea—on which political Zionism stakes all its moral authority—that any ethnic group can legitimately claim permanent formal dominion over a territorial state.

Whatever its pathos, romance, idealism, and depth of attached emotions, the mission of Jewish ethnic statehood has walked the same doomed course as ethnic nationalisms everywhere. No matter how legitimate they might appear to their adherents, all ethnic nationalisms confront the intractable problem of managing the presence of ethnic others within the state territory. Israel is an exemplar of this rule, rather than an exception. Early clashes between Jewish settlers and Palestinian peasants, three open wars, the military occupation of the West Bank and Gaza Strip, and now the ominous trajectory of violence promised by the settlements have all sprung from the Zionist mission to create a Jewish state, hitherto understood to require a permanent Jewish majority. In traditional Zionist doctrine, that mandate has granted moral authority to "cleansing" the land of non-Jews—although with considerable twisting of history to gloss over these measures (e.g., claiming that it was accidental but then blaming the Arab states for not completing it). As the Palestinians will not be "cleansed" without unacceptable trauma—and dreadful consequences for us all—those searching for peace must finally question that core logic of Zionism.

Such deep critique is obviously extremely sensitive. In Western mainstream political discourse, Zionism is normally considered untouchable for a cluster of reasons discussed shortly—and by strident and obfuscating Zionist arguments that any challenge to Israel's "right to exist" as a Jewish state implies genocidal intent toward the Jewish-national community itself.[1] While often made sincerely, that Manichaean argument—either a Jewish state will survive or Jewish annihilation will follow—must be seen as one discursive position rather than a definitive argument regarding essential conditions for collective Jewish survival. For one thing, arguments about what exactly constitutes a "Jewish state" play out even within Israel itself (e.g., the role of religion in being Jewish and whether Israel actually requires the West Bank highlands to fulfill its identity as the Jewish state). More important, a small but growing "post-Zionist" movement—articulated especially by Israeli intellectuals and human rights activists appalled by the occupation and what they perceive as looming disaster for Israel—is already proposing a very different configuration of Jewish statehood that would not require a Jewish majority.

This post-Zionist movement is not as radically innovative as it might seem. Zionism's own intellectual history includes early humanitarian Jewish thinkers who once argued passionately for sharing the land with the "Arabs." Today, such early ideas may seem superfluous or useful only as moral band-aids allowing modern Zionism to claim its early good intentions. Yet, revived in the writings of post-Zionists, those old ideas offer some venerable resources to unravel the present formula of destruction, by suggesting the only stable solution to the conflict—the same solution finally accepted by all the Western democracies: democratization in one secular, democratic, civil nation-state.

Why should policymakers push for an option presently deemed so marginal and unlikely—and possibly even distracting from such urgent needs as stopping terrorism, dismantling settlements, blocking the Wall, and forestalling the immiseration of the Palestinian people? Because a confrontation with Zionism's underlying philosophy of ethnic statehood is unavoidable. Prior efforts to resolve the conflict in ways that accommodate the mainstream Zionist premise of a "Jewish state" have proved unworkable. That they will remain unworkable can first be illustrated by comparing the Israeli-Palestinian crisis to conflicts elsewhere, such as South Africa and Northern Ireland, where racial or ethnic statehood was necessarily rejected and defeated. Zionist arguments that Israel must be held exceptional—that Jewish eth-nonationalism has a unique privilege in a world where ethnic statehood has become normatively obsolete and anathema—are then examined on their own merits.

ZIONIST EXCEPTIONALISM

By accepting the basic Zionist tenet of Jewish statehood—understood here as permanent Jewish-national dominion over state institutions and governance within a territorial state—well-meaning efforts have rendered the Israeli-Palestinian conflict uniquely resistant to peacemaking methods applied elsewhere. For example, people grappling with Israel-Palestine often look to the South African experience, where a similar depth of structural discrimination and oppression once prevailed. The case of Northern Ireland also arises, because of its binary ethnic clash and its suggestion that skilled mediation might allow a breakthrough. These comparisons are understandable, as both conflicts resembled Israel-Palestine in having settler-colonial dimensions, engaging rival discourses of indigeneity, and stubbornly resisting resolution due to mutual ethnic or racial fears and antipathy.

But taking these cases as models for conflict resolution in Israel-Palestine has only led efforts astray. First and most important, the South African and Northern Ireland conflicts were resolved not by creating two states but, rather, by democratization, on the premise that any ethnic or racial dominion is morally illegitimate. As long as Jewish ethnic dominion is accepted and validated for Israel-Palestine (through the two-state approach) rather than challenged and denounced, the relevant battery of political principles and conflict resolution methods brought to resolve these famous conflicts is here disabled. Second, the Israeli-Palestinian conflict is sustained not by social-psychological problems, such as fear and prejudice, but from structural conditions, focused on land control, arising from political Zionism's territorial imperative to secure a Jewish majority. Third, international pressure comparable to that which confronted apartheid simply cannot be brought to bear on Israel as long as Zionism and the historical "Jewish problem" configure so differently in European and

U.S. thought and moral geography—a problem calling for some hard self-critique in Western Christian Europe and North America.

Zionist spokespeople sometimes admit these differences and propose different parallels, such as the partition solution applied to the ethnic wars in the former Yugoslavia or the split of Czechoslovakia into two eponymous republics. They argue that these examples have freshly legitimized the principle of statehood along ethnonationalist lines. But these comparisons also derail rather than guide productive action, for the Jewish state does not operate politically as these Central European countries do, and reifying Israel's present ethnonational system within permanent borders will not generate a stable civil democracy like Hungary. Probing the differences among all these cases will lay these inapt parallels to rest.

South Africa

Today, although many Zionists heatedly reject the comparison, even some liberal Jewish-Israelis recall South African apartheid in observing Israeli government policy toward the Palestinians—and more frequently as people react to the Wall. The similarities do, at first brush, seem striking. Like the Zionist-Palestinian experience, the South African problem was structured psychologically and ideologically by a settler (Afrikaner) mytho-history of brave frontier settlement into empty land, even including a "chosen people" doctrine.[2] Just as Israel's laws secure Jewish-national dominion, white supremacy in South Africa was secured through discriminatory laws and white racial control of the state, deliberately excluding the native people. In both states, measures to cripple black and Palestinian economies secured the indigenous populations as cheap labor pools, building on and reinforcing stereotypes of their innate cultural (or racial) inferiority. Finally, mirroring Jewish-Palestinian tensions, apartheid South Africa was so steeped in mutual fears and antipathies that peaceful evaporation of its racial legislation long seemed unimaginable. Even the white sense of being under assault was greater than is now often remembered; in the 1980s, South Africa's white dominant society was greatly frightened by a series of terrorist bombings. Among many South African whites—as, today, among many Israeli Jews—a specter of intractable native hostility seemed to promise terrible retribution should racial restrictions be dropped.

Yet all these fears and legislative barriers were overcome: although not without upheaval, democratization of South Africa was achieved. Some people therefore invoke the South African comparison hopefully, finding apartheid's fall inspirational in suggesting that monolithic fears and prejudices in Israel-Palestine might also yield to a similar campaign of international moral suasion (publicity of human rights abuses, collective opprobrium, dialogue) coupled with trade sanctions to add the necessary elbow jab at Israeli state policy. In 2002, for example, a nascent "Divest from Israel" movement was launched from Harvard University on this premise and quickly spread to several U.S. and foreign campuses.[3]

Jewish nationalism in Palestine does replicate many dynamics of Afrikaner nationalism, but important differences pertain. Zionism actually takes the logic of ethnic separation one major step further. As did early Zionist settlement, white South African settlement involved expulsions and extensive land seizures (from Bantu and Khoikhoi peoples), as well as their permanent disenfranchisement. The Bantustan system also reflected some effort at genuine separation and, to a few Afrikaner dreamers, the possibility of securing an overwhelmingly white state. But apartheid was never seriously premised on complete ethnic (racial) cleansing. Rather, the black African population was incorporated as an integral element of the settler-colonial economy, and an enduring black majority was accepted both ideologically (albeit only as a subordinate racial caste) and as an empirical fact. Securing the black majority as a cheap labor force while politically excluding it—to ensure white dominion—accordingly presented a difficult challenge for white rule, generating apartheid's notoriously elaborate edifice of territorial and social division, composed of strict zoning and pass laws, the Bantustans, prohibitions on mixed-race sex and marriage, job restrictions, special laws to prevent any legal redress to these measures—and swift and brutal repression of any serious black dissent.

By contrast, although Palestinian labor was actually integral to Zionist settlement from the start, mainstream Zionism was shaped ideologically by the doctrine that Jewish nationalism (aiming for spiritual as well as political and cultural fulfillment) required restoring to European Jewry the spiritually healthy experience of laboring on "redeemed" Jewish-national land.[4] In this Zionist view, Jewish national life should embrace a complete society, engaging all realms of work and culture. To ensure Jewish labor in all sectors and to be truly Jewish in character, such a society required a permanent and overwhelming Jewish majority, a condition that necessitated "cleansing" the land of its majority Arab population. Hence, Zionist forces effected mass expulsions of Palestinians in the 1948 and 1967 wars. Today, Israel's strategic goals still reflect that basic logic: not stable incorporation of a subordinated native people (even if they were accepted temporarily as "hewers of wood and drawers of water")[5] but their physical removal—even, implicitly, their forced "transfer" out of the territory altogether—by any means that will not rebound too dangerously on Israeli security (and self-image). That this central ideology is fundamentally racist in its conception and effects is indicated by the language in which it is instrumentalized (e.g., "transfer," "cleansing," "Judaization").

The charge of racism is hotly rejected by Israel's defenders, on multiple grounds, including claims that Zionism, being a national liberation movement, cannot be considered racist; that Jews do not consider themselves superior to other races; that Israel is actually pluralistic; and that the Jewish nation is simply seeking the sovereignty enjoyed by other nations.[6] One thread of argument insists that, since Jews themselves come from all racial types and since Israel has absorbed all without exception, neither Judaism nor Zionism can be considered racist. (Israel's Ethiopian Jewish population and the Sephardic or Mizrahi Jews from Arab North Africa and the Middle East are often vaunted here.)[7]

This defense rings hollow to the Palestinians, however, as the designation "Arab" in the Zionist context clearly couples a group identity to notions of essential and intergenerational predispositions (e.g., backwardness, a propensity to violence, antidemocratic mentality), with all the crushing clout of any racist discourse. In short, in the Israeli context, "Arab" is a racial identity. Racist rhetoric surrounding "being Arab" in Israel is indeed sometimes astonishingly graphic. For example, prominent Israeli historian Benny Morris has referred to the

Palestinian people as "a wild animal there that has to be locked up in one way or another," for whom "something like a cage has to be built."[8] Brigadier General Effi Eitam, cabinet minister in the Sharm government and leader of the National Religious Party, has referred to the Arabs in Israel as a "cancer" in the state,[9] and in August 2002, Israeli Chief of Staff Moshe Ya'alon prescribed chemotherapy for that cancer.

> The characteristics of the threat [from the Palestinians] are invisible, like cancer. When you are attacked externally, you can see the attack, you are wounded. Cancer, on the other hand, is something internal. Therefore, I find it more disturbing because here its diagnosis is critical. . . . I maintain that this is a cancer. . . . My professional diagnosis is that this is a phenomenon that constitutes an existential threat. . . . There are all kinds of solutions to cancerous manifestations. Some will say it is necessary to amputate organs. But at the moment, I am applying chemotherapy. Yes.[10]

As discussed in chapter 2, however, racism in Israel consists not merely of attitudes. People defined as "non-Jews" are juridically unequal in Israel, being denied equal access to such resources as state and Jewish-national land. This discrimination, defended in the name of Jewish national "redemption," casts non-Jewish citizens at a major structural disadvantage—a racial formula in itself. The International Convention on the Elimination of All Forms of Racial Discrimination (which Israel ratified in 1979) deliberately defined "racism" intelligently to catch the crucial conflation of national, racial, and ethnic perceptions that drives anti-Semitism. It must therefore carry equal force when Jewish identity configures the designation "Arab" or even "non-Jew" in a manner that similarly

> has the purpose or effect of nullifying or impairing the recognition, enjoyment or exercise, on an equal footing, of human rights and fundamental freedoms in the political, economic, social, cultural or any other field of public life.[11]

In practice, however, arguments about whether "Zionism is racism" have tended more to polarize than to facilitate critical recognition of Israel's discriminatory practices. A more workable term today is *ethnic cleansing*, which, during the disintegration of the former Yugoslavia, was finally elevated in the international human rights lexicon to the status of an odious crime requiring international intervention. Zionism has clearly and openly adopted a logic of ethnic cleansing, most famously in the 1948 and 1967 mass expulsions of Palestinians from land claimed for the Jewish state. The same logic of "cleansing" pervades the explicit Judaization projects of the Jewish Agency, which continue inexorably to transfer Jews into Arab regions and public land to Jewish-only settlements (see chap. 2). Whether Arab identity is understood as racial or ethnic, the humanitarian impact of such treatment is the same.

Yet Israel has never received anything like the concerted international opprobrium and collective action that targeted similar doctrines in South Africa and Serbia, and not only because Israel has been impressively sheltered from such denunciations by strident Zionist accusations that any such criticism reflects anti-Semitism. Several enabling preconditions in European political tradition play in. First, Christian Europe's deep history of subordinating and persecuting Jews (terribly capped rather than defined by the Holocaust) has crippled the West's ability to denounce—or even to grasp—Israel's exclusion and abuses of "non-Jews" in the human rights terms so readily mobilized regarding South African apartheid or the former Yugoslavia. Even the language necessary to describe Israel's clearly discriminatory laws is stifled by this history, as phrases like "Jewish domination" or "Jewish-national supremacy"—ringing so ominously of the West's bloody and disgusting history of ascribing to Jews various fantasy conspiracies toward world domination—are almost unpronounceable to the morally conscientious. Hence, whereas Israel's abuses toward the Palestinians are frequently criticized, the basic premise of Jewish statehood that drives those policies is not being impeded by a hobbling sense of moral obligation (or at least uncomfortable reticence) regarding the Jewish experience. Zionist activists fully appreciate and stoke this brooding discomfort when they denounce any criticism of Israeli policy as anti-Semitic.

The South African case illuminates the political and moral inadequacy of Western critical reticence. It would clearly have been absurd to address South African government abuses of black Africans as arising merely from ethnic tension (calling for black-white "dialogue" and "reconciliation"), without understanding them as reflecting a structural inequality of wealth and power springing from the morally untenable premise of white rule. Grasping the immorality of white supremacy was also essential to grasping and denouncing apartheid's territorial "solutions," for it revealed the Bantustans and townships as extensions or elaborations, rather than redress, of white-settler dominion. Racism, coupled with gross black-white power differentials, precluded any fair division of land and resources in South Africa; apartheid as a whole was rejected by the African National Congress and the international community on precisely that basis.

Yet regarding Israel-Palestine, the generative premise of Jewish dominion over the state has been left sacrosanct; its epiphenomena are (uselessly) decried instead. This exceptional treatment is clearly inadequate on a purely pragmatic basis—in asking an overwhelmingly superior force to sacrifice valued land for peace. But it is also ethically inadequate, in ways that derail action. The goal of the international human rights movement for South Africa was full nonracial democratization and national unity, based on high-minded rejection of ethnoracial hierarchy in democratic government; the international goal in Israel-Palestine—the two-state solution—has been premised on *validating* ethnoracial (Jewish) domination in democratic government. Oddly, the West has not only understood the ethnic-exclusivist Zionist agenda but has endorsed it—and, in doing so, has disavowed the very human rights principles that elsewhere legitimize, empower, and guide international action.

The reasons for the West's exceptional treatment of Israel go beyond lingering sensitivity to the Jewish predicament, however, to a second precondition that calls for greater introspection in the West: Christian-ethnic understanding of Palestine as a biblical landscape. The West does not normally imagine Palestine as a Muslim landscape, despite fourteen centuries of Muslim history there. Rather, the Christian mythic narrative—animated in collective imagination by Hollywood-epic imagery of Moses and the Exodus, Samson and Bathsheeba, David and Goliath, Mary on the donkey, and the pathos of Golgotha, as well as by annual Christian pageants and the like—constructs Palestine as a proto-Christian landscape, naturalizing Jewish Israel as the geopolitical carrier of Judeo-Christian experience. This imagined landscape buttresses the otherwise ludicrous claim that ethnic Jewish indigeneity, dating back two millennia, legally and morally supersedes the ethnic Muslim/Arab indigeneity constructed over at least the past thirteen centuries. (A counterclaim has even been made that, having converted to Islam in the eighth century, the indigenous Christian and Muslim Palestinians are the actual descendants and cultural carriers of the Jewish and Christian societies of antiquity—or, minimally, are more so than European Jews.)[12]

The net effect of this framing and sentimental Christian narrative is to twist the settler-colonial paradigm off the table. By contrast, Afrikaner claims to indigeneity in Africa never successfully overcame the settler-colonial paradigm so glaringly evidenced by white skin and white rule. White ethnoracial domination over South African blacks was obvious, offensive, and easy to denounce—and otherwise-racist governments around the world gained a certain moral wash by doing so. Yet equally glaring juridical Jewish ethnoracial domination of Arabs somehow manifests as accidental fallout of a righteous cause, and its denunciation by outsiders is viewed as unfair targeting of a historically abused people (Jews) engaged in a semisacred mission of "return" to the Holy Land.

This disparity intertwines with the very different profiles that decolonized Africa and the decolonized Arab world have obtained in Western perceptions and on which Zionist propagandists play to foster freshly anti-Arab prejudices and stereotypes in the West. In plain fact, European-Jewish domination of native Arabs has not triggered the visceral moral revulsion in the West that, at least by the late twentieth century, accrued to white South Africans' domination of native black Africans. Again, multiple reasons underlie this distinction. Centuries of geopolitical rivalry between Christian Europe and the Muslim East (especially the Ottoman Empire) have left their legacy in lingering orientalism and its disparaging and exoticizing essentialisms.[13] (The problem has spilled over into the notorious prejudices heaped by Azhkenazi Jews, who dominate Israel's political system, on Sephardic and Mizrahi Jews, who came to Israel from Arab and Muslim regions.) The glutted wealth of Arab oil sheikhdoms also casts, in Western stereotype, a false aura of opulence and political capacity over the entire Arab world (although the combined gross domestic product of the entire Arab world does not total that of Canada).[14]

These discourses are aggravated by Western gullibility to the concept of Arab nationalism—that is, to the proposed existence of an "Arab nation" that shares a common cultural character and solidarity. Pan-Arabism has greatly facilitated Zionist efforts to lump Palestinians into the same basket with a monolithic (and unsympathetic) Arab other and to cast Palestinians as merely one peripheral group of labor migrants in an overprivileged Arab nation—which, simply out of hatred for Jews, democracy, and "freedom," is therefore reactionary and selfish in refusing Jews a homeland in one tiny corner of its vast territory. By contrast, the comparable Afrikaner moral claim—that the Afrikaner "chosen people" bravely settled the empty frontier despite bloody resistance by willfully backward black savages, who, although only roaming through land as hunters and with the rest of continent to sustain them, attacked well-meaning white settlers out of hatred for civilization and enlightenment—was always vastly less convincing.

In sum, looking to the South African experience for guidance or inspiration will avail little unless policymakers also adopt the principles, standards, and values that guided that struggle: that is, that ethnic supremacy is illegitimate and cannot generate a just political system and that formal civil democracy, for all its flaws and lingering injustices, is essential to permitting a more egalitarian and peaceful political competition for resources. Those principles—already incorporated by the Western democracies, to which Israel speciously claims political kinship—require that Palestinians also abandon reactionary notions of ethnonationalist statehood based on Palestinian ethnic, or "Arab," identity. But they certainly require the evaporation of the triggering doctrine, Israel's insistence on permanent Jewish ethnic dominion. The Palestinians have given at least lip service to the idea of a secular-democratic state, laying a groundwork for negotiations on democratic principles. But the very idea of ethnic equality or multiethnic democracy is explicitly rejected by dominant Israeli doctrine. If that rejection is actually *accepted* by the international community, the South African experience in eliminating apartheid must be considered irrelevant.

A second comparison often invoked by anxious observers of the flaccid Middle East "peace process" is the case of Northern Ireland. This case, too, is superficially similar: two ethnonationalist groups are juxtaposed in one small land; both have immovable ties to their communities, framed by competing discourses of ethnic rights and indigeneity; one ethnicity dominated the government to the clear disadvantage of the other; economic inequities gave one ethnicity (here, Protestants) clear incentives to sustain the status quo; and decades of violence framed by rival ethnic nationalisms had translated into crippling mutual hostility and suspicion, impeding even talks toward any power sharing. The Good Friday Agreement hinged on mutual sacrifice of long-standing rival ambitions to gain sovereignty over the entire territory (Protestant union with the United Kingdom or Catholic union with the Republic of Ireland). As rival territorial nationalisms also appear to drive conflict in Israel-Palestine, the relevance of the comparison seems strong.

Yet the difference between Northern Ireland and Israel-Palestine replicates the difference with South Africa. In Northern Ireland, rival ambitions abandoned claims for exclusive ethnic possession of the territory. Reconciliation therefore engaged the onus of democratization, after mutual admission by Protestant unionists and Irish republicans that—as neither nationalism could fulfill its ambition for full sovereignty in the territory—multiethnic democracy and power sharing must be faced as necessary. Israel has made no such admission: again, its stated program is to reject even the suggestion of ethnic equality. The stand precludes any accommodation of Palestinian residence, interest, or historical connection in the land of Israel; instead, it forces a two-state solution to accommodate the Zionist principle of permanent Jewish ethnic dominion. Moreover, especially in the right-wing Zionist worldview (now in control of the state and dominating diplomacy and U.S. Zionist discourse), Jewish ethnic dominion within Israel is not argued simply as a national right; it is claimed as an essential condition for Jewish national survival. Since democratic inclusion of Palestinians would wreck the Jewishness of the Jewish state, multiethnic democracy is seen by right-wing Zionists as a short path to Jewish national annihilation—possibly even Jewish physical annihilation. This discursive condition never pertained in Northern Ireland.

In both the South African and Northern Ireland conflicts, the correct assumption was that prejudice, fear, and suspicion were indeed primary obstacles to a stable peace, because they impeded the necessary trust and willingness to abandon old unworkable doctrines of ethnic or racial domination and negotiate toward power sharing in a fully democratic government. But the Israeli-Palestinian conflict does not hinge on attitudes (fears, hatreds, racism) in the same way. Exercises to bring both sides together—for example, high school camps where Palestinian and Israeli children learn to cook and sing together—have no significance. For although fear and loathing for Arabs concretizes popular Jewish-Zionist commitment to ethnic exclusion, the territorial exclusion central to Zionism was not born from fear or loathing of Arabs. Rather, antipathy toward Arabs is an accidental outgrowth of Zionist's fundamental nationalist premise, which is exclusive Jewish control over the land. Concomitantly, Palestinian antipathy toward Jews is not born of anti-Semitism (as pro-Israeli voices invariably claim) but has arisen from the stated mission of Israel to transfer Palestinian land to Jews, a project framed by the legal system, occupation policy, and Jewish-national privileges inspired by Zionist discourse and vested in the Jewish state.

This point is particularly relevant to Western Christians whose understanding of conflict resolution derives heavily from their belief in the transformative power of mutual human understanding. Certainly, breaking down negative ethnic or racial stereotypes is a potent achievement in all cases and can generate new energies toward peace within opposing parties. But in Israel-Palestine, two peoples learning to see each other as human beings is not the problem. Political Zionism is the problem, because it has always presupposed—and therefore seeks to manifest—an Arab-free landscape to enable full Jewish national "redemption." Of course, Palestinian society and nationalism can be held culpable for rejecting that project and for remaining rooted in and insisting on retaining their ancestral territory—and certainly the Palestinian leadership has been appallingly inept (as discussed in chap. 4). But such an argument condemning indigenous resistance would never be entertained elsewhere.

Accepting that human accord is here trumped by nationalist doctrine, international diplomacy has instead tried to accommodate both agendas through the ubiquitous formula "two peoples in one land." The formula is a sincere gesture toward evenhandedness and mutual recognition and has been dutifully adopted by voices on all sides.[15] Yet the "two peoples" concept has actually confused and derailed conflict resolution, because it recasts a settler-colonial conflict as a symmetrical rivalry between two peoples holding morally and politically equal claims and power. That formula cannot generate any successful peace process, because it obscures not only the extreme power differences at play (Israel's overwhelming strength) but also the Zionist ideology of ethnic exclusion that has shaped the Israeli-Palestinian conflict from its outset. Two rival national movements sharing comparable historical roots in one land—such as Croatian and Serbian nationalism—might find some workable compromise (political and/or territorial) if fears and mutual suspicions can be overcome. But a settler-colonial conflict requires substantively addressing native resentments about the injustice of their subordination and dispossession. The material and judicial dimensions of that project are daunting in themselves but they also engage a social-psychological dimension—that the settler society recant some basic elements of its own mission (as did South Africa), particularly its ideologies and practices of domination and dispossession, in order to steer fundamental changes in policy. That discursive step is one that Zionists have generally been unwilling to take—indeed, have rejected in the strongest terms—not least because it would entail sacrificing the myths of innocence and high-minded intent that, although important to all settler-colonist societies, are especially crucial to Zionism.

If this discursive dimension of the conflict seems trivial or superfluous to some, its political significance was demonstrated in the Oslo process. Oslo incorporated the "two peoples in one land" formula in emphasizing a historic reconciliation between two equally fearful and hostile peoples. Those observers entertaining the "two peoples" formula therefore sustained much misplaced optimism about Oslo, because they presumed that it was successfully overcoming the basic problem, an inability to compromise. By contrast, those observers viewing the Israeli-Palestinian conflict as a settler-colonial conflict foresaw Oslo's failure as inevitable, because Israel was never required (and never offered) to redress Palestinian dispossession in action or principle—for example, most obviously, through a settlement freeze or, more important, through formal acknowledgment that Israel is culpable for that dispossession. Such acknowledgment is the essential precondition for truly productive "final status" negotiations about Jerusalem and Palestinian return (whatever the actual details of the resulting agreements). In the absence of that admission, talks can only reproduce prior outcomes, which have accorded with the premise of Israel's innocence and fair dealing. Again, the South African case illuminates the political inutility of such talks.

Central Europe

Although pro-Israel spokespeople often claim that Israel is "the only democracy in the Middle East," civil democracy on the Western European or North American model—examples which guided the South African and Northern Ireland efforts—is, far from being a goal, not even an admissible option for Zionism. More apt comparisons are therefore those drawn by Zionists who point to ethnonationalist conflicts in which territorial division is the evident solution, such as partition in Yugoslavia or the split of Czechoslovakia into two ethnic republics. Indeed, early traditional Zionists took their inspiration from the Central European ethnonationalisms of the early twentieth century (e.g., Ze'ev Jabotinsky's primary model for nation-building was his native Poland). In partitioning the former Yugoslavia into independent states modeled roughly from historical ethnic territories (or ideas about them), the international community freshly revalidated the idea that, even in the twenty-first century, an ethnic nation can still claim a state territory as a legitimate and necessary condition for its survival and cultural expression. Why then, demand Zionists, should the world deny the Jewish nation a state in its historical "homeland" of Palestine—especially when the "Arabs" (accidentally in residence) have so vast a territory of their own? Is not Israel indeed simply replicating the history of any nation—for example, France—in establishing its own state?

But Israel operates on a model that none of the Balkan or Central European countries would entertain and it is certainly not reflected in France.[16] Technically, Israeli citizens (*ezrahut*) have equal rights: for example, all can vote. But according to its own laws, Israel is not a nation-state in the sense understood in all other countries—that is, the state of its citizens, who are nationals by virtue of that citizenship. Nor is Israel simply a Jewish state in the sense that Italy is a Catholic state or that Malaysia and Iran are Islamic states—in adopting religious teachings as guidelines for civil law. Rather, Israel is officially the state of the *Jewish nation*. Non-Jews can be citizens of Israel, but they cannot be nationals (*le'um*) of Israel, because no "Israeli" national identity exists under Israeli law.[17] Only the Jewish nation has juridical status, and a great body of civil rights and privileges are consigned to that nation. These rights are secured to Jews by limiting them to citizens who would qualify for Israeli citizenship under the 1950 Law of Return (as discussed in chap. 2). No non-Jewish nationality can gain comparable national rights and privileges, because no other nationality is admitted to hold legal rights within the country: "Arab," "Muslim," and "Christian" identities are considered only "pre-national formations." Thus Israel sustains the image and conceits of a universal democracy while preserving strikingly unequal access by Jewish and Arab citizens to the country's resources and privileges (land and building permits, educational and housing benefits, cultural services, and so forth).[18]

No resemblance to present-day Western democracies is evident in this formula. Certainly, France offers no similarity. "French" nationality is gained with citizenship. Moreover, in stark contrast to Israel, all residents of French territory were deliberately socialized into "French" identity through concerted education and market-integration programs in the nineteenth century.[19] The United States offers no similarity, either, despite racial inequalities that still obviously favor whites; no "Anglo nation" is inscribed in the U.S. Constitution, for example. Neither does Israel's model reflect governance in the Central European states or even in the ethnonationalist states that broke off from the former Yugoslavia—where, once carrying citizenship, anyone of any ethnicity is a national of the state and has juridically equal access to public resources. In all these states, discrimination among citizens on the basis of race or ethnicity is explicitly proscribed in their constitutions. By contrast, Israel's Basic Law proscribes *elimination* of the preferential rights granted to citizens of Jewish nationality. Within all the Western democracies, ethnic and racial tensions and inequality persist, but juridical and philosophical illegitimacy of any racial or ethnic hierarchy establishes the legal and political foundations for ongoing social struggles toward ethnic equality. In Israel, struggling for ethnic equality, at least in any way that would impugn the Jewish state (i.e., Jewish ethnic dominion over the government), is actually illegal.[20]

What underlies Israel's grim determination to secure Jewish ethnonationalist dominion by means so grotesquely at odds with Western liberal-democratic norms—in whose development, ironically, Jewish intellectuals were, historically, such important and inspired architects? Given Jewish history, so fraught with subordination and violence by ethnic others, the answer is obvious. A host of powerful emotions, beliefs, and collective experience indeed converge in Zionism, lending defense of Jewish statehood its passionate intensity. So passionate indeed are those feelings—reflecting, after the Holocaust, especially deep wells of fear and pain—that they are usually held exempt from critical examination. Yet if these feelings drive a doctrine of ethnic domination now leading Israel and the region toward unmanageable violence, they can no longer be held immune from a closer look.

One question especially remains murky, and in its vagueness lie hidden possibilities: if Israel must remain a "Jewish state," what exactly must be "Jewish" about the state? Israel's supporters may believe that preserving Israel's Jewish character is a cultural, ethnic, or religious mission, fundamentally a survival imperative, or all of these intertwined. But teasing apart these arguments may help to defuse— or at least differently illuminate—some of the strong emotions now surrounding them and to open new possibilities for their reassessment and reconception. The first step toward that project is to explore the central bastion of mainstream Zionism: its historical narrative—which is now under increasing strain.

Emotions about any national identity or national territory do not arise spontaneously. Embracing far-flung populations and territory beyond the immediate experience of any individual, nations are necessarily "imagined communities," conceptualized through images, historical narratives, ceremonies, and symbols developed specifically to inspire collective identity and political loyalty.[21] Related perceptions and beliefs then inspire and channel emotions—patriotic passion, collective hopes and fears, identification with the nation against its enemies—into behavior that serves the national project, such as willing military service. And a foundational component of any national identity is a shared understanding of its history.

The Palestinian-Israeli conflict is framed, above all, by competing versions of history, mythologized—as are all national histories—to mobilize mass loyalty and consensus in contemporary struggles. Already used in this book, the term *mytho-history* means not false history but a strategic and romanticized reading of historical events to suit later political agendas. Without such framing, material events (e.g., the Holocaust or the Palestinian *nakba*) would be politically indeterminate: people could take very different lessons from such collective experiences and be inspired to quite different political reactions. Nation- and state-building projects are therefore famous (or notorious) for generating mytho-histories that steer reactions toward supporting the state and its policies: for example, by incorporating some events while strategically omitting others; centering the narrative on one group (e.g., the "Jewish people" or the "Palestinian people") and sidelining or erasing others; retelling tortured national moments, such as a revolution, as noble and heroic; and casting as linear and visionary a nation-building process that was for decades internally fragmented, murky, and conflicted. In states the world over, school textbooks, national holidays, statues, monuments, maps, and scholarship are all organized to endorse "official" historical narratives created strategically to complement state legitimacy and authority, by affirming the nation's noble origins, its organic relationship to the territory, and its central values, character, and mission.

Thus a nationalist history gains mythic force in its pageantry of "legendary heroes and exemplary figures, dramatic events and golden epochs, immemorial lineages and durable traditions."[22] History also composes the landscape itself, giving it symbolic meaning. Individuals are then motivated to identify with that landscape—to defend and even die for it.

The ubiquitous formula "Israel-Palestine" reflects this dual historicized view of land, as, coexisting in the same terrain, the landscape perceived by Zionists differs profoundly from the landscape perceived by Palestinians. The latter is an Arab landscape, defined by Arab towns, fields, orchards, and roads, some of which have been razed and exist only in memory. On this Arab landscape, the Jewish settlements are alien objects, sterile and out of place—prefabricated orange-roofed invaders. The Palestinian interpretation of that landscape is straightforward: a settler-colonial movement has seized most Palestinian land and is incrementally seizing the rest, through brute force, slippery dealings, and the tacit backing of Western imperial powers. Zionist views are more varied and complicated (as discussed later in this chapter) but understand the landscape largely through the concept of "return": the land is Jewish; the Jews have come back to their ancient homeland after two millennia in exile and are raising lovely communities in which Jewish ideals of community and values can at last be fully articulated. That visionary mission is confronting a tattered and backward Arab presence that wandered into the land in some later era. And as Arabs are culturally unequipped to grasp the grand significance and national character of Jewish return, their ignorance and Muslim parochialism are translating into irrational and obdurate hatred, expressed in unspeakably brutal attacks.

Rival mytho-histories are mustered to defend these rival worldviews, in a struggle that plays out as a metaconflict (a conflict about the very nature of the conflict).[23] This metaconflict over history plagues and hamstrings any peace negotiations, bogs any discussion down in endless loops of argument, and polarizes the international community (while the Zionist narrative is endorsed by the U.S. government, the Palestinian view is increasingly endorsed by everyone else). Anyone who has dealt with the Israeli-Palestinian conflict has confronted long (often wearying) rival expositions. Palestinian mytho-history was composed largely in reaction to the Zionist narrative, through blow-by-blow refutations of Zionist claims about "empty" land and an immigrant Arab population. The Zionist narrative was therefore a launching point for resulting rounds of argument, and, in its present common form, might be summarized something like this.

Around the turn of the twentieth century, a small but gallant band of Jewish idealists, perceiving dangerous anti-Semitism in Europe, returned to the Jewish biblical homeland to create an ideal Jewish society. They mustered funds to buy some land from the Arabs in the mostly empty and unfertile territory, and by working hard and employing European techniques, they managed to turn desert and swamps into green and productive farms. Their success attracted Arab immigrants, who were drawn to the work opportunities, and the Arab population also rose. By the 1930s, Hitler's threat was driving desperate refugees to Palestine, and the Jewish homeland became a crucial sanctuary.

But the Arabs were jealous and resentful of the Jews' success and disliked Jews anyway because they were non-Muslims. Vicious and self-seeking Arab leaders agitated against the Zionists, who sought only peaceful coexistence in the biblical homeland. Arabs began to attack and kill Jews, and the Jewish community was obliged to defend itself. The United Nations tried to mediate by offering their partition plan (in which both peoples could be accommodated in part of the territory), which the Jews accepted. But the irrational and greedy Arabs refused the deal, instead attacking the peace-loving Jewish community. In the resulting War of Independence in 1947–48, the small Jewish force defended itself valiantly against five Arab armies, who sought to throw the Jews into the sea. By a miracle, the understaffed and underequipped Jewish forces prevailed. The Arab leadership had called on its people to leave their homes during the fighting, and although the Israeli leadership appealed to the Arab people to return, they refused to live under Jewish rule, and they remain in refugee camps today because surrounding Arab states callously refuse to grant them citizenship, instead using their plight as a political tool.

As the years went by, Israel repeatedly sought peace, seeking only recognition of the Jewish state by its Arab neighbors. But the Arabs always rejected all efforts, insisting that the only solution was the destruction of the Jewish state and expulsion of the Jews. In 1967, threatened by Egypt and Syria, Israel attacked to defend itself and again miraculously prevailed, taking the West Bank, Golan Heights, and Sinai. Israel was treacherously attacked without warning in 1973 by coordinated Arab armies but again survived through heroic effort. Finally, the great peacemaker, Egyptian president Anwar Sadat, stepped forward and signed a peace agreement, and optimism soared. But instead of following his example, the terrorist PLO sustained its adamant rejection of peace and, whipping up mass support through bribery, threats, and propaganda, ruined every diplomatic effort at a fair compromise. Israel remains on the defensive, supported by a loyal Jewish diaspora and its good friend and protector the United States, which is alone among the great world powers in truly appreciating the Jewish plight and its need for a state. The Palestinians speak about peace but continue to show their true colors by ghastly terror attacks on innocent civilians. Peace-loving Israel must therefore look to its own interests and protect its people somehow—by a firm hand in controlling these savages, by raising a terribly expensive security fence to defend itself against the terrorists, and even (perhaps, ultimately, out of sheer necessity) by transferring the Palestinians across the Jordan River into the true "Palestinian state," which is Jordan.[24]

The Palestinian mytho-history, of course, reverses much of this account, providing the mirror view of Jewish settlement.

Around the turn of the twentieth century, the Arabs in Palestine, living in their panoply of ancient towns and villages, were beginning to hope for independence from hated and crumbling Turkish rule. But just as the political conditions for an Arab state were coming together, a small group of Jewish-European fanatics arrived, backed by the colonial British, with plans to create a Jewish state in Arab land. Relations between Palestinian Arabs and Jews had always been friendly; they took tea on each other's porches. But the Zionist settlers began to buy up thousands of acres of village land, expelling tens of thousands of Arab peasants. With British support, they established their own government, which openly aimed to establish an exclusively Jewish state.

The Arabs protested, and even the British tried to limit the Jews' arrival, but they came illegally in ever greater numbers. The Palestinians began to fight against their own dispossession, but the Zionists developed terror squads (e.g., the Irgun) that murdered Palestinians and launched guerrilla attacks against the

British (e.g., blowing up the King David Hotel), proving their ruthlessness. The new United Nations, controlled by the great Western powers, proposed to hand over major portions of Palestine—including its great northern port cities and fertile northern coast—to the Jewish state, even though, in 1947, the Arabs were still the vast majority. The Palestinians naturally rejected the West's dismemberment of their country and tried to fight. But they were militarily weak and poorly organized, while the Zionists had Western weaponry and superior forces. Moreover, King Abdullah of Jordan struck a secret deal with the Zionists to allow them to take the land given them by the UN. In the fighting, the Zionists waged a campaign of terror and deliberate expulsion, massacring hundreds of Palestinian villagers and forcing 750,000 Palestinians to flee. The Zionists then bulldozed some five hundred Palestinian villages in the territory of the new Jewish state, to prevent the Palestinians from returning, and only the sabra cactus still marks where those villages once stood.

As the years went by, the Palestinians and Arabs repeatedly sought peace, seeking only to regain their ancestral homes and lands. Israel rejected all efforts, insisting that the Palestinians could never return and that the Arabs must recognize Israel's confiscation of the Palestinian homeland. In 1967, Israel aggressively attacked and seized the West Bank, Golan Heights, and Sinai, proving its expansionist character. In 1973, the Arabs managed a serious counterattack, which made no territorial gains but at least restored Arab pride. But Anwar Sadat treacherously made a private peace with Israel, leaving Israel free to continue its oppression of the Palestinians in the occupied territories. Under occupation, the Palestinians nevertheless sustained a heroic resistance, coordinated through the democratic PLO, their government in exile. Many governments and people around the world sympathized with the Palestinians, but the U.S. government, insulated from the truth by Israel, vetoed any UN resolutions that sought to end the occupation. Now Israel is consolidating its final control over the West Bank, imprisoning the Palestinians in fragments of their land and barricading them behind an enormous wall, the likes of which the world has not seen since the Berlin Wall.[25]

These narratives are not frozen but are continually adapted to suit changing times and factional differences. In recent years, the Zionist narrative has split bitterly into three camps, which, according to Israeli-Jewish historian Ilan Pappé, "seem to be in a battle over memory, reality, and vision, or over the past, present, and future." The main current—and Prime Minister Rabin's basis in negotiating the Oslo Accords—is what Pappé calls "traditional Zionism," which embraces both the Labor and Likud Parties. This current has underlain "the policies and plans of all Israeli governments since the creation of the state" and remains "the principal prism through which the political centre and the professional elites in Israel view the Israeli-Palestinian reality." Drawing on what he has experienced as "thousands of boring micro-histories" (supported, he notes, by a full flank of Israeli academic scholarship), Pappé sketches the more value-laden mytho-history through which traditional Zionism today constructs its own innocence while acknowledging internal troubles resulting from Israel's conflict with the Palestinians and the Arab world.

> In their [the traditional Zionists'] reconstructed view, Zionism was a national movement, humanist, liberal, and socialist, which brought modernization and progress to primitive Palestine, made the desert bloom, re-built the ruined cities of the land and introduced modern agriculture and industry to the benefit of everyone, Arab and Jew alike. Zionism was resisted by a combination of Islamic fanaticism, pro-Arab British colonialism and the local tradition and culture of political violence. Against all odds, and despite a most cruel local resistance, Zionism remained loyal to humanist precepts of individual and collective behavior and tirelessly stretched out its hand to its Arab neighbors, who kept rejecting it. Against all odds, the Zionists also miraculously established a state in the face of a hostile Arab world. A state that, notwithstanding an objective shortage of space and means, absorbed one million Jews who had been expelled from the Arab world, and offered them progress and integration in the only democracy in the Middle East. It was a defensive state trying to contain ever-growing Arab hostility and world apathy; a state that took in Jews from more than one hundred places in the diaspora, gathered them in and made one new Jewish people out of them. It was a moral, just movement of redemption, which unfortunately found another people in its homeland, but nonetheless offered them a share in a better future, which they foolishly rejected. This idyllic picture, so runs the reconstruction, was undermined and shattered by the evil consequences of the 1967 war and the political earthquake of 1977, which brought Likud to power. After, and because of,

1967, negative features have developed, such as territorial expansion and religious fanaticism on the right, and self-doubt and self-hatred on the extreme left. But it is a reversible development that can be stopped by returning to the traditional Zionist values of humanism, democracy, and liberalism.[26]

The "negative features" that Pappé identifies as challenging the "traditional" stream from the right and left are sometimes labeled "neo-Zionism" and "post-Zionism" (mentioned in chap. 3). Both reflect social change in Israel and, increasingly, discrete political camps. For instance, Pappé understands neo-Zionism as emerging from four "parallel processes":

> the fanaticisation of the national religious groups in Israel (whose strongholds are in the settlements and in a wide network of Yeshiva centres, funded by the state); the nationalisation or Zionisation of the previously anti-Zionist ultra-Orthodox Jews; the ethnic insulation of segments of the Mizrahi Jewish community caught in the geographical and social margins of society; and the fast integration of Israel into capitalist globalisation, which adds an intellectual neo-conservative centre, à la New Right, to the alliance.[27]

Gaining influence especially during the right-wing Netanyahu and Sharon governments, neo-Zionism is represented in a recent coalition of right-wing conservative and religious factions, which seeks to reconfigure Israel as an ethnoreligious theocracy, invoking the "glorious past" of the Second Temple period (200 BCE–70 CE). In this purified religious-nationalist order, traditional Zionists (and their liberal-secular tendencies) will be marginalized and voiceless; non-Jews of any stamp will, of course, be entirely excluded. The neo-Zionist appeal, according to Pappé, is not only its clear, uncompromising biblical vision, which promises national unity, but its hard rejectionist line toward the Palestinians—both doctrines being attractive to some Israelis struggling with a loss of political direction. Having gained control of the school system under the Netanyahu government and flourishing in a strategic alliance with hard-line militants in the Sharon government, the neo-Zionists are positioned to gain significant ground in Israeli popular political thought.

Neo-Zionists stridently denounce the "self-doubt" and "self-hate" of post-Zionists, who, on the opposite tack, are critiquing Israel's ethnonationalist mission from a liberal-secular position and with an emphasis on democratic values. Gaining force especially in the post-Oslo period and reacting to the violence of the occupation, post-Zionists promote a vision of Israel as a secular-democratic state that may preserve special accommodations for Jews (e.g., the Law of Return) but otherwise should serve all its citizens equally. For their part, post-Zionists dislike and reject the ethnocentrism of traditional Zionism and are appalled and repelled by the "fanaticism" and racism of neo-Zionists.

Still small and fragile, the post-Zionist movement has been freshly invigorated by recent archaeological conclusions, especially a wave of revisionist scholarship that, drawing on newly released documents from Israeli government archives, has uncovered a version of history much more in accord with the Palestinian account. Some of this work addresses the biblical foundations of the Zionist narrative. Israeli archaeologists have combed the area for decades attempting to confirm the Jewish historical narrative of the Exodus and Jewish conquest but have failed to do so. Instead, they have confirmed evidence of a more incremental Jewish arrival, smaller polities, and a pattern of shared lives by multiple peoples in the land. This unraveling of foundational Jewish-nationalist myths might be considered politically irrelevant; as Walter Laqueur has pointed out, few religions or nations fail to mythologize their origins.[28] But Zionist discourse invokes the biblical narrative not as myth but as historical fact, to support claims to exclusive Jewish sovereignty. These findings therefore unseat the Zionist claim of a natural right to "restore" exclusive Jewish sovereignty over a region that does not seem to have known such uncontested sovereignty in the past. Instead, the archaeological record would support a modern doctrine of cohabitation.

Moreover, the nationalist idyll of a peace-loving Zionist mission, forced to harsh measures by intransigent Arab hostility, has taken a series of body blows. Pappé himself is one of several "new historians" and sociologists—prominently including Avi Shlaim, Ephraim Nimni, Uri Ram, and (although rather against his will) Benny Morris—who have lent the imprimatur of their Jewish ethnic position to long-standing Palestinian claims and greatly rattled the official version of Israeli's history.[29] It was always known to scholars (as to the early Zionist settlers) that a hefty Arab society of some six hundred thousand people was well established in the territory when the first Zionists arrived in the 1880s. It was also known from published statements and writings by early Zionists that they understood the need to "spirit" or "transfer" those people out of the country in order to establish a Jewish state. But the "new historians" substantiated the most serious Palestinian grievances—that the Zionist forces launched a deliberate military campaign of massacres and terror to expel the Palestinians from their villages in the war of 1948; that the Arab states later offered peace proposals that Israel deflected or ignored; and that, far from reacting defensively, Ben-Gurion and other politicians provoked war with Jordan and Egypt in 1967 to permit further land acquisition, particularly of Jerusalem and the West Bank.

These revisionist histories are seriously challenging the classic Zionist mytho-history and engross large Israeli readerships for this reason.[30] Revelations about a deliberate expulsion of the Palestinians especially strikes at the self-image of a peace-loving and defensive Israel. For many, the hitherto rosy self-image of a righteous national effort is at least dimming with advancing doubt. But if the "official" mytho-history no longer so effectively casts a moral gloss over Israeli state policy toward the Palestinians, that policy must rest more heavily on other ideas. The rest of this chapter traces some common arguments for a Jewish state and explores their relevance to the two-state and one-state solutions.

THE ZIONIST MISSION

No short treatment of Zionist thought can do justice to it. For one thing, Zionism engages a depth of emotions often hard for outsiders to appreciate and not easily conveyed in print. It is also composed of many currents, which trace to disparate (and sometimes rival) doctrines formulated in the late nineteenth and especially the early twentieth centuries. Scholars have identified various typologies—"revisionist," "labor," "political," "religious," "spiritual," "culturalist"—

but each is subdivided by internal disagreements and evolving colorations. Politicians such as Yitzhak Rabin, Ehud Barak, Benjamin Netanyahu, and Ariel Sharon adapt and manipulate these currents rather than invent them. For example, Sharon regularly quotes from hard-liner Ze'ev Jabotinsky (1880–1940) and Sharon's policies toward the Palestinians strikingly mirror Jabotinsky's doctrine regarding the "iron wall," summarized in this 1923 passage:

> I do not mean to assert that no agreement whatever is possible with the Arabs of the Land of Israel. But a voluntary agreement is just not possible. As long as the Arabs preserve a gleam of hope that they will succeed in getting rid of us, nothing in the world can cause them to relinquish this hope, precisely because they are not a rabble but a living people. And a living people will be ready to yield on such fateful issues only when they have given up all hope of getting rid of the alien settlers. Only then will extremist groups with their slogans "No, never" lose their influence, and only then will their influence be transferred to more moderate groups. And only then will the moderates offer suggestions for compromise. Then only will they begin bargaining with us on practical matters, such as guarantees against pushing them out, and equality of civil and national rights. . . . the sole way to such an agreement is through the iron wall, that is to say, the establishment in Palestine of a force that will in no way be influenced by Arab pressure. In other words, the only way to achieve a settlement in the future is total avoidance of all attempts to arrive at a settlement in the present.[31]

Jabotinsky's view was, however, initially far from dominant; he was indeed writing to convince other Zionists, who shared little consensus about how to form a Jewish state. For instance, in philosophizing Jewish national revival, Ahad Ha'am emphasized spiritual and cultural renewal; aware of the Arab population, he decried Zionist settler abuses of Arabs and never fully endorsed Jewish statehood in the first place. Such prominent liberal Zionists as Martin Buber and Judah Magnes argued hard for a state shared equally by Jews and Arabs and denounced ideas of "transfer" (ideas enlarged in chap. 6) as inhumane and even sinful. But the school that triumphed in the formation of Israel, called "traditional Zionism" by Pappé and "political Zionism" or "mainstream Zionism" by others, took as its central imperative the project of establishing Jewish-national control over a state in Palestine.

Political Zionism itself is woven from disparate threads of argument, however, and individual Zionists hold more strongly to some threads depending on their own family history, religiosity, and general political worldview. This heterodoxy indeed allows Zionism the necessary flexibility to enlist diverse opinions behind the state-building project in the territory of Mandate Palestine. Resulting arguments, drawn from myriad public debates and writings, will be grouped here (with some abuse to their nuances and internal dissent) as they refer to ethnic sanctuary, geographic security, national expression, *Volksgeist,* and equal standing. Any peace proposal must engage these ideas, which deploy in complex and strategically shifting currents and engage disparate secular-nationalist, religious, and spiritual values about the land.

Ethnic Sanctuary

Among political Zionist arguments for a Jewish state, probably most familiar to readers is the claim that a Jewish state is necessary as a vital sanctuary for Jews in a world plagued by anti-Semitism.[32] This argument carries very broad force among Jews, who are keenly aware that their regular experience of ongoing anti-Semitism (whether serious or minor) resonates from a deep Christian and European tradition whose capacity for serious danger was irrefutably demonstrated by the Holocaust, or Shoa.[33] Nazi Germany, of course, murdered millions of Jews (among millions of others) in one of the greatest crimes against humanity of the modern era, nearly exterminating the old Jewish populations of Eastern Europe. That terrible experience crystallized once-ambivalent Jewish support for political Zionism almost overnight, in the 1940s, galvanizing passionate support (even what Hannah Arendt called a "suicidal impulse") for forming the new state. The trauma was imported into Jewish-Israeli discourse in a very immediate sense when Nazi terror triggered mass migrations of European Jews to Palestine in the 1930s and 1940s, greatly expanding the Jewish population in Palestine and providing the critical demographic mass for statehood. (In 1930, the Jewish population totaled only some 174,000, or just 16 percent of the population in Mandate Palestine; fourteen years later, it had tripled to 500,000, or about one-third of the population.)

Hence, the Holocaust became central to Israel's Jewish-nationalist iconography as (in classic nationalist fashion) the personal experience and lasting trauma of many Israeli-Jewish families were both commemorated and instrumentalized as a central moral legitimation for Israel's formation. The argument is undeniably powerful. Whether understood as a preventative ("never again") or as a political shelter in which a brutalized people could recover its collective psyche, a Jewish state can easily manifest as a necessary haven as well as the ennobled tragic carrier of European Jewry's culturally rich yet brutalized legacy. This discourse has been very broadly diffused through Holocaust literature, films, and in memorials (including the Holocaust Museum in Washington, D.C.), in which accounts of the horrific destruction of European Jewry by Nazi persecution commonly end with a Zionist tag, with some reference to the shelter or comfort that survivors found in Israel.

No minimization of these sentiments is intended here; they have been freshly validated within living memory and remain a backdrop validation for maintaining Israel as a Jewish state, even for Jews who do not anticipate any serious trouble in their home environments, in countries around the world. Still, the ethnic-sanctuary argument for sustaining Israel as an actual Jewish state is not as hegemonic as it might seem. Some Jewish critics protest that past brutalities, although never to be forgotten, no longer shape Jewish life or needs either in Israel or in the diaspora. (A small corpus of internal Jewish dissent even complains that a "Holocaust industry" has exploited and instrumentalized that terrible collective trauma to serve Israeli realpolitik.)[34] In this view, Jews today have better conditions in the Western democracies than anywhere else or at any time in history: anti-Semitism certainly persists but has dwindled to occasional irritants without serious substance. Passively supporting this argument are millions of Jews who live comfortably in European and North American democracies and do not want to live in Israel—not least because, far from gaining protection in Israel, they perceive that Jews are today nowhere subjected to more danger than in Israel itself.

From this perspective, while Israel is symbolically important as an ultimate Jewish refuge in case of catastrophe, the more strident project of a "Jewish state" is overdrawn. For some, Israel is even seen as vaguely corrosive to life within the Jewish diaspora—especially when its brutal occupation policies are deliberately identified by Zionists as reflecting the interests and will of Jews everywhere, tarring all with the same brush.[35]

All these objections are strongly contested by other Zionists, who protest and disparage the post-Zionists' naïveté about latent anti-Semitism.[36] Indeed, given a string of recent attacks in Europe on Jewish targets (synagogues, cemeteries, individuals), apparently in retaliation for Israel's policies toward the Palestinians, persistence of a pernicious anti-Semitic substratum in the West can hardly be dismissed. Still, post-Zionist Jewish views suggest that a different model for Israel might be even more efficacious on the question of sanctuary: to sustain the Jewish state as a durable haven for Jews (partly by retaining the Law of Return) but to relinquish the tenet of a Jewish majority, which presently entails discriminatory policies so painfully contradicting Jewish-liberal values. Zionists who see this formula as a quick route to Jewish annihilation (at the hands of an Arab majority) fiercely attack this suggestion, but the split in opinion indicates at least enough internal division to delegitimize any claim that it is unthinkable. (This debate is examined at more length in chap. 6.)

Precisely because Western democracies offer such relatively comfortable conditions for Jews, however, the Zionist ethnic-sanctuary argument today is redirected mostly toward the Arab world. In this view, it is primarily Arab hatred for Jews and Israel's constant threat of annihilation from Arab armies, which justifies Israel's well-fortified existence. Attacks by Hamas and other Palestinian suicide bombers targeting Israeli civilians have greatly reinforced this sense of intransigent anti-Jewish hatred and the belief that increasing Palestinian political power—for example, by democratization—would quickly doom Jewish Israelis to marginalization, oppression, and even expulsion. The Arabs, it is believed, have always sworn to "throw the Jews into the sea" and will do so at the first opportunity. Israel's remaining a Jewish state—in the sense of Jews dominating the state institutions—is therefore argued as an imperative against persistent Arab and Muslim hostility for which Palestinians would comprise a fifth column.[37] Coupled with memories of genocidal anti-Semitism in Europe, this perception of a monolithic and hostile Arab world assembles to comprise what one author called "the politics of fear."[38]

Although the revisionist histories mentioned earlier in this chapter have thoroughly discredited the stock Zionist claim that the Arab world has been intransigently hostile, certainly some Arab and Palestinian language supports this accusation when speaking of enmity toward "the Jews." But the Zionist argument (and genuine fears) play on a confusion. From the first major Jewish land purchases and political advances of the Zionist project, Arab and Palestinian communities and nationalists confronted "Jewish" not as an ethnic identity but as a rival national identity, deployed by Zionist politicians and military forces intent on taking Arab land for its state-building project. Although Arabs are certainly not immune from anti-Semitism, Arab language against "the Jews" reacts primarily to Zionist explicit promotion and privileging of "the Jews" and to the Palestinians' expulsion and dispossession in favor of "the Jews." (It behooves us periodically to recall that the label "Jewish settlements" is not simply descriptive but actually a legal formula: no non-Jew is permitted to live in these settlements.) Arab reaction therefore targets "Jews" not *qua* Jews but because "Jewish" is the political identity that Arabs confront in the fundamental conflict over the land. (For instance if, in some bizarre twist, the same project had been launched by a movement of, say, Southern Baptists, the enemy would be "the Baptists.")

To obscure this settler-colonial dynamic, political Zionism has sought to demonize Arab, Muslim, and Palestinian enmity for "the Jews" as deriving from the same anti-Semitic traditions and motives that plagued Jews in Europe.[39] Racism, orientalism, and Eurocentrism interlace this vision: Arabs are viewed as uncivilized, willfully backward, unscrupulous, and treacherous, with the barbarian's loathing of civilization and enlightenment.[40] Some recent pro-Israeli writings have traced Arab hostility to *resentiment* arising from envy of the golden and decadent Western life depicted on imported Western media or even—a notion pumped up in the Bush era—to simply a hatred for "freedom," emblemized by Israel, "the only democracy in the Middle East." Arabs are also portrayed as irrationally selfish as they have plenty of other places to go (Zionist rhetoric often cites "twenty-two Arab countries" at this point). In Zionist political thought, given the Holocaust backdrop, the Jewish nation would be foolish to sacrifice its own land and security to placate the same hatred for Jews now arising from Arabs, and it is naive and even morally reprehensible for others to ask them to do so.

This argument has heavily influenced swinging Zionist logics about the two-state and one-state solutions mentioned in chapter 3. As noted, a long-standing Zionist argument against the two-state solution was that a Palestinian state would only provide a proximate platform for murderous Arab intent regarding Jews and Israel. The same apparent threat has now been re-adapted to legitimize the two-state solution, by allowing Israel to reject growing pressure to incorporate the Palestinian population as citizens: for Zionists argue that, given the chance, the Palestinians would certainly seek Jewish destruction from within.

Aside from its glaring racial stereotyping, two factors complicate the Zionist argument that Arabs are intransigently hostile to Jews. First, it is by no means universally held within Israel. For example, suicide bombers have certainly terrified Israelis and reinforced fears that Palestinians sustain genocidal goals, but this interpretation is challenged by some Israeli groups, who trace the attacks instead to outrage and desperation arising from Israel's occupation policy. A proliferating number of joint Jewish-Palestinian initiatives reflect the mutual faith (e.g., The Other Israel, a peace initiative with one hundred thousand Israeli and sixty-five thousand Palestinian signatory supporters).[41] Second, relative to the scope of the military occupation and the size of the Palestinian population under occupation, suicide bombings and other attacks—despite their broadly terrifying impact—have remained a tiny fringe phenomenon. Writings and talks by Palestinian intellectuals of universally recognized integrity (whose representations of Palestinian sentiment cannot be dismissed) and the mass behavior by nearly 2.5 million Palestinians under occupation (which is simply to hunker down and get by) indicate that the vast majority of Palestinians remain impressively resistant to outright racial hatred. The enemy is Israel and Zionism, not Judaism per se. "The Jews" are feared and detested because they incarnate the occupation policy that oppresses Palestinians—for Israeli occupation forces act in the name of "the Jews." If Israel's occupation policy were to change and its actions in the name of "the Jews" were to shift toward sharing the land, Palestinian perceptions of "the Jews" as an incarnate threat would also change. Again, the South African experience suggests the dynamic. Prior to the fall of apartheid, many whites held the same confusion, failing to grasp that whiteness was targeted because it was coupled to repression, not because whiteness was hated in itself. Lingering anti-white racism certainly persists in South Africa, as racism would in Palestine. But it is defused into forms containable by a reformed democratic system.[42]

Of course, Jewish fears reflect a recent history of genocidal persecution not approached by the Afrikaner experience, whatever its own collective memory of abuse (by the English). But when Zionists conflate the ideologies of the Holocaust with Arab anti-Zionism, they obscure a very different dynamic. Although Arab and Palestinian rhetoric certainly called for expelling Jewish settlers from Palestinian land, they never seriously suggested their physical annihilation on anything like the racial terms of National Socialism. The Arab world as a whole certainly viewed mass Jewish settler immigration (overwhelmingly European until 1950)—which overran and demolished Palestinian society—as illegitimate, but it did so on the same grounds that French-settler society in Algeria, for example, was deemed illegitimate.

This is not to say that Arabs are immune from genuine Judeophobia: no population on earth appears to be immune from racism, and neither Arabs nor Israeli Jews escape this rule. Still, evidence of outright Arab racism against Jews is sufficiently thin that Zionist accusations of actual anti-Jewish racism commonly must center on just one genuinely racist figure: the incompetent and reactionary Grand Mufti of Jerusalem, Haj Amin al-Husseini. This figure, however, is unrepresentative. Installed as "Grand Mufti" by British colonial authorities (who also invented the position, which had not existed previously), al-Husseini reacted to Zionist state-building pressures by collaborating with Hitler (and Mussolini) in the 1930s, in the hope of reducing Jewish immigration to Palestine. He even endorsed Nazi persecution of Jews and seems entirely to have adopted Nazi racial doctrines. But his maneuvers remained both ineffectual and isolated, and he was never a leader of more than a few reactionary Palestinian factions. His primary accomplishment was to sideline and obscure for history those Arab factions that sought coexistence with the Jewish-Zionist movement. (Not to excuse al-Husseini but to contextualize him, we also might recall that various Zionists, including the Haganah, also attempted ineffectually to collaborate with Hitler in the 1930s, on the opposite agenda. The Nazis were then, after all, becoming an immense power, with a central role regarding European Jewry and most other issues in Europe. In their early years, they attracted many ill-conceived overtures, including British, American, and Russian ones.)[43]

In any case, the flamboyant rhetoric used by Arab leaderships in the 1960s to encourage expelling "the Jews" is long gone; it had not been heard in any public forum for twenty years, until, ominously, it was whipped up among extremist Islamic sectors by the U.S. occupation of Iraq in 2003 (which led some to believe that U.S. and Israeli occupation policies were linked). As noted earlier, the Arab states have made repeated peace overtures to Israel, and indeed desperately seek peace with Israel, as discussed in chapter 4. Even the PLO recognized Israel in 1988. Zionist charges that the Arab world intends Jewish annihilation manifest today as unacceptable. Israel's inability to respond to that political change by altering its own rejectionist foreign policy is indeed the urgent matter now under international scrutiny.

Indeed, rather than promising Jewish annihilation, the history of Arab rhetoric regarding Israel signals hope for the one-state solution. Arab statements denouncing Israel (or the "Zionist entity") have commonly been heard by Zionists as targeting Jews per se. In the formulas of Arab League statements, however, such denunciations clearly targeted the "state" portion of the formula. It is the Jewish-national *state* that was deemed unacceptable by the Arab world, as a violation of Palestinian political rights. This distinction suggests a flexibility that mainstream Zionist discourse prefers to reject: that some profound modification of the state's Jewishness, as in a binational or multiethnic formula, would unravel that objection and permit the Arab world to accept the (now normalized) Jewish-national presence in Palestine.

The second common argument for a Jewish state builds from the ethnic-sanctuary argument in arguing that Israel is geographically so small (and vulnerable to impending Arab attack) that a Jewish state— understood here as securing absolute control by Jews over Israel's formidable security forces—is essential to Jewish survival in the country. In this argument, Israel's small size and vulnerable shape themselves are rationalizations for a posture of adamant Jewish-ethnic defense, as well as for rejecting any land-for-peace settlement. Much is made, for example, of the narrow "waist" of Israel—just nine miles at its narrowest point, between the Green Line and the sea—and of the short distances between Israel's major cities and surrounding Arab territory. In tours of this geography regularly extended to visitors, the West Bank highlands are pointed out as obvious vantage points for enemy artillery attacks onto the coastal plain; the deeper land buffer provided by the West Bank is therefore argued as necessary to defend Israel against sudden Arab attack or invasion. The same risk, from Syrian missiles, is cited to justify retaining the Golan Heights. Hence, Menachim Begin asserted that Israel's withdrawing to the 1967 border would be "national suicide," Golda Meir denounced such a withdrawal as "treasonable," and Abba Eban said that the 1967 border carried "a memory of Auschwitz."[44]

Many visitors to Israel are quickly persuaded by these arguments. For instance, the whole package cropped up unvarnished in a 2004 address to the Anti-Defamation League by John Kerry, in his campaign for the U.S. presidency.

> But I never understood this fragility and vulnerability more than when I first visited Israel on an ADL mission so many years ago. For days, my inner–Top Gun sought out a ride in an Israeli Air Force Jet. And when I finally got one, my inner-politician convinced the pilot to let me take control of the plane for awhile. But after a few minutes in the air—a few minutes—the pilot yelled for me to turn the plane around. "We just got in the air," I told him. "I know," he said. "But if we flew in any other direction for two minutes more, we would be flying into enemy territory." From that moment on, I felt as Israelis do: The promise of

peace must be secure before the Promised Land is secure on a thin margin of land.[45]

Still, the geographic-security argument is more ambiguous than a helicopter or jet flight might suggest. Primarily, it does not clarify precisely how a Jewish territorial state is protecting the Jewish people or even what territory is required for that protection: e.g., whether Israel's security requires control over the West Bank. The latter question is already controversial in Israel. Evolving military technology has made the added buffer of West Bank territory increasingly superfluous: its short span would take only seconds off a missile attack from any territory beyond the Jordan River and modern missiles do not require heights (as Saddam Hussein's scud-missile attacks in 1991 demonstrated). Indeed, some Israelis argue strongly that the West Bank is actually a security detriment, partly because Israel's occupation generates such dangerous Palestinian and Arab reaction and partly because the occupation is seen to corrode Israel's "national soul." In this view, handing over some portion of the West Bank to a Palestinian state would serve Israeli security not just adequately but better.

Recently, Jewish-Israeli inclinations toward giving up the West Bank have gained ground for a different reason: the perceived "threat" of Palestinian citizenship. The Peace Index report in January 2004 found that as many as 66 percent of Israel's Jewish population believe the West Bank should be given over to Palestinian control, but the ostensible public reason, to contain terrorism, did not seem to drive this sentiment. Rather, the designers of the survey, working closely with the data, concluded that "The broad support for separation [the two-state solution] apparently stems from the very widespread fear (73 percent) that if a solution to the conflict is not found in the near future and Israeli control of the territories continues, the Palestinians will eventually become a demographic majority west of the Jordan and a de facto 'binational state' will emerge."[46] In other words, respondents wanted to hand over the West Bank not so much to contain Palestinian violence as to contain the "threat" of the one-state solution.

This willingness to give up the West Bank reflects another glaring fact that also erodes the geographic security argument: that the actual risk of any major military ground invasion or assault on Israel has become nonexistent given Israel's overwhelming military strength. Israel's air force (incorporating the latest technology), its sophisticated surveillance systems and its excellent ground forces (tanks, artillery, superbly trained personnel) comprise a defense and war-making capability several times greater than those of all its neighbors combined. The threat of any devastating mass Arab attack was also permanently eliminated when Israel became a nuclear power. As noted in the previous chapter, no Arab army has ever existed or will exist that could begin to overrun Israeli territory, even discounting U.S. interference. Even by the 1980s, no Arab force could dent Israel's military sway in the broader Middle East and Arab world: e.g., its capacity to bomb a nuclear reactor in Iraq (in 1981) or PLO headquarters in Tunisia (in 1985). The only implicit rival to Israel's regional military hegemony was, briefly, Iraq under Saddam Hussein in the late 1980s, but that threat was tidily eliminated.

These strategic realities, coupled with internal Jewish-Israeli disagreements about Israel's most appropriate borders, illuminate the deeper logic of the security argument. It is not precisely any specific geography that is deemed strategically vital to the Jewish state, for geography is no longer determinative to security. Rather, security rests on permanent Jewish control over the state's impressive defense forces, through which Jews can secure the safety of Israel's Jewish-national population. This logic is actually circular, however, in arguing that Jewish statehood is essential to protect Jews from the consequences of Jewish statehood. For the awkward fact is that, if Palestinians came to enjoy democratic rights as citizens in one secular-democratic state, the threat of Arab attack would disappear entirely, as Arab states would have no motive to attack such a state.

Indeed, considering a one-state scenario, Zionist fears about Jewish security focus not on any external Arab threat (which would evaporate) but on domestic Palestinian hostility: that a future Palestinian electoral majority might change the constitution or otherwise seize control of the security apparatus to subordinate, dispossess or persecute the Jewish minority rather than respect constitutional provisions for its protection. One immediate weakness of this doomsday argument, as noted before, is that Israel presently has an Arab citizenry of some 19 percent and, given the Arab sector's higher birthrate, cannot count on a Jewish majority forever in any case. Yet the precise nature of the peril resulting from this indigenous "demographic threat" is not clear. Some do imagine that anti-Jewish hostility by a Palestinian-Arab majority within a secular-democratic state would take the form of outright military attack and/or mass traumatic expulsion of the Jewish population. Many constraints would impede such actions, however, not least the new state's dependency on international trade and the Palestinian population's own anxieties for the country's stability. A more realistic fear is that a still-resentful and Judeophobic Palestinian majority would launch a more insidious attack on Jewish interests and cultural life—e.g., by orchestrating massive Palestinian return, appropriating Jewish homes for returnees, progressively demoting Jewish cultural concerns, seizing control of holy sites, and otherwise callously eliminating the conditions for Jewish culture, economic security and the free expression of Jewish spiritual values and national life. Hence Jewish-Israeli resistance to a one-state solution is expressed as rejection of becoming vulnerable to majority tyranny by historically hostile others, replicating the uncomfortable and sometimes disastrous historical conditions of Jewish communities in other countries.

At this argumentative juncture, defense of the Jewish state therefore shifts to center not so much on the physical safety of Jews as the preservation of a robust and healthy Jewish cultural and national life. Hence arguments for sustaining Israel as a Jewish state come to focus not on Jewish physical survival but on Jewish-*national* survival, in the sense of comprising a vigorous cultural and political community able to control its conditions and destiny.

National Expression

In most Zionist thought, a Jewish state is deemed the essential condition for the Jewish nation to flourish as a cultural and political community. In this view, mere physical security for Jewish individuals, which they may find as well or better in the diaspora, is not sufficient to authentic Jewish life. Rather, Jewish national life has precious and unique social and spiritual qualities that can be experienced only collectively, that have been stifled or attenuated in the diaspora, and that life in the Jewish state has enabled and reinvigorated. As loss of the Jewish state would signify the dissolution of Jewish national life, its defense is paramount, fundamental to Jewish national survival.

This classically ethnonationalist argument inspired and steered much of the Zionist movement in the early twentieth century and has remained central even after the Holocaust. For instance, the Jerusalem Program (a set of foundational principles developed at the Twenty-Seventh World Zionist Congress in 1968, discussed in more detail in chap. 6) mentioned "survival" as a central concern—but primarily in the sense of the national community of "the Jewish people," which was understood to be at risk of dissolving due to assimilation in the diaspora. Four "basic values" of Zionism were understood as fundamental to restore ethnonational cohesion:

1. The recognition of the basic solidarity of the Jewish people, with a common destiny, which transcends geographical and cultural barriers. We are One People—Am Echad, with each of its parts responsible for the others.
2. The recognition that the survival of the Jewish people is a supreme and absolute Jewish and universal value, and that this nation is worthy and obligated to exist forever. Hence, the absolute rejection of any form of assimilation.
3. The recognition that the Jewish people must achieve national sovereignty in its historic homeland. Hence, the overriding obligation of every Zionist to strengthen the State of Israel through personal Aliyah to Israel.
4. The recognition of the centrality of the State of Israel in the life of the Jewish people because Israel alone is the living expression of all these values, and because she constitutes the focus for worldwide Jewish identification.[47]

This ethnonationalist argument also steers the claim to the state's territory. Conceivably, Jewish-national survival would not require a state in Mandate Palestine (famously, in his foundational text *Der Judenstaat,* Herzl mentioned Uganda and Argentina as options). But the deeper Zionist claim on the territory, also expressed in the

Jerusalem Program, is that the biblical land of Israel is actually the "historic homeland" of Jews as a people or nation, which sustains primordial spiritual or even cultural ties to it. In this view, "Jewish" is not simply an ethnic or religious identity but an ethnonational identity that originally arose in this land, with a lineage tracing to Abraham (some threads emphasize that it was granted to Abraham, Moses, and Joshua by God). Over the centuries, the "Jewish people" as a national totality took its fundamental values, character, myths, and symbols from that land. Israel's Declaration of Independence opens with this claim: "The land of Israel was the birthplace of the Jewish people. ERETZ-ISRAEL was the birthplace of the Jewish people. Here their spiritual, religious and political identity was shaped. Here they first attained to statehood, created cultural values of national and universal significance and gave to the world the eternal Book of Books."[48]

Mainstream Zionist mythohistory stresses that since they were unjustly expelled from Palestine by the Romans in 72 CE, the Jews have sustained a collective psychological longing for and attachment to the homeland that sustained their national character (hence, ritual formulas such as "next year in Jerusalem"). Other Jewish scholars, however, have insisted that this "longing" was actually an abstraction. European Jews did not literally wish to return to underdeveloped Palestine—which individuals, in any case, could and did visit (hence a steady trickle of Jews moved in and out of the Jewish community in Jerusalem). Some ultra-Orthodox Jewish thought even argued that any collective return was spiritually unwise or prohibited, as it would pre-empt the messianic redemption that could come only through spiritual practice or miraculous intervention. Rather, "Jerusalem" was a concept more than a literal place, the just world in an imagined future when anti-Semitism would be overcome and Jewish culture and religious life could be freely and fully expressed.[49] But Zionist doctrine maintains that this theological concept was a more literal nostalgic longing and that the Jewish nation has a natural right to reconstitute itself in that homeland. Hence, the symbolic narrative underlying political Zionism is neither migration nor settlement but return.

One spin on this argument is that Jews are indeed the indigenous people of the region, a claim that deliberately reverses the settler-colonial paradigm. A corollary claim is that Palestinians are actually later immigrants—even twentieth-century ones attracted by Jewish labor opportunities—with no legitimate claim to what is truly Jewish-national land.[50] The latter notion is transparently specious: any glance at Ottoman tax, trade, and census records shows a hearty and growing Arab society in Palestine in the nineteenth century. But in any case, a claim to "original" sovereignty in Palestine is unworkable for any group, given the region's very old history. (The Hebrew conquest of inhabited cities in Palestine—"the place of the Canaanites, the Hittites, the Amorites, the Per'izzites, the Hivites, and the Jeb'usites"—is, of course, a central element of the heroic narrative of the Exodus.)[51]

The claim that Jewish indigeneity supersedes Arab indigeneity has indeed required a comprehensive remapping of history and the Palestinian landscape, to erase the Arab presence and recenter the Jewish-national presence as a defining continuous thread (a maneuver too readily swallowed by Western Christians, as noted earlier). Open machinations were undertaken on this agenda. For example, in the 1930s, the Jewish National Fund formed a Naming Committee to expunge Arab place-names (cast as mere carriers of "original" Hebrew names) from the regional map; in the 1950s, Israel's Government Naming Committee carried the project to fruition, providing a Hebraized map that became the authority for Israeli textbooks, civil law, literature, and tourism.[52] Hence, a seemingly complete—or at least self-contained—body of scientific, linguistic, literary, historical, and biblical authorities was invented to foster impressions of Jewish belonging and natural rights in a Jewish homeland reproduced from biblical legend.[53]

Biblical legend is indeed the primary authority invoked to support a special Jewish right to this land, which clearly has been occupied, through the millennia, by many peoples. In its simplest form, this right is cited simply as a divine gift (as discussed shortly). A more complex argument is that the land was given to the Jewish people (Hebrews) by God so that Jews—whether consciously religious or not—could collectively fulfill God's will by constituting the just society that God commanded. This idea of a sacred bond between the

Jewish people and the land, which has always had great epic appeal, was eloquently elaborated by (among others) Martin Buber.

> The story of Abraham, which connects the gift of Canaan with the command to be a blessing, is the most concise résumé of the fact that the association of the people with this land signifies a mission. The people came to the land to fulfill the mission . . . This land was at no time in the history of Israel simply the property of the people; it was always at the same time a challenge to make of it what God intended to have made of it. . . . It was a consummation that could not be achieved by the people or the land on its own but only by the faithful co-operation of the two together and it was an association in which the land appeared not as a dead, passive object but as a living and active partner. Just as, to achieve fullness of life, the people needed the land, so the land needed the people, and the end which both were called upon to realize could only be reached by a living partnership.[54]

But as modern Zionism gelled into a movement in the late nineteenth and early twentieth centuries, it also drew on imagined links between territories and peoples then simmering in contemporary racial-nationalist thought. In that period, transnational ideas about nationalism were heavily influenced by the new racial "sciences," which conceived a determinative relationship of territory to race, race to collective mentality, mentality to culture, and culture to national character—thus legitimizing the nation's primordial claim to statehood in the territory that gave it life. While emotionally compelling to many, these logics had grim implications in implying that any strong nation required racial purity, sanctioning the elimination of ethnoracial others from the state territory. Hopefully, no further discussion is needed here to discredit racial nationalism: its outcomes have been graphic on both a global scale (e.g., in Japanese and German racial imperialism and in British colonialism) and a local one (e.g., in the extermination of Native Americans and in the various forced population transfers in Central Europe). Still, although long discredited, some of those same logics still vaguely infuse most nationalisms and even some putatively scholarly work today: e.g., Samuel Huntington has freshly endorsed them in a recent analysis of U.S. foreign policy imperatives and they ring through anti-Muslim analyses in the West that extend to racial essentializing. Thus classic racial-nationalist doctrine feeds the Zionist assertion, otherwise drawn from biblical myth, that Jews collectively sustain an organic relationship to their homeland of origin, which has shaped the Jewish national character, has legitimized their return, and makes moral sense of expelling ethnic others who are not recognized to have any comparable relationship to the land.

However emotionally appealing such ideas of an organic link between land, race, and nation might be, they have no credence in themselves. Certainly, they cannot be held to constitute any legitimate defense of the Jewish state. Indeed, reading them literally, few people would endorse them. But they lurk within more subtle arguments, such as concepts that the Jewish people as a whole share some transcendental spiritual Jewish quality, or *Volksgeist*.

Volksgeist

Zionist rhetoric often alludes to the idea that the Jewish people and the land of Israel are bound by a spiritual or metaphysical connection. In modern Zionism, this has always been a strategically murky concept, reflecting great disagreements on its nature. For religious Zionists, the idea obviously invokes the sacred relationship of the Jewish people to the land granted them by divine ordinance. Notions of Israel's spiritual mission also pick up ideas that Jews everywhere share a common spiritual charge by God (or burden), as the "chosen people." But the idea of a spiritual connection has also imported newer nationalist logics, again connected to European racial theory, which drew on Hegelian notions that each race (or people or nation) has a spiritual existence, or *Volksgeist,* whose fullest expression is the state's primary charge and is the true locus of identity, pride, and loyalty by its members. In the early twentieth century, nationalists around the world were entranced by this idea, writing about the "Argentine spirit" or "Chinese spirit" spirit, which manifested as a collective will and energy in a people as a whole yet was expressed and translated into action by the state, which the people accordingly had a higher obligation to serve (obviously a fascist logic). This package was deployed to argue an incontestable claim for independent statehood in whatever territory was deemed to have generated the nation's cultural (*cum* racial, *cum* spiritual) character. Zionism was by no means immune to its appeal. David Ben-Gurion wrote much on the concept, and his ideas have lingered, cropping up as a quote in a recent speech by Ariel Sharon.

> We have one secret weapon, which is perhaps the main one which promises the chance of victory, and we must strengthen it. This secret is in your hands—in the hands of those who are here and in the hands of those who are not here—the spirit, and that is what will be decisive in the war in which we find ourselves. The spirit will be decisive but not when it is alone. All of the artillery and airplanes will be of no help if a spirit does not rise up in us; until today, this spirit has given us the power to endure and with it, we will be victorious.[55]

Unfortunately, this emphasis on a unique national spirit tended to reinforce logics of racial purity. "Every race has a different spiritual mechanism," wrote Jabotinsky in 1933. He continued:

> Let us draw for ourself the ideal type of an "absolute nation." It would have to possess a racial appearance of marked unique character, an appearance different from the racial nature of that nation's neighbours. It would have to occupy from time immemorial a continuous and clearly defined piece of land; it would be highly desirable if in that area there would be no alien minorities, who would weaken national unity. It would have to maintain an original national language, which is not derived from another nation.[56]

Prior to modern Zionist thought, Jewish identity in Europe had always coupled religious practice and spiritual values to ideas of descent and kinship. The sense that Jewishness was also intergenerational, passed through maternal lines, was one foundational premise for Jewish solidarity (and, terribly, for violence by anti-Semites). With the advent of modern Zionist thought, new transnationalist discourses fusing "people" and "spirit" struck a *Volksgeist* tone, supporting the claim that the Jewish nation shares an ineffable spiritual character (or spiritual condition or spiritual burden) of which Israel is the territorial expression—or at least, in extremis, the ultimate protector. When modern Zionist writings allude to a "spiritual dimension" to Zionism and the Jewish state, something of this spiritual quality—not literally religious or dependent on specific practices—infuses the allusion. Jews everywhere inherit and share a special charge of spiritual labor that they "come up" to Israel to fulfill—from which developed the concept of *aliyah,* or "ascending," to Israel. In practice, *olim* may be entirely secular in their views; their "ascent"—a spiritual notion—is here to the nation itself.

Of course, some Zionists make an outright religious claim on the land, particularly on the West Bank ("Judea and Samaria"), on the grounds that God granted the land to Abraham (and to Moses and Joshua). In this view, the Jewish people are now rightly reclaiming that divine bequest, and no one else's opinion matters. Such biblical authority is indeed far from confined to the fancies of a fundamentalist or zealot fringe, appearing in ostensibly secular and moderate sites as an unstated or tacit backdrop for Israel's sacred national mission. (For instance, former defense minister Ezer Weitzman titled his book on the Israeli Air Force *Thine Are the Heavens, Thine Is the Earth,* using a verse from Psalms praising God; when questioned about the propriety of using language directed toward God for a secular military force, he asserted that as God and the Jewish people are the same, the same references hold for both.)[57]

More famously, the religious settler movements claim divine sanction for the settlements and for their militant resistance to any withdrawal. As related internal Israeli tensions were discussed in chap. 2, religious arguments need no further discussion here. The only real surprise about such claims is that the international community accords such arguments the slightest credit, in accepting that the Jewish people indeed has a special spiritual claim on the land which somehow mitigates its brutalization and expulsion of the indigenous population—a slippage that again, calls for some introspection in the Christian West. Religious zealots exist in most major religions, and it is normally the chore of the international community to contain their more ravaging ambitions—if as politely as possible.

But *spiritual* is a vague term that can evoke deep feelings in a broad spectrum of people, including those who would find openly religious claims distasteful. To some, it seems clearly to invoke religious teachings and biblical myth. To others, it translates, in more secular modes, as referring to a high-minded moral mission to create a just society. In practice, Zionist language of "in-gathering," "redemption," and "return" conflates religious, ethnic, and nationalist modes, allowing internal flexibility to accommodate a wide range of individual views but also strategically blurring secular and spiritual ideas, facilitating their emotional synergy. Hence, in abstract and sometimes only semiarticulate ways, even non-Zionist secular Jews may retain a strong sense that some precious, ineffable, Jewish-spiritual quality or mission has at last found its free expression and realization in Israel. If Israel were converted to a binational state, chock full of Muslim and Christian Arabs, that spiritual imaginary would be swamped and dissolved—a loss far more heart-wrenching to contemplate than the loss of political dominion alone.

Yet to what extent can the international community support a spiritual quest that has translated into such ruin for a Palestinian population of millions and is now leading to regional instability?

Equal Standing

One quick Zionist answer to the question of international concern in the Israeli-Palestinian conflict is that while Palestinian suffering is regrettable, the Muslim and Christian worlds hold vast territories and can just make room for one tiny Jewish state. Zionism is hardly alone in attaching statehood to religion: some Islamic, Christian, and Hindu nationalisms do the same, and similarly strong emotional attachments accrue. Zionists argue, then, that given the world's acceptance of these other states, why should it not accept the Jewish state?

This argument fails on three counts. First, it overstates its case. Religious governments everywhere are problematic, and where they are openly brutal (as in Iran) or where religious nationalism generates convulsions of mass violence (as in Hindu attacks on Muslims in India), they receive world opprobrium. Second, all other religious states can claim titular affiliation with the majority society in the territory, drawing from a religious tradition embedded in the territory through centuries of practice. Israel crafted that majority by force, having formed through a twentieth-century campaign of mass Jewish immigration coupled with mass expulsion of an indigenous Christian/Muslim majority. Israel's ethnoreligious identity is therefore premised and sustained through a graphic project of ethnic cleansing; it stands in Palestinian and regional eyes as an old-fashioned religious invasion or "crusade" rather than a consensual mass expression of majority indigenous religious sentiment.

Third, although officially a "Jewish state," Israel is not precisely a religious state—that is, a state whose basic laws affirm Jewish religious principles as an informative system of ethics for its laws and citizenry. Indeed, as discussed earlier, Jewish identity has never been simply a religious affiliation but powerfully incorporates ideas of lineage, culture, and, with Zionism, nationhood. Eternal arguments about "who is a Jew" signal this complexity, and Jews transnationally are used to navigating a very wide spectrum of opinion on the question. But so many crucial privileges and political rights attach to being Jewish in Israel that formal lawmaking has necessarily formulated a definition. Enshrined in the Law of Return, Israel's legal definition of a "Jew" is "a person who was born of a Jewish mother or has become converted to Judaism and who is not a member of another religion."[58] Additional provisions have become necessary, however, which suggest the controversies.

> In addition to defining a "Jew," the new law [Amendment 5714] created a new class of immigrants who would have the "rights of a Jew." These individuals would be able to immigrate under the Law of Return but would not be recognized as Jews by the state. These individuals include any child or grandchild of a Jew (male or female), the spouse of a Jew, the spouse of a child of a Jew, and the spouse of a grandchild of a Jew. . . . "a person who has been a Jew and has voluntarily changed his religion" is exempted from the Law of Return. . . . individuals enjoying the "rights of a Jew" would be eligible as citizens of Israel under the law, but could not be registered as Jews either by "ethnic affiliation or religion if they do not fulfill the definition of Jews." Thus, those individuals who immigrated to Israel under the Law of Return but who are not Jewish could not be registered by the Ministry of Interior as Jews. As non-Jews, these individuals would be barred by the Ministry of Religion from marrying Jews or being buried in a Jewish cemetery in Israel.[59]

These elaborate legal provisions signal the care with which Israeli law guards the Jewish national identity and its major package of special rights and privileges. But even the purely religious issue of conversion is a ticklish question. To gain consensus that Israel is indeed the "Jewish state," Zionism's national pact granted authority over "who is a Jew" to Orthodox authorities who believe that Halacha law determines the question. As a result, until 2002, to the endless irritation of Reform and Conservative Jews, anyone in Israel who had not converted to Judaism under Orthodox or ultra-Orthodox auspices could not gain legal standing in Israel as Jewish. When Israel's High Court declared that Reform and Conservative converts must be recognized as Jews (for registration purposes, but still not for marriages or burial), a storm of controversy ensued.[60]

Given all this complexity and tension about Jewish identity and conversion, it is not surprising that no state or private Jewish missionizing agency is out working Arab-Israeli neighborhoods—particularly the occupied territories—seeking to convert Muslims and Christians to the national religion. Missionizing has never been a Jewish tradition, but in Israel, the conflation of ethnic, religious, and national dimensions in "being Jewish" translates into a tribalism that permanently and deliberately holds non-Jews outside the only nationality to which the state grants rights. In fact, Israel is unique among religious states in holding as neither conceivable *nor desirable* any general conversion to the national religion by citizens in the state's territory. For, again, Israel is not precisely a Jewish state in a narrowly religious sense; it is the "state of the Jews" (the literal translation of Herzl's *Der Judenstaat*), a community strongly bound by internal understandings that its identity, while open to conversion, is primarily rooted in ideas of ancestry and descent. No similarity to other religious states is evident here.

CONCLUSION: THE ONUS FOR ZIONISM

In Zionism, as in any nationalist discourse, disparate argumentative threads combine to lend the nationalist project pathos and mystique while providing the philosophical diversity crucial to enlisting a broad spectrum of followers. The threads critiqued in this chapter normally appear not in isolation but in such a conjunction, blurring into a larger affective claim on Jewish loyalty while able to meet any challenge with a strategic shift of ground. By separating and examining those threads, this discussion has attempted to show their actually contested and uncertain hold on Jewish Israelis as well as their dismal standing relative to international human rights norms. The discussion generates two conclusions. First, the fundamental problem plaguing the Israeli-Palestinian conflict—its origin, its enduring basis, its stubborn resistance to resolution—has been the Zionist tenet that to be a Jewish state, Israel must sustain a Jewish majority. Second, the threads of that argument are deeply frayed, and despite the passion with which it is argued, the whole construction stands on rapidly eroding sand.

Given the advancing crisis in the Middle East, those fraying threads must now be addressed more quickly than the normal pace of political evolution might make comfortable. Western democratic thought has come to consider ethnic dominion over a state morally repugnant: hence, when Milosevic's "Greater Serbia" efforts led to massacres and forced population transfer (the first such crisis in Europe since World War II), stumbling international action was at least steered by a clear moral compass. Yet, although contributing to a far larger crisis, Zionist argument has successfully cast "Greater Israel" as a moral project, deserving—indeed, morally requiring—fulfillment and protection. This argument maintains that Israel must be held exceptional, as falling outside the bounds of civil-democratic norms applicable elsewhere. That premise has morally confused international diplomacy, by appropriating Jewish culture and a history of persecution—especially the compelling moral legacy of the Holocaust—to legitimize ethnic statehood. Given looming disaster, however, such moral confusion must now be laid aside. The origins of the Israeli-Palestinian conflict trace not to mid-twentieth-century persecution but to a late nineteenth-century nationalist movement—inspired by anti-Semitism but also by the rampant ethnonationalist ideologies of the period—to create a Jewish-national state in a territory that, unluckily, already held an ancient and politicized indigenous Arab society. The formula was always unworkable, as Zionism's

earliest architects recognized. Zionism's success was always understood to require the Arabs' mass transfer or exit—a goal twice sought
by force (in 1948 and 1967) but not achieved. Israel's continuing
efforts to realize that vision are now generating untenable regional
dangers.

To some extent, Israel suffers from unlucky timing in attempting
to expel indigenous Arabs some half century after the region's decolonization. Its settler-colonial conceits—of bringing development and
"civilization" to a blighted backward land—confront their normative
obsolescence even as white supremacy found itself an embarrassing
anachronism in black-majority South Africa. Moreover, the rest of
the Western democracies have learned their own lessons (albeit
slowly) from past sins. In the nineteenth century, white settler armies
pushing across the Great Plains of what eventually became the United
States were able to attack and destroy the native peoples—even place
bounties on their ears or noses—and be lauded for their noble efforts
to spread civilization and Christianity. No more. Israel does not have
the privilege, as Zionists often claim, of replicating these terrible
offenses of the past.

Finally, self-styled as "the only democracy in the Middle East,"
Israel remains the only ethnic democracy claiming membership in the
Euro-American international community. That claim is becoming an
intolerable embarrassment, as the model is long obsolete elsewhere.
For instance, the "White Australia" project sustained a racial democracy in the early twentieth century, banning Asian immigration and
excluding Aborigines on the belief that only racial homogeneity could
permit whites to freely enjoy a democratic practice brought from
Europe. Southern states in the United States used a host of methods,
official and unofficial, to exclude black voting and secure white
dominion well into the 1960s. But the civil movements that challenged and defeated these systems carried with them more than local
or national change; they campaigned for and consolidated an international normative discourse that rejected ethnoracial supremacy as an
inherent source of injustice, dehumanization, and human suffering.
The shift rose to catch South Africa and quickly discredited apartheid;
Milosevic's Serbian ambitions also came too late and hit the cresting
wave. The lessons from World War II had at last come to fruition:

ethnic nationalism generates unacceptable discourses of ethnic supremacy and inferiority, grants moral authority to ethnic cleansing, and precludes equal rights before the law, which is the foundational principle of Western democracies. If a state is to be fully democratic—with all its citizens held equal before the law—it cannot be based on ethnic dominion. Whatever Israel claims based on the past sins of Europe or on its own mythologized past of peaceful resistance to ferocious Arabs, if the Jewish state claims membership in the Western club, it cannot expect to be held exempt from these principles.

As Mark Twain once pointed out, it is good when nations lie about their actions, because it shows that they know they are doing something bad. Pro-Israeli discourse acknowledges the Jewish state's moral difficulty—and the normative shift in international human rights—in its elaborate promulgation of two self-exonerating myths: the myth of Palestine as an empty and barren land, to which immigrant Arab labor was drawn by the accomplishments of hardworking Jewish settlers who made the desert green, and the myth of hostile anti-Semitic Arab leaderships who ordered the Palestinians to flee in 1948. That mytho-history reflects an affirmation that justice and fair dealing are also fundamental values for the Jewish state. It remains for Zionists to marshal those values to confront their revised understanding of their past with fresh honesty. To some extent, that process is already underway: the histories are being rewritten, old racial stereotypes are collapsing before the graphic abuses of the occupation, and settler-colonial rationalizations are waxing too stale. The flagging mytho-history is losing its audience. Debates within Israel have always acknowledged the tension between a Jewish state and a democratic state, but dominant voices have urged that the Jewishness of the Jewish state must be prioritized. That contradiction must now be resolved differently.

6. The
One-State
Solution
The Expanding Debate

After a century of dreams and conflict, the Zionist dream has run on the shoals of its own contradictions. Israeli-Jewish, Israeli-Arab, and Palestinian populations are so interdependent and intertwined that their forced partition promises only a downward spiral toward disaster. Culture, ideology, and a century of conflict divide them. But they are embedded in each other, inextricably linked—conjoined twins in a narrow and delicate landscape. Perhaps at some earlier time, two states were still possible. But the two-state option evaporated years and perhaps decades ago. Perhaps, as some voices have always argued, it never existed at all. Whatever the past possibilities for partition, they are now lost. Today, no ideology, no planning, no new "peace process," and certainly not the snaking apartheid Wall can make sense of carving this small land into two states.

The dilemma now facing both sides is therefore becoming obvious to all. Far too large and too politicized simply to crumble quietly within the Wall, the Palestinian people will fight against national ruin and immiseration. In the two-state formula, Israel must either confront Palestinian reaction with unprecedented repression or capitulate to Palestinian demands for a substantial withdrawal. Yet an Israeli withdrawal from the West Bank sufficient to allow a viable Palestinian state is no longer imaginable, for the settlement grid has become equally immovable, anchored by its massive demographic, financial, and ideological weight. Israel's only other option—forced mass transfer of the Palestinian population out of the West Bank into Jordan—would trigger catastrophic political reaction throughout the region and the world and again bring crisis. No existing political force can alter that face-off. Internal Israeli politics is not capable of resolving the ideological tensions that would escalate at any serious attempt by the Israeli government to withdraw the West Bank settlement grid, and no Israeli government has any capacity or reason to launch such a showdown—at least not in the absence of overwhelming external pressure. Yet no present external actor or coalition of actors possesses both the political will and the raw power (economic, political, or military) to exert that pressure.

Crafted under these terms, the impending two-state option only carries this long-burning ethnic conflict toward explosion, and widening circles of people are realizing it. In response, within both Jewish and Palestinian politics, a major shift is brewing. With increasing clarity and insistence, people are beginning to speak of a different future for Israel and the Palestinian territories: one democratic state, in all the territory of Mandate Palestine, shared by Jews and Palestinians alike. "The time has come to think the unthinkable," wrote New York University professor Tony Judt in October 2003, breaking public U.S. political ground in the *New York Review of Books*. "The two-state solution—the core of the Oslo process and the present 'road map'—is probably already doomed."[1] In a *Ha'aretz* interview in 2003, longtime Israeli peace activist Haim Hanegbi, a leftist journalist born in Israel, calls for everyone to face facts: "Everyone with eyes to see and ears to hear has to understand that only a binational partnership can save us."[2] Israeli journalist Daniel Gavron makes the same point flatly in *The Other Side of Despair* (2003): "We are left with only one alternative: Israeli-Palestinian coexistence in one nation."[3] Gavron made *aliyah* to Israel with his family in 1961, in wholehearted pursuit of the Zionist dream; in proposing the one-state solution, he knew very well how deeply his transformed views challenged the mainstream. But he and others are speaking and writing as voices among a growing cluster of Jewish and Palestinian journalists, activists, and intellectuals who have accepted—many with inner pain and moral turmoil—that the two-state solution is already unworkable.

Meron Benvenisti, former deputy mayor of Jerusalem, came to the binational solution only after decades of research on his native land and with a sense of deep sorrow. "It is not easy for me to part with my father's dream of a Jewish nation-state. It's hard for me. For most of my life that was my dream, too," he said. But he, too, sees no alternative.

> The conclusion is that the seemingly rational solution of two states for two nations can't work here. The model of a division into two nation-states is inapplicable. It doesn't reflect the depth of the conflict and doesn't sit with the scale of the entanglement that exists in large parts of the country. You can erect all the walls in the world here but you won't be able to overcome the fact that there is only one aquifer here and the same air and that all the streams run into the same sea. You won't be able to overcome the fact that this country will not tolerate a border in its midst. . . . There is no choice but to think about western Palestine [Eretz Israel, or the land of Israel] as one geopolitical unit. . . . What we have to do is try to reach a situation of personal and collective equality within the framework of one overall regime throughout the country.[4]

And so Israel faces a fateful decision, which Ariel Sharon has accelerated and which now confronts all. "We are postponing an inevitable harder choice," says Tony Judt, "that only the far right and far left have so far acknowledged, . . . between an ethnically cleansed Greater Israel and a single, integrated, binational state of Jews and Arabs, Israelis and Palestinians."[5]

Some from the center and the right wing also understand that a choice is imminent: for example, Israeli historian Benny Morris, who—apparently to his own political trouble—was responsible for wrecking a founding myth in Israel's national narrative by documenting the Zionists' deliberate expulsion of hundreds of thousands of Palestinians from their villages in 1948.[6] To the amazement of a recent interviewer, Morris endorses those cruelties as morally legitimate in permitting Israel's formation as a Jewish state: "There are circumstances in history that justify ethnic cleansing." But Morris also believes that, ultimately, the effort was fruitless, given Arab hostility. "It was a mistake," he said toward the end of the famous *Ha'aretz* interview that first publicized his logics, "to think that it would be possible to establish a tranquil state here that lives in harmony with its surroundings." Journalist Avi Shavit bleakly returned, "Which leaves us with two possibilities: either a cruel, tragic Zionism, or the foregoing of Zionism." "Yes. That's so," replied Morris. "You have pared it down, but that's correct."[7]

These voices, few but growing in number, are generating a sense of rising pressure and eliciting scathing Zionist reactions. "The idea of the Jewish state is under systematic attack," warns Yoram Hazony (president of the Shalem Center in Jerusalem) in *The Jewish State: The Struggle for Israel's Soul.*[8] "The debate is raging," protests Yoel Esteron, managing editor of *Ha'aretz,* denouncing the one-state solution in passionate terms.[9] For these Israelis as for many Zionists, the very suggestion of a binational state represents an unconscionable betrayal of the Zionist dream and an inadmissible capitulation to Arab rejectionism—even a self-hating or autogenocidal delusion. For a binational state would mean an Arab majority, a condition presumed to spell the end of the Jewish state and of Jewish national life—even national suicide, resulting from genocidal Arab attack and/or expulsion of the Jewish people from their "historic homeland." Willingly inviting that condition manifests as unfathomable. "Can an idea be ludicrous and dangerous at the same time?" says outraged Esteron.[10]

But insurgent Jewish voices are refusing to be silenced, out of deeply held principles of their own. The two-state solution now seems to promise Israel only the most dismal future—permanent war, ongoing terrorism, and a domestic political culture increasingly dominated by militarism and neo-Zionist theocratic (or at least ethnocratic) chauvinism. Statements from the right wing have aggravated this terrible vision. Israeli geographer Arnon Soffer, a major voice arguing that Israel must forcefully confront the Palestinian "demographic threat," speaks bluntly about the immediate consequences of "unilateral disengagement" to the two-state solution he urges.

First of all, the fence is not built like the Berlin Wall. It's a fence that we will be guarding on either side. . . . when 2.5 million people live in a closed-off Gaza, it's going to be a human catastrophe. Those people will become even bigger animals than they are today, with the aid of an insane fundamentalist Islam. The pressure at the border will be awful. It's going to be a terrible war. So, if we want to remain alive, we will have to kill and kill and kill. All day, every day. . . . If we don't kill, we will cease to exist. The only thing that concerns me is how to ensure that the boys and men who are going to have to do the killing will be able to return home to their families and be normal human beings.[11]

Such a Dorian Gray portrait of the Zionist dream is deeply upsetting to Jewish liberals and leftists—suggesting a version of Israel not worth preserving. For peace activists like Hanegbi, not only Israel's security but Israel's very character therefore rests on creating a binational state.

In essence, the binational principle is the deepest antithesis of the wall. The purpose of the wall is to separate, to isolate, to imprison the Palestinians in pens. But the wall imprisons the Israelis, too. It turns Israel into a ghetto. The wall is the great despairing solution of the Jewish-Zionist society. It is the last desperate act of those who cannot confront the Palestinian issue. Of those who are compelled to push the Palestinian issue out of their lives and out of their consciousness. In the face of that I say the opposite. I say that we were apparently too forgiving toward Zionism; that the Jews who came here and found a land that wasn't empty adopted a pattern of unrestrained force. Instead of the conflict foisting moral order and reason on them, it addicted them to the use of force. But that force has played itself out, it has reached its limits. If Israel remains a colonialist state in its character, it will not survive. In the end the region will be stronger than Israel, in the end the indigenous people will be stronger than Israel. Those who hope to live by the sword will die by the sword. . . . In general, we have to shift to a binational mode of thinking. Maybe in the end we have to create a new, binational Israel, just as a new, multiracial South Africa was created.[12]

Hence, sentiment toward establishing a binational or secular-democratic state is incrementally gaining force not because a one-state solution is deemed more fair or more just—although it is argued to be—but because, empirically, it manifests as the only alternative to a doomed future for Israel. But what about the Palestinians? Would they not reject any idea of joining with Jews in a multiethnic state?

Strikingly, Palestinian voices are raising the same prospect. Palestinians are, of course, most keenly aware that the mottled ethnic demography created by the settlement grid spells certain doom for Palestinian nationalism within the "cage" or "ghetto" of the promised Palestinian "state" or Bantustan. "The problem is that Palestinian self-determination in a separate state is unworkable," wrote Edward Said, as early as 1999, "just as unworkable as the principle of separation between a demographically mixed, irreversibly connected Arab and Jewish population in Israel and the occupied territories . . . I therefore see no other way than to begin now to speak about sharing the land that has thrust us together, sharing it in a truly democratic way, with equal rights for all citizens."[13] Professor 'Ali Jarbawi, of Birzeit University in the West Bank, believes that broader Palestinian sentiment is moving toward the same conclusion: "Most Palestinians prefer the idea of separation, because they want their own state. But Sharon's idea of a two-state solution is to squeeze us into cantons. . . . Given a choice between cantonization and one state, Palestinians will go for the latter."[14]

Given overwhelming Jewish-Israeli and Zionist antipathy to any idea of dissolving the Jewish state, Palestinian talk of the one-state option might manifest simply as a ploy to leverage a meaningful Israeli withdrawal from the occupied territories. PA Prime Minister Ahmed Qurei indicated as much, in wielding the one-state solution as a kind of threat: "This is an apartheid solution to put the Palestinians in cantons. Who can accept this? We will go for a one-state solution. There's no other solution. We will not hesitate to defend the right of our people when we feel the very serious intention to destroy these rights."[15] PA official Hani Al-Masri offered a similarly strategic message in January 2004, in a column in the West Bank Arabic daily *Al-Ayyam*. Considering the likelihood that Israel will not reverse its policies in the West Bank, he wrote:

> we will have no choice but to abandon the choice of establishing
> a Palestinian state on the territories occupied in 1967 and revert

to the option of establishing a secular, democratic state in the entirety of Palestine where Jews, Muslims and Christians live on equal footing. . . . The goal we must pursue, and Israel can't prevent us from pursuing it, lies in dismantling the Palestinian Authority and abandoning Palestinian statehood.[16]

The threat has worked. Precisely on grounds that the binational state is otherwise imminent, a rash of Jewish Israelis, such as Israeli government official Ehud Olmert, have intensified support for Sharon's "unilateral disengagement" strategy. For they understand that the greatest risk to Israel is indeed a Palestinian demand for full democracy. "We don't have unlimited time," Olmert says. "More and more Palestinians are uninterested in a negotiated, two-state solution, because they want to change the essence of the conflict from an Algerian paradigm to a South African one. From a struggle against 'occupation,' in their parlance, to a struggle for one-man-one-vote. That is, of course, a much cleaner struggle, a much more popular struggle—and ultimately a much more powerful one. For us, it would mean the end of the Jewish state."[17]

Arab-Israeli Knesset member and professor 'Azmi Bishara—an early proponent of a binational state, who still argues forcefully for Arabs' equal citizenship within Israel—has pointed out that these PA statements ring false, as political maneuvers. If one really wants an outcome, he observes, one does not threaten one's opponent with it. But Olmert's concerns accurately reflect the moral power weaving through Palestinian writings on the one-state solution, for most are clearly principled calls. At its 2004 convention (16–19 April), the U.S.-based Palestinian group Al-Awda (Palestine Right to Return Coalition) adopted "by an overwhelming consensus" several "points of unity," the first of which was establishment "of an independent, democratic state for all its citizens in all of Palestine . . . which encompasses present-day 'Israel', the West Bank and Gaza Strip."[18] A Palestinian imam wrote in the *Denver Post*, "If we truly want to create a model for freedom and democracy in the Middle East, we should be encouraging a one-state solution in Israel, the West Bank and Gaza where Jews, Christians, Muslims and everyone else have equal rights, responsibilities and opportunities."[19] In a March 2004 essay, Chicago professor Raja Halwani wrote passionately of the one-state option as an ennobled political mission.

> It might be true that we are "pushed" or "forced" into the one-state solution because of facts on the ground, such as the wall that Israel is building and the fragmentation of Palestinian land due to the Jewish settlements. . . . Nonetheless . . . the real reasons for the one-state solution are moral, not practical (or not just practical) ones. They stem from our recognition of the importance of the justice of the right of return, and they stem from our recognition that the land of Palestine, all of it, is important for both Jews and Palestinians. And these are not reasons that "push" or "force" us into the one-state solution. They are reasons that ought to lead us to it with our heads help up high and with smiles of pride and joy on our faces. Sharing Palestine is not a lesser of two evils. It is a high—indeed, given the conflict, the highest—good.[20]

What underlies this tectonic shift among Palestinian intellectuals toward the one-state solution? The immediate reason is their appreciation of the pragmatic reality—that the national land base is now inadequate; that the peace process is futile; and, not least, that the Palestinian protogovernment remains debilitated and unable to leverage a settlement withdrawal. Surveys of Palestinian disillusionment with Palestinian nationalism are still lacking, and journalist Khalid Amayreh believes that support for one state is "still confined to elitist segments within Palestinian society." But as the settlement grid continues to advance, he believes that "these ideas will spread quickly and gain momentum among Palestinians as many of them are already discovering that the PA has become more of a national liability than a national asset."[21]

Electronic Intifada cofounder Ali Abunimah believes the shift reflects a deeper evolutionary change in Palestinian politics, tracing to three factors. First, he considers that fatalism has taken hold: "despite the bitterness of the conflict, the vast majority of Israelis and Palestinians accept the permanence of the other, and on each side only a few really fantasize about the disappearance of the other."[22] Second, he argues that the midcentury decolonization ideology of indigenous nationalism, which shaped doctrines in the PLO Charter, has "lost its luster." As decolonized states in Africa and the Middle East have conspicuously "failed to deliver the prosperity and freedom they promised," Palestinians living in the Arab world have especially become disenchanted with the old native-nationalist discourses. Third, Abunimah argues that decades in diaspora life throughout the Middle East, Europe, and North America have cultivated in Palestinians a faith in civil multiethnic democracy and dwindling interest in forming a state on the old nationalist terms "embodied by a flag and a marching band." What they do want, Abunimah believes, is "freedom of movement, of expression, and equal access to the benefits of a democratic society." Focusing on these basic democratic goals "makes it much easier to contemplate a multi-ethnic future in Palestine without experiencing it in any way as a loss of Palestinian-ness."

So, in his turn, Abunimah asks, "If Palestinians can be convinced, then what about Israelis?"[23]

Some among the Jewish "post-Zionist" few, observing this shift in Palestinian intellectual thought toward endorsing one multiethnic state, are discovering cross-ethnic intellectual synergy and a nascent political coalition. Gavron speaks confidently of his sense of a Palestinian consensus: "Many Palestinians have told me that they would prefer a single state but accept a two-state solution because that is what the Jews want."[24] Professor Haim Bresheeth, from the University of East London, senses the same convergence.

> This is not something I find easy to say, as an Israeli and son of Holocaust survivors. I would like to be able to argue for an Israeli-Hebrew entity—not a Zionist militarist enterprise, of course, but a democratic, autonomous political and cultural entity twinned with a similar Palestinian entity. But after four decades of military rule and all the desecration of political, human, civil, property and other forms of rights by the occupation regime, most reasonable people will agree that no support can be given to this outdated, violent, immoral and inefficient mode of domination of one people over another. . . . Many Palestinians are now returning to an earlier, more principled stage of their political development and argument—the PLO solution of a secular, democratic single state in the whole of Palestine; one state that allows equal rights to Jews and Arabs alike. It is ironic that through failing to grasp the nettle which

would have enabled them to keep a separate Israeli state in the pre-1967 borders, Israeli leaders have forced a change in Palestinian thinking: "if we are not allowed to live as a free people in 22 per cent of our country, or come to that, even 10 per cent of it, maybe we should go back to fighting to liberate the whole country, for both people to live in peace, as equals."[25]

In Jewish-Israeli thought, too, the shift has been maturing, for broader reasons. First, more effective legal and political challenges by Arab Israelis to Israel's two-tiered citizenship system, which has always contradicted Israel's own democratic principles, have been cultivating (if unevenly) liberal and "post-Zionist" momentum toward reform. Second, after half a century of nation-building, a more robust Israeli national identity has gelled, generating a deeper cultural rift between Jews in Israel and Jews abroad. In mixed cities like Haifa, Arabs and Jews have much more in common with each other—language, cultural references, social norms—than they do with their ethnonational kin outside the country. Third, recognition that the Western democracies are indeed proving stable and safe environments for Jews is progressively dimming the sense that the Jewish state is vital to Jewish ethnic or cultural continuity. At the same time, the resurgence of multiculturalism in those once-assimilationist Western democracies has opened new public spaces where diaspora Jews can develop forms of ethnic community and cultural expression more in tune with their local circumstances.

As a result, the late nineteenth-century Zionist project to "normalize" the aberrant situation of the stateless Jewish nation by establishing a Jewish state is transmuting into ambitions for a new "normalcy"—a stable, safe, and culturally rich life for Jews in a multiethnic, democratic, "Israeli" civil nation.[26] The security crisis—and the horrific Wall—are bringing all these sentiments into sudden focus: many Jews are concluding that it is better to have one civil state, whatever its ethnic tensions, than to have the Zionist dream corroded past recognition.

The psychological obstacles to the one-state solution, however, remain huge on both sides. For the vast majority of Jewish Israelis and Zionists abroad, the idea violates beliefs and loyalties to Zionism that run deep in their personal worldviews, internalized historical narratives, and most heartfelt values. Some who have made the intellectual journey to endorse the one-state solution have done so only with inner anguish and sorrow for lost Zionist visions, as well as great and anxious hopes for new ones. Those who foresee Jewish disaster and destruction in a one-state solution are equally driven by deep emotional and philosophical commitments. The bureaucracies associated with the Jewish-national institutions—the Jewish Agency, the World Zionist Organization, the Jewish National Fund—are also well armed to feed the collective consciousness of those commitments and are working to strengthen every psychological obstacle. Any serious proposal for the one-state solution will galvanize broad new energies to oppose it—indeed, the idea has already done so.

Shaking off the "Palestinian state" formula will surely shock or jar many Palestinians as well, many of whom will fear or reject any alternative formula. Although the old native nationalism may be fading, Palestinian activists who have dedicated their lives to Palestinian self-determination (directly or vicariously) may view a one-state solution as a national betrayal. Some will genuinely believe that only through Palestinian statehood can the Palestinians find full ethnonationalist expression—the mirror image of Zionist logics. Others will fear permanent political subordination in Israel: so great is the power differential between Jewish Israel and Palestinians that a multiethnic state may seem to promise only permanent second-class citizenship, as has been imposed on Israeli Arabs. More lumpen nationalists may simply find unfathomable the prospect of losing the symbolic lexicon of Palestinian political dignity—the flag, the stirring rhetoric—and will resist dissolution of an imagined future Palestinian nation-state utopia. Of course, some elements have much to lose from a multiethnic state; not least, the old-guard Palestinian elite and their clients in the PA would lose the fat sinecures of their much-abused positions. But political doctrines and incentives are not the only obstacles. Many Palestinians, especially in the Gaza Strip, will feel visceral aversion to sharing a national life with the Jewish society that has wrecked their culture and immiserated their families, especially as anger and hatred for Jewish Israel has crested in recent years with peaking Palestinian death counts, mass house demolitions, and a sense of betrayal following the collapse of Oslo. A zealous few will believe that the one-state solution would betray God's will—that is, the defeat of the Jews by the Muslims, prophesied in some Islamic traditions.[27]

Shifting both Zionist and Palestinian national consciousnesses toward the radically new path of one multiethnic state will therefore require both soul-searching and fortitude to weather the political turmoil and some bitter splits, both of which must be pursued within the opposing communities with renewed courage and honesty. The effort might seem as unviable as the two-state solution, except that the two-state solution cannot possibly work. As no Jewish withdrawal from the "Holy Land" would be required, the challenge here is to share the land rather than abandon it—a more difficult formula for right-wing and religious Zionists to reject (as Olmert pointed out). Unfortunately, facing a fateful historical juncture, these great historical challenges must now be pursued faster than such a momentous transition would seem to require.

The last task attempted in this book is to lay some foundation for those necessary debates, by focusing on the Zionist logics that have precluded the one-state solution from the outset. But first, the debate itself needs to be normalized. Even sensible discussion of the one-state solution has been largely blocked by strident Zionist charges that it is innately anti-Semitic or even genocidal in its motive or at least its implications. Initial consideration must also be given to the challenge that the one-state solution would contradict international consensus supporting a two-state solution and therefore be somehow illegitimate. Addressing these two objections will allow political space for an initial discussion of the burning substantive questions: what the one-state solution would mean for the Jewish national home and whether an alternative future might be found to salvage the Zionist dream.

INTO THE BREACH:
THE ANTI-SEMITISM CHARGE

Over the past few years, any attempt to discuss the one-state option for Israel-Palestine has primarily suffered from fierce Zionist denunciation that any such idea represents a covert assault on the Jewish people. Zionist discourse has long defined any criticism of Israel as "cover" or "code words" for anti-Semitism, and in the past decade, a wave of publications has emphasized afresh that talk of a multiethnic state reflects this "new anti-Semitism" or "anti-Semitism without Jews."²⁸ Under this banner, Zionist networks (e.g., those described in chap. 4) are commonly mobilized to target even Jewish advocates of the one-state solution as witting or unwitting architects of genocide. Professor Tony Judt, a senior scholar at New York University, met such an onslaught after publishing his landmark "Israel: An Alternative" in the *New York Review of Books,* as he attested in a later *NYRB* letter exchange.

> Much of the American response verged on hysteria. Readers accused me of belonging to the "Nazi Left," of hating Jews, of denying Israel's right to exist. "Distinguished professors" at American universities cancelled their *NYR* subscriptions (in marked contrast to Israeli correspondents who welcomed the disagreement, "basic to freedom" as the director of the Yad Vashem Archives put it). Andrea Levin, executive director of the "Committee for Accuracy in Middle East Reporting in America" [CAMERA], accused me of "pandering to genocide" and being "party to preparations for a final solution." Alan Dershowitz of Harvard made the analogy with Adolf Hitler's "one-state solution for all of Europe." David Frum, a former speech-writer for President Bush, charged me with advocating "genocidal liberalism": characteristically, he attributed my opinions to my origins, which he mistakenly took to be Belgian. *The New Republic* described my essay as "crossing a line": in a broad hint to readers for whom anti-Zionism and anti-Semitism are indistinguishable, it dubbed my views "anti-Zionism with a human face."²⁹

A review essay in *The Nation* in which Brian Klug attempted to critique this "new anti-Semitism" charge³⁰ met similar disparagement in a published letter from Gidon Remba. Insisting that "binational advocacy" is indeed "inherently anti-Jewish racism," Remba predicted that the "malign binationalist nightmare" implied by Klug's secular-democratic ideas would inevitably reduce the Jewish population to "a tolerated, subjugated minority, most likely recapitulating the tragic fates of multiethnic polities like Lebanon, Bosnia and Yugoslavia." Hence, proposals for a one-state solution are only "a fig leaf for depriving Israeli Jews of their basic civil and human rights in a new Arab state. In this regard, it is anti-Jewish discrimination, satisfying standard definitions of anti-Semitism as a form of racism against Israeli Jews." Remba finished in apocalyptic mode.

Such misbegotten noble intentions will help pave the road to perdition, bolstering the Israeli right, feeding Jewish fear and paranoia and Arab chauvinist triumphalism. If successful, they will sweep Israelis and Palestinians down to the next rung of the raging Middle Eastern inferno, engulfing them in the great and intimate flames of civil war.[31]

Several themes (discussed in previous chapters) converge in this vision of debacle: a frightened Jewish society and a demonized Arab society (which, hating Jews, will seek minimally to deprive Jews of basic civil and human rights), settler fear of native revenge (Remba's "chauvinist triumphalism"), and a turned-table assumption that Zionist ambitions to expel Arabs must inevitably translate into Arab ambitions to expel Jews. That Israel is already replicating the "tragic fates" of other ethnonationalist states does not seem to register in these formulas. That Israel might successfully democratize as a multiethnic civil society—albeit with some tortuous process of adjustment, as occurred in South Africa—is not considered remotely realistic. In any other setting, such transparent racial stereotyping against Arabs and histrionics about certain genocide at the hands of recidivist natives would trigger instant derision by critical readerships. Instead, for reasons discussed in chapters 4 and 5, Zionist defenses have strangely succeeded in confounding and delegitimizing even academic discussions of a binational or secular-democratic state, by casting them into the pit of the morally inadmissible, as portents of the "raging inferno" and a new "final solution."

This shrill rejection of one-state arguments as anti-Semitic builds on several themes. First and most simplistically, it equates the Jewish state with Jewish people and regards any criticism of the state (or its Jewishness) as an attack on Jewishness per se. This argument is often devastating when dealt as brute hammer strokes in public polemics but is actually very feeble, being speedily set aside by the retort that states everywhere are prone to certain sins, that the state of Israel is no exception, and that it should not be held uniquely immune to human rights standards and the norms of modern civil democracy simply because of its Jewish ethnonationalist connection. The standard Zionist non sequitur is that many states treat their domestic minorities far more badly than does Israel, so singling out Israel must be motivated by some special agenda, which can only be anti-Semitism. An impressive blindness to the scale of Israel's abuses levied on the Palestinians is evident here, as well as equally impressive denial of the conflict's configuration in the Middle East, which lends it such dire implications for global security. But Israel's proud claim to be part of the Western democratic community is the particular logical failing. Claiming that its democratic character and moral authority warrant its special patronage by the United States, Zionists cannot then convincingly argue that Israel be judged favorably in comparison to the brutal regimes of, for example, Saddam Hussein or the Sudanese government.

But the anti-Semitism charge also reflects genuine concern that eliminating Israel as a Jewish state would leave Jews vulnerable to discrimination and even physical attack, particularly by Arabs but also elsewhere. This perspective is fraught with racism in its demonization of Arabs and "Arab society." But it also constitutes a genuine fear that requires discussion up front.

THE SPECTER OF ARAB HOSTILITY

Commonly, the first argument against even considering a binational or secular-democratic state is that it is self-destructive on its face, due to intransigent Arab hostility to Jews and murderous intent. Remba's apocalyptical vision (cited earlier) made this assumption, as did the U.S. writers who levied charges of "genocidal liberalism" against Tony Judt. Intertwined within this fear are racist assumptions of an innate cultural predisposition in "Arab society" toward authoritarianism and dictatorship, which would lead the Palestinians to eradicate democracy itself. Hence, one implied meaning of the common Zionist formula "Israel must remain Jewish and democratic" is that if democracy brought power to Arab majority, Israel would soon cease to be democratic. (The counterfactual position of Israeli Arabs, who are full players in Israeli democracy and have clearly indicated no desire to lose that status, somehow does not confound this assumption.)

To the extent that it is mere racial stereotyping, this argument might be derided—particularly as some of Israel's most inspired liberal-democratic politicians are Israeli Arabs. But to the extent that it reflects genuine Jewish fear of Arab hostility, this argument is an edifice not easily breached—not least because, at this unhappy point in history, it has more validity than previously. Arab and Muslim anger and frustration with Israeli policies have reached a point where genuine anti-Semitism (demonization of "the Jews") is being whipped up to new intensity, as a classically racial-reactionary explanation. Of course, as noted in chapter 5, Arab rhetoric about "the Jews" responds directly to Israeli rhetoric and Zionist ideology promoting "the Jews" as a national identity in the Middle East, especially as Israel's defense of "the Jews" extends to authorizing the subordination of Palestinians in the name of "the Jewish people." Although invoking old racist references, Arab rhetoric does not spring from some primordial or deep-historical tradition of hating Jews. Nevertheless, no special Jewish sensitivity is required to glean racial hatred from Palestinian suicide bombings of Jewish civilians, bombings and defacing of synagogues in Europe, hostile rhetoric about "the Jews" from such Islamic groups as Hezbollah and Hamas, and decades of Arab-state rhetoric about "the Jews" and the "Zionist entity." Even promises of outright Jewish expulsion have occasionally reemerged from such posturing tyrants as Saddam Hussein, and, in more millennialist terms, from Hamas, suggesting a larger substratum of sentiment and brooding intent. Fine-tuned distinctions between anti-Zionism and anti-Semitism especially become too nice regarding some of the language in Hamas's charter: for example, when invocation to action—such as "Our struggle against the Jews is very great and very serious. It needs all sincere efforts"—are coupled with Islamic aphorisms about exterminating Jews. All this language reinforces Jewish understandings of Israel as a beleaguered enclave in a sea of hostile Arab Muslims bent on Jewish destruction—a view that taps into the deeper experiential well of the Holocaust.

The PLO charter also plainly rejected residency rights in Palestine to Jews who could not trace their ancestry to Jews "who had normally resided in Palestine until the beginning of the Zionist invasion," implying expulsion or at least an uncertain future for the rest. Oslo raised a brief hope of reconciliation, but the intensity of violence since the second intifada has greatly reinforced popular Jewish certainty that Palestinians still hope to rid the land physically of "the Jews." In this view, if Palestinians came to comprise a majority in a single state, they could at best be expected to demonstrate callous disregard for Jewish interests, which over time would progressively erode the expression and freedoms of the Jewish community and end the function of Israel as a Jewish national home. This fear is sometimes expressed in predictions of a "staged" takeover of the country by Palestinians if they are given any opening. That these fears have been instrumentalized and inflated by right-wing ideologues to reject even modest Palestinian political claims makes them no less genuine, and they will not easily be assuaged. In short, fear of Palestinian vengeance is a political factor in itself.

But Jewish impressions of Arab hatred did not obtain their present configuration simply through collective Jewish experience of Arab rhetoric and recent violence. Political Zionism has a long-standing tradition of constructing the Arab other as an irrational hateful enemy, partly to exonerate and legitimize the Jewish state and partly to support a hard-line rejectionist posture toward the Palestinians—a view stoked by interlaced doctrines of racial stereotyping and Israel's idealized mytho-history. Those convinced of this tenet readily cast various Arab peace initiatives based on "land for peace" (e.g., the Saudi peace proposal of March 2002) onto the diplomatic trash heap as mere ploys toward positioning Arab armies on Israel's borders.[32] Yet the tenet of intransigent Arab hostility might still be softened in some genuine peace process. Brightened Jewish-Israel hopes in Oslo's early years indeed indicated that greater openness toward Palestinians has lain latent within Israel's body politic through those same decades. Palestinian hopes and enthusiasm impressively reciprocated that brief goodwill, indicating the same resilience.

Truly considering that Palestinians might share the state without seeking Jewish destruction will, however, require more than epiphenomenal Jewish mood swings regarding Arab and Palestinian intentions. It will require a serious project to reconceptualize Palestinian anger as born of specific injustices perpetrated by Zionist state-building, as well as a demonstrated shift in policy and rhetoric to reflect that realization, both to elicit meaningful reciprocity from Palestinians and to lay a conceptual basis for crediting Palestinian peace gestures, which are now too often dismissed as hypocritical. But that step requires that Jews both in Israel and abroad engage in a profound collective reconstruction of Israel's founding myths—no easy task on any level, political or emotional, especially regarding the myth of a peace-loving and enlightened Zionist movement that sought to share the land and was instead viciously attacked by "five Arab armies." (Fully grasping that the Palestinians were deliberately expelled in 1948, to "cleanse" the land for Jews, recasts Palestinian-nationalist resistance in a very different light, as reflecting the just anger of a dispossessed native population.) Similarly, if Jewish Israelis and Zionists could accept that Arab states made apparently genuine peace overtures in the early years of the state and that these offers were actually rejected by Ben-Gurion and later prime ministers, a better climate might be created for crediting recent peace initiatives by Arab states (e.g., the 2002 Saudi-led offer). Only if Jewish understanding of Palestinian resentment can alter to appreciate its origins can sufficient political will be found to reconsider state policy. As in South Africa, even diplomatic language to this effect could trigger meaningful Palestinian reciprocity and lay the long-missing basis for genuine peace talks.

Indeed, far from displaying a deep history of rejectionism, the Arab world has long indicated its substantial interest in a shared state. Until the 1947–48 war, Zionists who sought a "national home" for Jews in Palestine (e.g., Judah Leib Magnes, Martin Buber, and Hannah Arendt) were firmly convinced that an Arab-Jewish state could be formed in coordination with willing Arab partners. Some critics have derided this view as naive, sometimes noting that the Arab partners for a shared state were never identified. But a 1947 subcommittee report from the UN, calling for a binational state, provides unique support for their views.[33] The General Assembly had convened a special committee to consider options in Palestine and later formed a subcommittee to examine the resulting proposals. Ultimately, the majority view won out: on 29 November, the General Assembly passed UN Resolution 181, which endorsed partition of Palestine into an "Arab state" and a "Jewish state."

But a second subcommittee was formed to examine alternatives to partition. This committee was composed by representatives from mostly Arab-Muslim states: Afghanistan, Colombia, Egypt, Iraq, Lebanon, Pakistan, Saudi Arabia, Syria, and Yemen. Its report arrived at a very different conclusion: that the only legal and just solution in Palestine was a binational state. The subcommittee found that a "national home for the Jewish people" (as provided for by the Balfour Declaration of 1917) was indeed admissible under the terms of the British Mandate but that a Jewish *state* was not. In its final draft resolution, the subcommittee called instead for a unitary democratic state with several provisions to ensure ethnic rights. First, the legislature should secure proportional representation for "all important sections of the citizenry," yet provide "wide discretion" for local authorities "in matters connected with education, health and other social services." Management of holy sites and freedom of religion should be practiced "in accordance with the *status quo*." A constitutional provision would secure group rights for Jews no matter what proportion of the country's population they constituted.

> The guarantees contained in the constitution concerning the rights and safeguards of the minorities shall not be subject to amendment or modification without the consent of the minority concerned expressed through a majority of its representatives in the legislature.[34]

The subcommittee also held, presciently, that if a Jewish state came into being "against the bitter opposition of the Arabs of Palestine and of the inhabitants of the adjoining countries," it would only "jeopardize peace and international security throughout the Middle East" and "give rise to an outbreak of hostilities which it may become extremely difficult to check and bring under control."

> It is a matter for regret that the Special Committee, instead of finding ways and means to ensure greater co-operation between Arabs and Jews in a single State, should have evolved a scheme

which would, in fact, destroy whatever prospects still exist of friendly co-operation between the two communities and lead to most tragic consequences.[35]

Today, Jewish fears of Arab hostility will not be assuaged simply by recalling this midcentury diplomatic history—not least because several wars and rounds of violence subsequently redefined all relationships for the worse (as the subcommittee predicted). Yet this Arab-Muslim intervention in 1947 does address the generic racist assumption that Arabs per se have been intransigently opposed to the Jewish presence in Palestine or to any compromise toward a stable solution. The "Zionist entity" later denounced in Arab rhetoric was the Jewish state, not the Jewish presence. As discussed in chapter 5, early Arab and Palestinian rhetoric did denounce Jewish settlement, much on the model of French settlement in Algeria, and pompous Arab public rhetoric has indeed sometimes included rhetorical flourishes about expelling "the Jews," much as occasional Israeli public rhetoric has always flourished propositions to expel "the Arabs." But interpreting long-standing Arab League rejection of the Jewish state as monolithic rejection of the Jewish people is a Zionist propaganda maneuver.

The UN subcommittee's carefully drawn constitutional provisions (see app. A) also demolish the racist myth that Arabs are innately anti-democratic and, if absorbed into Israel, would make short shrift both of Jews and of Israel's democratic system. Dignifying that myth by contradicting it can be confined to a few curt references, to the Arab political theorists of the late nineteenth and early twentieth centuries, who argued eloquently for democratic systems for their new states; the democratic opposition movements in Egypt, Jordan, Algeria, Tunisia, Lebanon, Iraq, and the Persian Gulf in the past century (some partly successful, others suppressed with help from Western imperial powers); and, hardly least, the democratic Israeli Arab population already integrated into Israeli politics and its eloquent Arab representatives to the Knesset.[36]

Under more legitimate question here is the democratic character of Palestinian politics. Palestinian society, lacking a central government, has shown the same political diversity that any population might experience under such conditions. The spectrum has run the gamut from Marxists, through social democrats and liberals, to Islamic totalitarians (the last, unfortunately, increasingly eclipsing the others in media coverage). But even in conditions of exile and fragmentation, this spectrum has been addressed pluralistically. Indeed, Palestinian nationalism has entertained a democratic philosophy from its earliest stages, a political foundation that now shapes Palestinian struggles to establish a legitimate elected leadership after the death of Arafat.

That democratic tradition has not been apparent to those who believe Palestinian politics have historically been defined entirely by Arafat's inept personality cult or that Palestinian democratic rhetoric is belied by the suicide bombers. Hamas especially has even led some analysts to propose Palestinian politics as driven primarily by Islam. But that portrait is strikingly ahistorical, even strategically amnesiac. As anyone familiar with Palestinian politics can attest, the Islamic tendency is a recent and still minority twist for a national movement that, through its first half century, was overwhelmingly secular. Palestinian politics were long structured by famous party rivalries between the right-wing Fatah, the left-wing PFLP and DFLP, and the tiny Palestinian Communist Party. The PLO accommodated this spectrum in the Palestine National Council (PNC), the Palestinian "parliament" organized on democratic principles. Such Palestinian intellectuals as Ibrahim Abu Lughod and Edward Said were at times representatives to the PNC, which provided seats for writers, students, workers, women, and diaspora populations, as well as guerrilla groups. The PNC was never an ideal democratic system; Arafat and the major Palestinian parties always manipulated and competed over its memberships, and Palestinian politics (not surprisingly) suffered heavily from the internecine rivalries typical of exile politics. (Ironically, some parallels to preindependence Zionist politics might be drawn.) Still, that lasting ethos of democracy runs deep and frames all Palestinian political discourse except the very recent and frightening rise of Islamic totalitarian doctrines. Indeed, because of this democratic tradition, Palestinians have admired Israel's democracy and hoped for something similar for the Palestinian state. The same democratic values now drive the shift among some Palestinians to favor the one-state solution, in the hope that the Palestinians' democratic values can find expression in Israel's ruggedly democratic institutions.

Israel's sturdy democracy should be entirely capable of remaining democratic while absorbing this democratically oriented population. Its Basic Law would need to be retooled, and its state institutions would require dramatic adjustment (as discussed later in this chapter). Early work to establish a new constitution and stabilize a new party system can lay a firm groundwork for civil democracy, and a truth-and-reconciliation process might help to clarify and embed a new consensus on the country's history, forming a new basis for civil nationalism. None of this implies a sudden collapse of democracy or serious loss of political power for the Jewish population. Gavron points out: "In its early years, the new state will be dominated by Israeli Jews. We will form a majority of its parliament, run its government, lead its army, head its judiciary, and administer its education system."[37]

In short, Israel can adjust as South Africa is adjusting and as many other states have adjusted. The fall of apartheid is indeed suggestive here, as that process was famously presaged by overwrought white fears of black irrationality, violence, and vengeance. Yet Afrikaners discovered that they could share the state with blacks and not only live to tell the tale but preserve their society, neighborhoods, homes, and jobs. The rule of law held, as the black population had an equal stake in it. The mutual need of whites, coloreds and blacks for democratization, coupled with a sense of historic achievement with white political capitulation, stabilized what many had believed an impossible transition. For blacks, whatever the delayed rewards and ongoing difficulties, the fact of democracy ultimately displaced old resentments onto the political process itself, while defusing and discrediting black militancy. Other transitions, such as that in Guatemala, have shown similar high-minded indigenous response. (The consistency shown by historically devastated populations in extending forgiveness to their settler conquerors is endlessly astounding to this writer.) In this vision, the Jewish people will join the experience of other groups who once held dominant positions in Western democracies: they will become one ethnic group sharing a civil democracy, with persisting group interests but also, eventually, crosscutting ethnic ties. Just how that transition might be orchestrated is discussed briefly here, but no one is better positioned to orchestrate it than the Jews themselves, whose collective history as architects of civil democracy and human justice comprises a far deeper well of experience than does the Holocaust.

INTERNATIONAL CONSENSUS

A second Zionist argument preempting discussion of the one-state option is that the two-state solution is supported by a deep tradition of international consensus endorsing partition and a Jewish state. That claim sometimes cites the Balfour Declaration of 1917, a letter conveying formal British approval for the Zionist mission to establish a "national home for the Jewish people" in Palestine. But the claim relies especially on UN Resolution 181 of 1947—the "Partition Resolution"—which divided the land and provided for two states (in economic union) and was resurrected vaguely in the Oslo process, although on radically different geographic terms. Hence proposing a one-state solution is argued to contradict nearly a century of expert judgment and to digress unacceptably from that consensus. Given Israel's otherwise impressive disdain for UN resolutions and international opinion—and the actual content of Resolution 181 itself, which called for equal ethnic rights that Israel will not now consider—this argument may ring ironic, but it still warrants brief attention.[38]

The Balfour Declaration has been subjected to extensive historical study, which any summary here would abuse.[39] Two aspects of its politics can, however, be highlighted. First, some people—both British and Zionist—centrally involved in its design were clear that the Zionist movement sought to establish a state and that the declaration's phrasing regarding a "national home for the Jewish people" was simply a diplomatic fig leaf for that goal. Second, others involved in its design were equally certain that a Jewish state should not be formed in a land holding so large an Arab majority and that the provision for a "national home for the Jewish people" signified no more than a right for Jews to settle and form a coherent ethnic community in a land whose political future was still to be determined. Later rival analyses have argued that one view trumped the other. But close studies leave the question at least contestable, having shown a complicated interplay of views and argument on which the Zionist movement had to play carefully to wrest the concession.[40] In any case, no clear international consensus about Jewish state-building can be found in either the language or the intent of the Balfour Declaration.

Assessing the UN partition plan of 1947 requires a preliminary note about the UN's role in making international law. (It might also call for considering lopsided UN politics at the time—for example, its contemporary dominance by the United States and Western European powers and deep splits between core and recently decolonized countries, as suggested earlier—but those dynamics will be set aside for the moment.) General Assembly resolutions especially fall into a hazy area of lawmaking: they may be considered to direct collective international action, to codify or express "common law," or to express international consensus on some matter of international concern. Given the UN's intentionally weak enforcement capacity, General Assembly resolutions regarding peacemaking are considered guidelines or statements of principle rather than binding orders or law. (For this reason, Palestinian rejection of the UN partition plan in 1947 did not precisely violate "international law," nor did Israel's subsequent rejection of it as outmoded.) Failure to implement such a resolution, even over decades, does not render it invalid, as its validity derives from the principle of consensus rather than compliance. But neither do its provisions necessarily hold if that consensus changes with evolving conditions. In other words, General Assembly resolutions are not international statutes: for example, the General Assembly need not repeal a past resolution to render "legal" some state action that contradicts it.

For this reason the UN partition plan of 1947, although still available for reference by either side, by no means precludes a decision by Israelis and Palestinians to form one state if they wish to do so. The intent of UN peacemaking resolutions is hardly to prevent two peoples from making peace. Resolution 181 reflected a political assessment that both the Jewish and the Palestinian peoples had legitimate claims on the land, which could not be reconciled in one state; if those claims can in fact be reconciled, the condition for the resolution is obsolete.

Later UN action on the conflict remained indeterminate on the question of a one- or two-state solution. Diplomacy would eventually concentrate on two Security Council resolutions, considered to have much greater legal authority, although never implemented: Resolution 242 (22 November 1967) and Resolution 338 (15 October 1973), both of which were reaffirmed in the Oslo Accord's Declaration of Principles (1993). These resolutions reduce to three principles: (1) that Israel shall withdraw "armed forces from territories occupied in the recent conflict" (the 1967 war, when Israel took the Golan Heights, the West Bank, the Gaza Strip, and the Sinai Peninsula); (2) that Israel shall do so while "achieving a just settlement of the refugee problem"; and (3) that negotiations should be pursued "between the parties concerned under appropriate auspices aimed at establishing a just and durable peace in the Middle East."

Together, these provisions established the basis for the interminable and unproductive "peace process," while leaving the actual goal of that process unclear. Neither resolution mentioned the Palestinians, who appeared only as the "refugee problem" and, for decades, were not even granted a seat at the negotiating table. (The "parties" or "States" mentioned in the resolutions were Egypt, Jordan, Syria, and other concerned Arab and Western states.) Moreover, the actual territory from which Israel was to withdraw remained unspecified. Due to hard Israeli lobbying, the English translation of Resolution 242 strategically omitted the definite article from the crucial phrase "territories occupied in the recent conflict." (Every other official translation included the definite article, indicating that Israel must return *the* territories—that is, all territories—occupied.) Hence Israel could claim to have fulfilled the intent of Resolution 242—at least according to the English version—by withdrawing from Egyptian territory in the Sinai. Certainly, neither resolution recognized any Palestinian right to a state; neither mentioned the Palestinians at all.

As a consequence, no juridical formula in the post-1967 "peace process" provided that territory ever be turned over to Palestinian sovereignty or suggested that the outcome would be two states. The

Oslo Accords, which invoked that history, took as its own "goal" only the creation of the "Palestinian Interim Self-Government Authority," which would assume responsibility for such matters as electricity, water, and policing in the West Bank and the Gaza Strip. The occupied territories were to be considered "a single territorial unit whose integrity would be preserved during the interim period." Most Palestinians and observers believed that these provisions foreshadowed a true independent state. But the provisions strategically left out exactly what kind of political entity that "unit" might ultimately be—an independent Palestinian state, some kind of autonomy zone, or part of Israel—and whether the unit's "integrity" would be sustained after the interim period.

Only the U.S. "road map for peace," presented by President George W. Bush on 24 June 2002, spoke directly for the first time of a two-state solution. But the road map did not say exactly where those states were to be. A subsequent "letter of understanding," issued by the Bush administration to Prime Minister Sharon on 14 April 2004, spoke of "two states living side by side in peace and security." The Palestinian state should be "viable, contiguous, sovereign, and independent"—somewhere.[41] The Israeli government endorsed the plan, and on 14 April 2004, the Sharon government issued a letter formally admitting the two-state solution. But within Sharon's letter was also the final annexation formula—that while Israel would withdraw all or most settlements from Gaza, only "a small number of villages" would be withdrawn from "Samaria" (roughly, the northern half of the West Bank).[42] Bush's letter offered a lethal endorsement.

> In light of new realities on the ground, including already existing major Israeli population centers, it is unrealistic to expect that the outcome of final status negotiations will be a full and complete return to the armistice lines of 1949, . . . any final status agreement will only be achieved on the basis of mutually agreed changes that reflect these realities.[43]

None of this language suggested any U.S. commitment to a viable Palestinian state in the West Bank. By endorsing the settlement grid as immutable "realities," the Bush administration instead was endorsing Sharon's enclave plan.

In sum, no deep history of diplomacy or international consensus offers any normative obstacle to a binational or secular-democratic state. The two-state solution itself carries a greater burden of legitimacy, having lacked formal endorsement by the Palestinians until 1988 and by Israel and the United States until 2002. The true obstacles to a one-state solution, then, are the views of the two protagonists—their national ideologies, internal politics, and mutual antipathies. Given the psychological burden of a half century of violence, dispossession, mutual fears, and stereotypes, these obstacles are formidable.

Central to those views is the Zionist doctrine that the Jewish state represents a collective project by all world Jewry, providing the main body of the Jewish nation with shelter and providing diaspora Jewry with crucial cultural and spiritual resources whose loss would damage Jewish communal life everywhere. That doctrine supports the mission to ingather the Jewish people to its homeland of antiquity. But that mission has also generated trouble in being translated into a particular understanding of the "Jewish state" that has mandated a Jewish majority and therefore the expulsion and exclusion of the indigenous Palestinian people.

JEWISH NATIONAL UNITY: TERRITORIAL OR TRANSNATIONAL?

As the "Jewish state," Israel is supposed to represent and advocate for Jewishness, Judaism, and Jews everywhere. Reimagining the Jewish-national state as the "*Israeli*-national state" (or the "State of Jerusalem" or some other formula), serving all its territorial citizens equally, could therefore be seen as eliminating a vital Jewish cultural and spiritual center for Jews domestically and in diaspora, imperiling Jewish ethnic cohesion. Disputes have arisen, however, as to exactly how (or whether) Israel serves the Jewish diaspora community, and in these disputes lie new possibilities for rethinking Israel as the Jewish national home.

Early political Zionism assumed that the Jewish diaspora would "ingather" to Israel, as life within the state would provide the "normalcy" for Jewish national life shared by other nations. But even by the 1967 war, limits to mass *aliyah* had become clear; a sizable Jewish diaspora located especially in the United States seemed permanent, and diaspora Jews themselves took ill the suggestion that their lives were less ethnically legitimate or ultimately faced anti-Semitic ruin that they did not themselves anticipate. Political Zionist doctrine accordingly reconfigured to emphasize a stable interdependence between the state and enduring diaspora communities, through transnational connections. "We must act as one people," affirmed the Jerusalem Program, a set of Zionist principles drawn up in 1968.

> The Diaspora cannot maintain its true Jewish identity without the spiritual inspiration, cultural creativity, and educational resources of Israel, and Israel must continue to draw on the human resources and political support of the Diaspora. Indeed, in the course of Israel's three decades of independence, the Jewish State and the Diaspora have become increasingly inter-related, and this trend appears likely to characterize their mutual relations in the years ahead.
>   . . . The emergence of the Jewish State has breathed a new spirit into Jewish life all over the world, and caused a significant transformation in the status and prestige of Jewish leadership in Diaspora. The centrality of Israel has, therefore, become an integral part of Jewish life in the Diaspora, as has their inter-dependence mentioned previously. Israel is indispensable to Jewish existence; without Israel, world Jewry would turn cold and hollow.[44]

"Cold and hollow" was a very negative read of life within the Jewish diaspora, represented in the Hebrew word *Galut* (the common Zionist translation of *diaspora*). "Galut" connotes the alienation and inauthenticity of Jewish life under foreign rule, adapting the religious concept of exile from the biblical homeland as having been divinely ordained for sins of the Jewish people.[45] In 1968, assimilation still had a very negative connotation of ethnic suppression; U.S. and Western European political doctrines confined ethnicity to the private sphere, asserting a putatively neutral but actually mono-ethnic normative climate (Anglo-Saxon Protestant) in the public sphere. Confined to private homes and in the shadow of anti-Semitism, Jewish and other ethnic lives could not find full expression. Under these stifling conditions, a full Jewish cultural and religious life in Israel was understood to provide a font of cultural and spiritual resources to the diaspora, through WZO networking, family ties, and a transnational Jewish-nationalist identity.

Still, the problem recognized in the Jerusalem Program (point 4) as being the most serious for world Jewry was not precisely assimilation under anti-Semitic pressures but "cultural obliteration," resulting from relaxed Jewish solidarity in the liberal democracies.

> Assimilation is the law of existence in the Diaspora in ancient Jewish history and in the modern history of our people. Never was the Jewish people so geographically dispersed, so culturally and linguistically fragmented, and subject to such powerful pressures making for assimilation, as in our time. The bonds of the traditional protective forces have in some cases been weakened and in others entirely vanished. We are faced today with the bitter spectacle of shedding limbs of the Jewish body through religious assimilation and cultural abandonment.
>
> Under these conditions, the Jewish people needs a great national ideal and a comprehensive national movement which will unite it in dedication to historic values and traditions.
>
> The establishment of a Jewish State was a major aim of the Zionist Movement, but the ultimate goal was always the preservation of the identity of the Jewish people, and the regeneration of Jewish vitality and creativity. Today more than ever before, it is clear that every available force must be enlisted to fight the tendency towards cultural obliteration, and the Zionist Movement—as the most representative group of the Jewish people—must assume the leadership of this struggle through an elaborate and extensive system of high quality Jewish education.

The problem of assimilation persisted, although it was soon complicated by changing conditions. On the one hand, the shift to multiculturalism in the Western democracies allowed Jews greater freedom to express a vigorous Jewish cultural and religious life, permitting Jewish cultural centers to flourish with new vigor. On the other hand, that climate actually fostered assimilation by softening ethnic defenses: the Jewish population in the United States, for example, has declined significantly over recent decades, through intermarriage and low birthrates, falling below Israel's Jewish population in 2003 for the first time in history. For some in the United

States, apprehension about this "J2K problem" (vanishing Jewish ethnic identity after the millennium) has led to much discussion and some alarmist measures (e.g., in the Internet age, Web sites like www.whymarryjewish.com).[46]

By contrast, others hold that Jewish diaspora life has found new richness and distinct forms of local expression—an experience better conveyed in the Hebrew word *T'futsoth*, which connotes the more positive "dispersion" of Jews into Western democratic life both as individuals and as distinct collectivities.[47] From this perspective, the Jewish state is not so vital to Jewish continuity and is even a hindrance, in asserting one model of "being Jewish" not necessarily appropriate to Jewish communities in far-flung world regions.

Whether Jewish assimilation is indeed a problem warranting collective Jewish action is considered here a matter for internal Jewish discussion. The question raised here is whether, for those who do see assimilation as a problem, Jewish *statehood* is truly necessary to sustaining Jewish cultural and religious continuity. On the *Galut* model, the Jewish state still manifests for Zionists today as a vital force for Jewish ethnic continuity everywhere. The concern to sustain Israel's connection to the Jewish diaspora is indeed one reason why no "Israeli" nationality is permitted under Israeli law, as an Israeli national identity would imply a division between Jews in Israel and abroad.[48] But could the "Jewish national home" be maintained in Israel, serving ethnic and spiritual functions for Jews globally, without having to maintain the discriminatory juridical apparatus now entailed by Jewish *statehood*?

Significant here is that open disagreement on this precise point was once very common within the world's Jewish communities and even within the Zionist movement. Through the 1930s, even Jews who were enthusiastic about building a Jewish "national home" in Palestine—including some of those who came to Palestine and labored for it—did not necessarily endorse a specifically Jewish state, and some passionately opposed it. Some opposed statehood on spiritual grounds: Jews living as minorities had, through the centuries, cultivated an enlightened universalist ethos posed as a counterweight to the materialist excesses of states, and statehood seemed a betrayal of that unique spiritual legacy. Others believed that the true value of the

Yishuv (the Jewish settlement) lay in its communal and socialist values, which the material incentives of statehood would burden and corrupt. Some were sensitive to the Arab civilization in which the Yishuv was nested; enlightened self-interest seemed to mandate sharing sovereignty with the Arab society, and ethnic accord seemed morally incumbent upon the true "light unto nations" that the Yishuv might constitute. Hence, while such political Zionists as Ben-Gurion and Yitzhak Shamir were mustering political and military resources to establish the state of Israel, among their principal opponents were indeed a plethora of Jewish organizations and intellectuals in Jerusalem, Europe, and the United States, who lobbied hard against the Jewish-state project.

One chronicler of those early Zionist battles is Yoram Hazony, who offers a historical exposé in his irate but engrossing political history *The Jewish State: The Struggle for Israel's Soul.*[49] Hazony sees post-Zionism as an insidious danger to Israel; plumbing its intellectual antecedents is his way of exposing their nefarious role in opposing the Jewish state from its earliest stages. Yet in assembling a dense history of those early political battles, he offers an illuminating reminder that Jewish disagreement about establishing a Jewish state was once rife and competed closely for dominance in Palestine. In the United States, for example, bitter battles surrounded the Zionist project. Through the 1930s, the Orthodox organization Agudat Israel opposed the idea of a Jewish state, as did B'nai B'rith, the American Jewish Committee, and, for a time, Hadassah. The central Beth-El congregation in Houston rejected it, as did the main San Francisco Jewish congregation and the wealthy and influential Emanu-El congregation in New York City. Reform Judaism remained anti-Zionist into the late 1930s and was deeply divided on the question through the 1940s. In 1942, a group of one hundred Reform rabbis met in Atlantic City to sign a public statement rejecting the creation of a Jewish state; the initiative led to the formation of the anti-Zionist American Council for Judaism, which in its first years included *New York Times* publisher Arthur Hays Sulzberger, who helped write its manifesto. Albert Einstein famously opposed Jewish statehood, considering a state's temporal power antithetical to his more spiritual understanding of "the essential nature of Judaism": "I would much rather see reasonable agreement with the Arabs on the basis of living together in peace," he wrote, "than the creation of a Jewish state."[50]

In Palestine, the climate within the Yishuv was mostly favorable to statehood, but deep divisions persisted. Pitched against such state-builders as Ben-Gurion and Yitzhak Shamir (and others grouped under the Jewish Agency) were a plethora of leftist and liberal voices. The important settlement movement Hashomer Hatzair, for instance, was firmly anti-state. In 1925, a cluster of activists and intellectuals formed Brit Shalom (Covenant of Peace), which lobbied domestically and internationally for a binational Arab-Jewish state and included some of the most important intellectuals in Palestine. None of these intellectuals could be accused of ignorance regarding Arab intentions or political goals; their arguments for an Arab-Jewish state were based on their immediate experience of conditions in the country and their commitment to building a Jewish national home, based on inclusion and democracy, in a land holding an indigenous Arab society.

Among the most famous intellectuals lobbying for a binational state were Rabbi Judah Leib Magnes and theologian Martin Buber. Magnes could not imaginably be deemed "self-hating" (a term not applied to anti-state Zionists at the time). In 1906, Magnes, who had been trained at a Reform seminary, became associate rabbi at New York City's Temple Emanu-El, which served the wealthy German-Jewish families of the city and was one of the most important congregations in the United States. Later, he represented both B'nai B'rith and the Jewish Joint Distribution Committee in Palestine and was intimately involved in the grand project to establish a Jewish homeland in Palestine. Yet he found the whole project of a Jewish state anathema, advocating instead an Arab-Jewish state that could blend the interests of both peoples. "We must once and for all give up the idea of a 'Jewish Palestine,'" he wrote. "Jews and Arabs . . . have each as much right there, no more and no less, than the other: Equal rights and equal privileges and equal duties. That is . . . the sole ethical basis of our claims there." But his concerns were not merely ethical; he also feared the consequences of a Jewish state, writing in 1920: "Your Balfour Declaration decrees a Jewish ruling class from the outset. This gift of political primacy to the Jews in Palestine rather than political equality contains the seed of resentment and future conflict. . . . When I think that Palestine was conquered by force of arms, and that it was made 'Jewish' by the iniquitous [Versailles] Peace Conference, I am reminded of the well-known Jewish description: 'Conceived and born in uncleanliness.'"[51]

Martin Buber, too, cared deeply about the Jewish national home. But he also harbored a deep distrust of ethnic nationalism and argued passionately, for most of his professional life, for just dealings with Palestine's Arab population and for a binational state. In 1942, with Magnes and others, he cofounded the organization Ichud, which became an important voice in the Yishuv and in international lobbying efforts. "We describe our programme," he wrote in 1947 (on the brink of war), "as that of a bi-national state—that is, we aim at a social structure based on the reality of two peoples living together." Buber continued:

> The foundations of this structure cannot be the traditional ones of majority and minority, but must be different. . . . This is what we need and not a "Jewish state"; for any national state in vast, hostile surroundings would mean pre-meditated national suicide, and an unstable international basis can never make up for the missing intra-national one. . . . The road to be pursued is that of an agreement between the two nations—naturally also taking into account the productive participation of smaller national groups—an agreement which, in our opinion, would lead to Jewish-Arab co-operation in the revival of the Middle East, with the Jewish partner concentrated in a strong settlement in Palestine. This co-operation, though necessarily starting out from economic premises, will allow development in accordance with an all-embracing cultural perspective and on the basis of feeling at-oneness, tending to result in a new form of society.[52]

The Ichud formulated this view as a formal program to build the Jewish national home in Palestine in the form of a binational Arab-Jewish state, based on universalist principles.

  1. The Association Union (Ichud) adheres to
      a. The Zionist movement insofar as this seeks the establishment of the Jewish National Home for the Jewish People in Palestine.

b. The struggle throughout the world for a New Order in
international relations and a Union of the peoples, large
and small, for a life of freedom and justice without fear
oppression and want.

2. The Association Union therefore regards a Union between
the Jewish and Arab peoples as essential for the upbuilding of
Palestine and for cooperation between the Jewish world and
the Arab world in all branches of life—social, economic, cultural, political—thus making for the revival of the whole
Semitic World.[53]

Most such opposition to a Jewish state evaporated in the mid-
1940s, with the horrifying revelations about the Nazi death camps and
the postwar Jewish refugee crisis. In 1947, the new UN also aston-
ished the antistate camp by granting its imprimatur to the "Jewish
state" in UN Resolution 181. All remaining objections to Jewish
statehood were abruptly discredited as reprehensible dithering, a
profile that lasts to this day. Hannah Arendt, writing at this fulcrum,
was staggered by the "amazing and rapid change in what we call
national character. There is now no organization and almost no individual Jew that doesn't privately or publicly support partition and the
establishment of a Jewish state." But that opinion shift also brought
a militancy and a totalitarian ethos that Arendt deplored.

Jewish left-wing intellectuals who a relatively short time ago still
looked down upon Zionism as an ideology for the feeble-
minded, and viewed the building of a Jewish homeland as a
hopeless enterprise that they, in their great wisdom, had
rejected before it was ever started; Jewish businessmen whose
interest in Jewish politics had always been determined by the
all-important question of how to keep Jews out of newspaper
headlines; Jewish philanthropists who had resented Palestine as
a terribly expensive charity, draining off funds from other "more
worthy" purposes; the readers of the Yiddish press, who for
decades had been sincerely, if naively, convinced that America
was the promised land—all these, from the Bronx to Park
Avenue down to Greenwich Village and over to Brooklyn are
united today in the firm conviction that a Jewish state is needed,
that America has betrayed the Jewish people, that the reign of
terror by the Irgun and the Stern groups is more or less
justified, and that Rabbi Silver, David Ben Gurion, and Moshe
Shertok are the real, if somewhat too moderate, statesmen of
the Jewish people.[54]

Arendt also chronicled the sudden repression of dissent. She herself had ardently supported the project of creating a "Jewish homeland" in Palestine; by 1948, the Yishuv's achievements and the accomplishments of the kibbutzim were, in her view, "the great hope and the great pride of Jews all over the world."[55] She viewed as a dramatic shift, however, the switch from seeking a "homeland" to the militant drive for a "state," in which "Terrorism and the growth of totalitarian methods are silently tolerated and secretly applauded." She continued:

> [Jews in the United States and Palestine] are essentially in agree-
> ment on the following more or less roughly stated propositions:
> the moment has now come to get everything or nothing, victory
> or death; Arab and Jewish claims are irreconcilable and only a
> military decision can settle the issue; the Arabs, all Arabs, are our
> enemies and we accept this fact; only outmoded liberals believe
> in compromises, only philistines believe in justice, and only
> *shlemiels* prefer truth and negotiation to propaganda and
> machine guns; Jewish experience in the last decades—or over the
> last centuries, or over the last two thousand years—has finally
> awakened us and taught us to look out for ourselves; this alone
> is reality, everything else is stupid sentimentality; everybody is
> against us, Great Britain is anti-Semitic, the United States is
> imperialist—. . . in the final analysis we count upon nobody but
> ourselves; in sum—we are ready to go down fighting, and we
> will consider anybody who stands in our way a traitor and any-
> thing done to hinder us a stab in the back.[56]

Arendt cautioned that this extremist ethos conveyed a climate of "mass unanimity [which] is not the result of agreement, but an expression of fanaticism and hysteria."[57] She herself still believed firmly that the Jewish "national home" must be realized through "close cooperation" between Arabs and Jews in Palestine. She closed her 1948 essay—subtitled "There Is Still Time," though written as the Arab cities had already been emptied by war—with a last anguished call for Arab-Jewish cooperation, through such provisions as "local self-government and mixed Jewish-Arab municipal and rural coun-cils" (see app. A). "The only way of saving the reality of the Jewish homeland," she insisted, was by sharing it.

> The idea of Arab-Jewish cooperation, though never realized
> on any scale and today seemingly farther off than ever, is not
> an idealistic day dream but a sober statement of the fact that

without it the whole Jewish venture in Palestine is doomed.
. . . Many opportunities for Jewish-Arab friendship have
already been lost, but none of these failures can alter the basic
fact that the existence of the Jews in Palestine depends on
achieving it.[58]

Even in this charged climate, arguments for a shared Arab-Jewish
state were seen by their critics not as anti-Semitic but as misguided
visions of the best path toward Jewish welfare, whether cultural,
physical, or spiritual. Those same arguments, appearing in later
decades, became seen as anti-Semitic in the hindsight assessment that
had there been a Jewish state during the Nazi terror, to absorb unlimited Jewish immigration, millions of Jewish lives might have been
saved. Hence, opposing the Jewish state today is seen, at best, as
morally irresponsible in ignoring that history and, at worst, as geno-
cidally motivated in inviting the enabling conditions for Jewish
slaughter again. The same assessment argues that the Western
democracies, while superficially comfortable for Jews, did not provide
the crucial sanctuary in the 1930s and 1940s and cannot be relied on
to absorb Jews in any future crisis unless a Jewish state exists to
deploy crucial political leverage, if not literal sanctuary. With so many
Jewish dead invoked to support them, arguments for the one-state
solution may appear as willfully blind to lasting risks that the Jewish
people have no moral responsibility to invite again.

These arguments may seem unassailable; the question raised by
post-Zionists is whether they are correct. Does an ethnically exclusive
Jewish-national state in Palestine best address Jewish needs? Is ongoing anti-Semitism sufficiently serious to require that such a "Jewish
state" continue—particularly when that state is premised on ethnic
cleansing and massive human rights violations of its own, which are
arguably inspiring far more hostility and resentment toward Jews
than any other world factor? After half a century, Jewish life in the
Western democracies has normalized to a point where physical sanctuary seems to reside more securely there than in Israel. Life in the
West is also materially more attractive. (Even massive Russian Jewish
emigration in the late 1980s initially targeted the United States overwhelmingly; only elaborate visa restrictions and a travel-debt system
imposed by Israel eventually funneled the emigrants to Israel.)[59] Jew-

ish diaspora institutions have also gained political and social influence to a point that their frequent disjunction with Israel's interests sometimes actually complicates their local services. As mentioned in chapter 5, Israel's ethnic exclusivity is now glaringly out of step with the Western liberal-democratic values that now frame and enrich Jewish diaspora life.

In sum, consensus is lacking. The "never again" lesson of the Holocaust does not clearly prescribe what kind of political conditions world Jewry now requires in Israel. Since 1948, a collective (and coercive) ethic to support Israel has tended to forestall and stifle new internal discussions of Israel's role. Yet that conversation can no longer be rejected prima facie as intrinsically hostile to Jewish cultural and national survival; it can as reasonably be defended as essential to it.

Indeed, given the impending security crisis, fresh conversations about the Jewish state must now be joined. The question now confronting Zionism is precisely what would be lost for the Jewish national home if one state were to form in all of Mandate Palestine and if the "Jewish state" were thus to become something else—a binational Jewish-Palestinian state or simply a multiethnic state offering some provisions for ethnic group rights. That question centers on one logistical fact (or "nightmare," as Zionist objectors cast it): reunification of Mandate Palestine as one state would quickly translate into an Arab majority in Israel. This result is seen by political Zionists as disastrous in itself, because, even in a peaceful transition, Israel would thereby cease, in some unspecified way, to be a "Jewish state." Exactly what is meant by the formula "Jewish state" therefore becomes the crux of the Israeli-Palestinian conflict.

THE JEWISH STATE

There is no single definition for the formula "Jewish state." The phrase does suggest that the state is somehow the political expression of the Jewish people or has some special guardian role for the Jewish people. Either interpretation implies that Jews are in control of the government and, because the government is democratic, that the country's majority is and must remain Jewish. These associations have generated the circular logic that Israel must preserve a Jewish majority to maintain control of the government and preserve Israel as a "Jewish state." But precisely what "Jewishness" does that majority secure? Does the formula "Jewish state" simply mean a state where Jewish religion is practiced freely? That condition pertains in all the Western democracies. Does it mean that Jewish holidays determine the public rhythms of national life—of public services, work, and vacations? Israel is unique in offering that precious normalcy for Jewish life, but such a condition could also be sustained in a binational state, and in any case, a "Jewish state" cannot be simply a matter of the religious calendar; it must have some deeper meaning, reflecting its roots in Jewish religion and values. But what is the exact public character of that religious identity, and what are those defining values?

In other words, what qualities of "Jewishness" would necessarily be lost if Israel ceased to have a Jewish majority? One answer is that Jews would immediately be at risk from vicious anti-Semitic Arabs, but, as discussed earlier, that fear is assumed here to be greatly exaggerated. If, with some hard work toward the transition, a stable civil-democratic state could indeed be constituted in all of Mandate Palestine, what diminution or evaporation of the Jewish national home would automatically ensue?

The first and most obvious answer is that in a single secular-democratic state, the whole apparatus of Basic Law and public policy that now privileges Jewish nationality in Israel would have to be dismantled. As discussed in chapter 2, Israeli law establishes a two-tiered system of citizenship that provides the Jewish nationality with special rights (e.g., regarding land, housing, and education benefits) and denies those privileges to Arabs and all non-Jews. This clearly discriminatory system would have to dissolve in favor of laws that provide all the state's citizens with equal rights to the country's resources. The urgent question posed by the one-state solution is therefore how the core spirit and functions of the Jewish national home—sanctuary, national expression—can be preserved while providing Palestinians and all non-Jews with full political equality. Given the conflict's history, a completely ethnic-blind system would not suffice; mutual guarantees would have to ensure both Arab and Jewish collective interests, particularly in the transition. Zionist Jews, understandably, view any suggestion of "guarantees" with great skepticism. But if Jewish life could sustain meaningful expression in a country so stabilized, the benefit to Zionism would actually be enormous, for it would defuse Israel's daunting "demographic threat" permanently, by making it meaningless. Motives to sort out some workable system should therefore be high.

Analysts of a one-state solution are already debating very nascent proposals that can be briefly flagged here. Binationalist proposals attempt to secure equal rights for Jewish and Palestinian individuals by ensuring ethnic group rights independently of people's location—for example, by securing ethnic language rights, the religious calendar, cultural production, and ethnic control over holy sites and local school curricula. Federalist proposals usually envision ethnic territorial designations based on demographic densities. The extravagantly twisting borders that would be required to accommodate Israel's present ethnic mosaic argue against any attempt to carve out actual ethnic districts, but federalism might still work on a regional basis. The territory of Mandatory Palestine does sustain historical regions, such as the Galilee, the northern West Bank highlands, and the Negev, which might be delineated as electoral provinces or districts. Such districts might be granted local governments, subordinated to federal constitutional authority (as in Canada and the United States), which could accommodate local politics and administration. Each would have Jewish or Palestinian majorities, but each would also have sizable ethnic minorities whose electoral clout would still matter to party politics at the district and national levels.

Debating the state's exact design is, however, premature at this stage. As in South Africa's transition, the protagonists must sort out the new state's design themselves through legitimate forums. In those discussions, myriad mutual fears and concerns about safety guarantees, stability, and cultural expression will doubtless be debated in full. At this juncture, the specific model for government is less important than the idea that framing laws must somehow guarantee equal standing by Arab and other non-Jewish citizens while securing convincingly durable protections to the (sizable) Jewish minority. To be durable, such laws would probably include some version of the following provisions.

- Sustain the Law of Return for Jews, reflecting the special historical relationship of Jews to the state of Israel and confirming Israel's permanent function as a sanctuary.
- Detach any additional privileges (e.g., automatic citizenship and special housing benefits) from immigration status under the Law of Return. Revise the Citizenship Law to include ethnic-neutral criteria for naturalization.
- Curtail the activities of the WZO and the Jewish Agency regarding the active promotion of Jewish *aliyah,* while sustaining their activities regarding *olim* absorption and supporting Jewish diaspora life.
- Establish some parity principle for Palestinian return: for example, provide for some initial adjustment period to repatriate Palestinian refugees who wish to return, then, if the state feels compelled to limit immigration for logistical reasons, insure that annual quotas for Palestinians at least match annual Jewish immigration numbers. Second- and third-generation Palestinians not born in the territory should be held to the same naturalization criteria applied to prospective Jewish citizens.
- Eliminate and prohibit all ethnic provisions regarding land tenure, allowing Arabs and all non-Jews full access to the state's lands.
- Abolish ethnic differences regarding military service and attached tertiary privileges (e.g., subsequent educational, health, or housing benefits).
- Transfer public authority over planning and development to non-Jewish-national state agencies. Restrict the domestic activities of the Jewish Agency to managing and promoting Jewish ethnic and religious matters, such as promoting cultural events and managing ethnic resources (e.g., libraries, historical projects).
- Insure free access by all citizens and foreign pilgrims to holy sites, with norms of respect established and enforced by their respective religious authorities.
- Eliminate all national identities except the state identity as a status recognized under state law. Through the usual modes of public iconography, a new mytho-history, and new textbooks and schooling, affirm and inculcate in the population a sense of the dignity, viability, and vision of the state identity as a cohesive multiethnic national identity that embraces all the state's citizens equally and in which all citizens experience a sense of common national character and destiny.

In a state incorporating such formulas, the Jewish settlements could remain in place. Jews would retain full access and residency rights in the territory of biblical antiquity so important to multiple currents of Zionist thought. Yet elimination of special incentives to live in the settlements (e.g., low-interest loans) and dissolution of preferential access by Jewish communities to land, water, and transportation would reduce the allure of the settlements as bedroom communities and ease demographic pressures in the West Bank highlands. Working toward ethnic parity would obviously take years, and the process would doubtless be saturated with political battles over a major reconfiguration of the country's resource allocation. Ethnic politics will persist into the imaginable future. But competition would now be channeled into democratic mechanisms. As in other Western democracies, ethnic divisions would gradually be complicated by crosscutting political alliances based on class, gender, subregional agendas, and other interests.

Multiple fears challenge easy optimism, however. For example, both equal access by Palestinians to the state's resources and reform of immigration laws might suggest to Israeli Jews that their communities would be rapidly swamped by Palestinians, especially Palestinian returnees seeking to restore their family residences in their old neighborhoods. Particularly unsettling might be the prospect of Palestinians moving into Jewish settlements themselves, as they would then have the legal right to do. Jewish apprehension about these possibilities reflects partly simple racism (antipathy toward Arabs moving into the neighborhood) and partly fear that mass return will translate into expelling Jews from their (sometimes formerly Palestinian) homes. Some prior agreement must secure people's homes—a delicate subject for negotiation. But, as happened in South Africa, mass demographic flows would be moderated by many factors, including individual choices regarding ethnic "comfort zones," availability of housing and jobs, kin ties to present-day Arab communities, and income levels.

A greater Jewish fear is that a Palestinian majority would eventually use its electoral clout to dismantle constitutional protections (as discussed earlier in this chapter), but that risk can be addressed by, say, making any constitutional change affecting minority rights contingent on approval by a majority of that minority (see the UN subcommittee proposal in app. A). Any temptation to abuse or suspend the constitution itself would be further mitigated by mutual Palestinian interest in a successful transition, as has been true for blacks in South Africa. Economic interests would further feed mutual cooperation, as the already dense economic ties between the now-divided sectors could be properly integrated and rationalized, offering major and mutual economic benefits to both sides. Indeed, it is almost certain that, as Jews have for so long overwhelmingly dominated the state's politics and businesses, Jewish ethnic dominance will endure for decades, just as white advantages have persisted in South Africa. Stability of the new constitution might initially have to be guaranteed by the international community (most obviously by Europe and the United States)—for example, by making international trade contingent on mutual compliance. Such a determinative outside role regarding domestic politics would contradict a basic Zionist doctrine of independence and self-reliance, but under current conditions, Israel is heavily dependent on the United States anyway. As the constitution stabilized and a multiethnic political culture normalized in the new nation, that international role would cease to be relevant and could be formally terminated.

But would some vital quality of "Jewishness" not be lost in this formula, as seems intuitively clear? If so, those concerned to preserve Israel as a "Jewish state" must specify more precisely just what dimension of Jewishness would be risked or lost in conditions of a non-Jewish majority—aside from the fear of persecution (a fear requiring respectful consideration but deemed exaggerated here, as already discussed). Forecasts of trouble should at least be sufficiently specific to open their debate in more clear and frank ways than the normally vague and circular Zionist reasoning has hitherto permitted. Otherwise, the Zionist argument would appear to be that Israel should simply function as an exclusive Jewish ethnic enclave—that is, that "Jewish statehood" should be understood as a "gated community." No ethnic group today has a right to this "dream."

A note of caution on this question should precede its further discussion: ethnic experience often eludes concrete description and is not tidily reducible to specific customs or privileges, even if some can be cited as important or emblematic. Moreover, an ethnic or racial group remembering the constant feeling of otherness that accompanies life as a permanent minority may consider the simple change to being a majority itself so vast a collective relief as to transcend description in terms of specific fears, privileges, or customs. (Some nonparallel analogies include Native Americans, African Americans, and women—groups who often experience this relief when they obtain, even briefly, some homogeneous social space.) But again, the comfort of ethnic homogeneity itself, rendered as a physical living space, tends to emulate the "comfort" of a gated community. When one ethnic group makes the extraordinary claim to an entire state, some specifics about that group's more substantive needs can reasonably be demanded. Mainstream Zionist doctrine does not simply call for Israel to serve as a center for Jewish life; it insists on preserving Israel as a "Jewish state" by actually fixing Jewish ethnic dominion in its government, with jurisdiction through the state's territory.

So what is and must remain "Jewish" about the "Jewish state" in order to preserve its Jewish society? Is a Jewish majority truly essential to sustaining Israel as the Jewish national home? Can the state be shared with the indigenous Palestinian people and still provide sufficient social and political space for the Jewish-national project? Must Jewish-national self-determination still be understood on the early twentieth-century model—which emphasized the nation-state formula, promoted for peoples under crumbling Ottoman rule—or can it be understood on the late twentieth-century model? The latter has recognized endemic dilemmas plaguing territorial states holding multiple nationalities, and has shifted to develop the concept of the multinational state, in which different groups sustain their national character through local autonomy over education and other vital concerns, reflecting their distinct social institutions as well as their unique cosmological and moral frameworks.[60] Could Israel be redefined on such multiethnic or multinational grounds? Could it even be a progressive examplar for multicultural democracy, as some early Zionists urged?

One point of departure on questions about the requirements of Jewish nationalism might be the most recent resolutions of the Thirty-Fourth Zionist Congress (held in October 2002), which repeatedly emphasized—with an undertone of defensive urgency—that Israel is a "Jewish and democratic state." The tortured tension between ethnic-chauvinist and universal-democratic values was obvious here.

> The 34th Zionist Congress calls upon the elected institutions of the State of Israel to properly apply the principles of the Declaration of Independence, so as to ensure that the State of Israel will be a Jewish and democratic state, which represents a spiritual national center, as well as a source of inspiration for Jews worldwide. . . . The State of Israel grants equal rights to all its citizens, with no difference regarding religion, race or gender. . . . The combination of the universal principles of Judaism on the one hand, and of the principles of democracy on the other, create the basis for the balance that is necessary for relations between majorities and minorities within the State of Israel. . . . At this time, the Zionist Congress views the issue of demography as of being of critical importance for the Jewish-Zionist future of the State of Israel today; ensuring a large and stable Jewish majority is necessary. Present tendencies threaten this majority, and therefore it is necessary to urgently act in order to ensure a Jewish majority.[61]

Yet if Israeli citizens have equal rights, "with no difference regarding religion, race or gender," why is ensuring a Jewish majority so "urgent" a matter? Clearly, Jewish citizens are deemed to require some special demographic advantage, which requires sustaining Israel as a "Jewish and democratic state." Yet the congress never defined that formula, affirming only that it should accord with "Zionist principles." What precisely are the "Zionist principles" that a Jewish majority secures?

The Twenty-Seventh World Zionist Congress, held in Jerusalem in 1968, offered an often-cited formula of four principles that became known as the Jerusalem Program (mentioned in chap. 5). These principles were (1) that the Jewish people comprise one unified nation, (2) that cultural "survival" and resisting assimilation is a collective

Jewish imperative, (3) that Jewish-national sovereignty is essential and that *aliyah* is incumbent, and (4) that Israel is central to Jewish life everywhere. The Jerusalem Program also affirmed, however, that establishing the state of Israel on these principles was only the beginning. "The majority of the Jewish people is still in the Diaspora," the program noted, "where their spiritual survival is increasingly threatened, while Israel is in need of mass immigration to assure its continued growth and economic independence." The Jerusalem Program therefore operationalized these four principles as a "mission" for every Zionist, comprised of five major "aims":

1. The unity of the Jewish People and the centrality of Israel in Jewish life;
2. The ingathering of the Jewish People in its historic homeland, Eretz Israel, through Aliyah from all countries;
3. The strengthening of the State of Israel which is based on the prophetic vision of justice and peace;
4. The preservation of the identity of the Jewish People through the fostering of Jewish and Hebrew education and of Jewish spiritual and cultural values;
5. The protection of Jewish rights everywhere.[62]

But these five points still left unclear exactly how the state of Israel is supposed to function in all these ways or how a Jewish *state* intersects with the Zionist project of building a Jewish national home in Palestine. Point 1, for example, proposed that Israel is central to Jewish life but did not explain how. Nor did it explain what comprises "Jewish life." This is a difficult question, given religious, cultural, and ethnic diversity among Jews; its answer is intuitively obvious to diverse Jewish readerships only if "Jewish life" is left vague. In later elaboration on this point, Jewish diversity itself is acknowledged as a point of pride—although the discussion conspicuously omits the deep social and political divisions between Ashkenazi Jews (from Europe and North America) and Sephardic or Mizrahi Jews (from the Arab world).

We are one people:
This concept dominated the history of our people and the development of modern Zionism. One of the distinctive charac-

teristics of Zionism was its ability to unify all vital forces of the nation, religious or secular, socialist or bourgeois-liberal, as well as the proponents of diverse Zionist political ideologies, in a common political and economic effort to build a national home. Without its pluralistic character, the Zionist Movement would not have been able to unite all Zionists into a single national and social liberation movement of the Jewish people.

Hence the Jerusalem Program does consider that Jewish liberation requires a "national home." But point 1 does not offer any reason why Jewish unity and cohesion or even its "liberation movement" could not be sustained and flourish in a national home configured within a shared multiethnic state. Nor does point 2, which also proposes that Israel is central—but now in a geographic sense, providing a "homeland" where the Jewish people can assemble and enjoy a cultural autonomy not possible elsewhere. Point 2 emphasizes the predicament of the Jewish diaspora discussed earlier—that Jews, being dependent on the tolerance of non-Jewish majorities, must constrain the full expression of their Jewish identity to parameters tolerable to non-Jews. Ingathering is therefore deemed the central "function" of Zionism, because the revitalization of Jewish culture, valuable in itself, will also enable individual fulfillment.

> All Zionist Federations and organizations recognize that the real function of Zionism as a national liberation movement is the ingathering of most, if not all, Jewish people into the land of Israel, and liberate them from daily dependence on the good-will of others. With the ingathering of the exiles, will come the creation of appropriate conditions for the regeneration of the cultural activity, and the continuity of the spiritual heritage of the nation, in which the new immigrant will find his historical identity and self realization—for himself and for his family, and the opportunity to contribute as a Jew and as a Zionist to one of the most dynamic national and social enterprises of the century.

Yet ethnic fulfillment might also be pursued in a shared multiethnic state. Is exclusively Jewish statehood essential to providing the conditions necessary for Jewish "cultural regeneration?" Point

3 of the Jerusalem Program argues that the state is indeed an "essential instrument" that enables the highest realization of "distinctively Jewish values"—although, again, "Jewish values" are not defined.

> Zionism is striving for the realization of the prophetic ideas of justice and equality among all men.
>
> Zionism strives for the creation of a new Jewish society in which social ideas as well as distinctively Jewish values are achieved on their highest level.
>
> While Zionism has aspired to Statehood, it has sought a particular kind of statehood consonant with the ideals of the Jewish people.
>
> In Zionism, the State and the land are the essential instruments through which the building of a higher moral and national order can be undertaken.

According to the Jerusalem Program, the "State and the land" and its "new Jewish society" would allow the personal transformation that is affirmed to be "central to the Zionism dream."

> An important part of this vision has been the development of a new Jewish person who is an upright citizen, a soldier when necessary, a cultured man, and a devoted Jew inspired by a sense of idealism and a sense of mission. It is an image created by the founding fathers of modern Israel, and carried out by the Chalutzim of each generation who have come to Israel from all corners of the earth.

But precisely why is Jewish dominion over the state necessary to this mission? It would seem that these high ideals and personal transformations might be pursued just as fully—and in the long run, even more durably—in a Jewish national home in Palestine that does not require a Jewish electoral majority to sustain its character. Point 4 affirms that only a Jewish state can provide the essential conditions for this revitalization of Jewish national life, but does not specify just what the state will accomplish besides preserving the Jewish people from its chief danger. Yet in this formula the chief danger is not anti-Semitic violence but rather the *lack* of it—that is, cultural and religious assimilation in the diaspora, leading to the dissolution of Jewishness.

Assimilation is the law of existence in the Diaspora in ancient Jewish history and in the modern history of our people. Never was the Jewish people so geographically dispersed, so culturally and linguistically fragmented, and subject to such powerful pressures [elsewhere clarified as liberal democracy] making for assimilation, as in our time. The bonds of the traditional protective forces have in some cases been weakened and in others entirely vanished. We are faced today with the bitter spectacle of shedding limbs of the Jewish body through religious assimilation and cultural abandonment.

Under these conditions, the Jewish people needs a great national ideal and a comprehensive national movement which will unite it in dedication to historic values and traditions.

Among the idea and movements that have appeared on the Jewish horizon in recent generations, there is none but Zionism and the Zionist Movement that are capable of fulfilling this function. The establishment of a Jewish State was a major aim of the Zionist Movement, but the ultimate goal was always the preservation of the identity of the Jewish people, and the regeneration of Jewish vitality and creativity. Today more than ever before, it is clear that every available force must be enlisted to fight the tendency towards cultural obliteration, and the Zionist Movement—as the most representative group of the Jewish people—must assume the leadership of this struggle through an elaborate and extensive system of high quality Jewish education.

But why could this grand project to regenerate "Jewish vitality and creativity" not be pursued in a multiethnic state, as such Zionists like Hannah Arendt, Martin Buber, Judah Magnes, Albert Einstein, Elmer Berger, and others once so passionately urged and as new, "post-Zionist" visionaries urge today? Would not a Jewish national home within a state based on multiethnic principles be even more stable through the generations, having successfully obviated the "demographic threat"? Could not the Palestinian and Jewish peoples, after all their torment, indeed discover their greatest national missions in forging a binational future?

Would not that future be the true "realization of the prophetic ideas of justice and equality among all men"?

Fixed at a sensitive nerve center of the Middle East—the "holy land" of three religions—the Zionist project of Jewish statehood has culminated in a powder keg for international security and a course of doom for Israel. This project, so tightly bound to mytho-histories of Arab hatred and intransigence, still sustains such emotional power that it remains locked in gear as it rolls toward the precipice. Yet voices are raised to avert that disaster, calling up potent currents of thought from democratic traditions, Jewish thought, and even Zionism itself, to offer Zion a more genuine "redemption."

Defenders of Israel have long evaded the dreadful contradictions of Jewish statehood through the collective fiction that the Arabs were responsible for Palestinian suffering and that the Jewish state did not bear the moral burden of dispossessing the Palestinian people. But the "new historians" have demolished that enabling illusion, and increasing numbers of Israelis and Zionists are facing the implications—that ethnic cleansing has been intrinsic to the state-building project from the start. The Jewish state now confronts the consequences, in the need to lock a subordinated people into a walled enclave, violating every tenet of justice that the Jewish state ever hoped to realize.

Still, the idea of a Jewish state holds such cognitive force that it remains conceptually inseparable from the dream of a Jewish national home. Israeli novelist David Grossman, for example, sees the two as one: "With all the terrible and atrocious things here, and with all the criticism I have of this state, I know that if I find myself living in a period after the state has ceased to exist, it will be a tasteless life."[63] But Israeli journalist Daniel Gavron laid down the gauntlet: "I believe in Zionism. I'm just saying that Zionism, like everything else, has to adapt itself to reality."[64] If that "reality" is indeed the need to create one democratic state, adds Haim Bresheesh, "The question seems to be: Must we have a bloody showdown, massacres and ethnic cleansing before it emerges?"[65]

Earlier discussions in this book have emphasized the darker implication of recent surveys: the increasing polarization between a liberal-democratic post-Zionist tendency and a right-wing neo-Zionist tendency, which paralyzes any settlement withdrawal by threatening civil war. Yet those same surveys discredit the Zionist tenet of unanimity on Jewish thinking about the Jewish state, suggesting that a robust minority could form the nucleus of a new nationalist imaginary. In one 1995 survey of Jews in Israel, for example, nearly 30 percent believed that Israel is "the shared homeland of the Jews and the Arabs." While 45.8 percent of Jews believed that the state "should give significant preference for Jews," a substantial 25.6 percent believed it should give "no preference for either Jews or Arabs." Most important, responding to the question "What would you prefer in the event that the democratic-egalitarian character of the state comes into contradiction with its Jewish-Zionist character and you are forced to choose between them?" 21.9 percent replied that they would "certainly" support a democratic-egalitarian character, and 23.8 percent thought they would but could not be certain. Hence, nearly half of Israeli Jews would lean toward a more egalitarian political system for Israel if conditions were right.[66] Comparable numbers emerge in Palestinian surveys (see app. B). Whole nations have been imagined and created from a smaller social base than this.

In the project to reimagine Israel as a civil society embracing the Jewish national home, Jewish thought and Zionist history have much to offer. Nothing truly alien to the Zionist project (if taken in the full philosophical breadth of its history) resides in a revived Jewish program to share the land with indigenous Palestinian people and craft a just society in a shared society. Indeed, the Declaration of the Establishment of the State of Israel laid the basis for Israel's "righteousness," in its most substantial passage.

> [I]t will foster the development of the country for the benefit of all its inhabitants; it will be based on freedom, justice and peace as envisaged by the prophets of Israel; it will ensure complete equality of social and political rights to all its inhabitants irrespective of religion, race or sex; it will guarantee freedom of religion, conscience, language, education and culture; it will safeguard the Holy Places of all religions; and it will be faithful to the principles of the Charter of the United Nations.

This passage was not merely a tag to placate international opinion, as some have accused; the Zionist movement always took justice as its banner creed, and the formation of a just and enlightened society is foundational to the Zionist dream, if not the reality.

But even for its longtime supporters, the Zionist dream seems to be dying from its failure to fulfill this mission. Zionism has accomplished what it could; it has established a Jewish national home in Palestine. But it has not created a stable Jewish state, and it can never do so in a land that holds another people. It has created not justice but a structure of injustices, which scandalizes the region and many of its own Jewish citizens. Israel is by no means unique in this failure; no ethnic nationalism can do otherwise. Some Palestinians, too, have picked up the ethnic state-building mission to their own grief. The Zionist mission of state-building has achieved something unintended but inevitable, which some early Zionists foresaw and Ariel Sharon has unintentionally furthered. One nation, sharing a "joint origin, common destiny and history" in the land of Israel-Palestine, is now terribly split by bitter racial anger, as one population grapples to preserve its dominion and another struggles for survival and dignity.[67]

On 9 May 2004, Israeli conductor and pianist Daniel Barenboim stood in the Knesset to receive Israel's prestigious Wolf Prize, awarded to artists and scientists who have contributed notably to "the benefit of mankind." Lauded by the prize committee as "a person of profound musical and humanitarian commitment, who has distinguished himself as one of the great musicians of our time," he gave a short speech that startled and even offended some present, in which he asked the great existential question now facing Israel.

I am asking today with deep sorrow: Can we, despite all our achievements, ignore the intolerable gap between what the Declaration of Independence promised and what was fulfilled, the gap between the idea and the realities of Israel? Does the condition of occupation and domination over another people fit the Declaration of Independence? Is there any sense in the independence of one at the expense of the fundamental rights of the other? Can the Jewish people, whose history is a record of continued suffering and relentless persecution, allow themselves to be indifferent to the rights and suffering of a neighboring people? Can the State of Israel allow itself an unrealistic dream of an ideological end to the conflict instead of pursuing a pragmatic, humanitarian one based on social justice?[68]

Another path exists. In every country that has attempted modern nation-building, change in the national ideology has always been launched by a few inspirational voices who periodically reimagined the national community and gave it new direction. Such a process of national reconstruction can now begin in Israel-Palestine. The land needs and deserves a more noble mission: real democracy, through a bridging of peoples and their histories. It has been done elsewhere against staggering odds, and it can be done here.

A. One-State Proposals from the 1940s

I. PROGRAM OF THE ICHUD (1942)

In 1939, alarmed by the conflict they foresaw in the political Zionist movement to establish a Jewish state, a group of antistate intellectuals and activists in Palestine formed the League of Arab-Jewish Rapprochement and Cooperation. Rejecting both the Jewish state sought by the political Zionist movement and the Arab state proposed by a British white paper of 1939, the league proposed a binational for-mula—"that the Palestine question [be] solved on the basis of economic advance-ment and freedom of national culture and social developments of both nations— Arab and Jewish—together."[1] The league embraced an unwieldy political spectrum, and in 1942, some members sought to establish a more cohesive political group. The founding members of the new Association Union—in Hebrew, the Ichud or Ihud—included Henrietta Szold (founder of Hadassah, the Women's Zionist Organization of America), as well as Judah L. Magnes and Martin Buber. The program of the Ichud is provided here from Paul R. Mendes Flohr's edited volume A Land of Two Peoples: Martin Buber on Jews and Arabs *(New York: Oxford University Press, 1983), 148–49.*

1. The Association Union (Ichud) adheres to
    a. The Zionist movement insofar as this seeks the establishment of the Jew-ish National Home for the Jewish People in Palestine.
    b. The struggle throughout the world for a New Order in international relations and a Union of the peoples, large and small, for a life of freedom and justice without fear, oppression and want.
2. The Association Union therefore regards a Union between the Jewish and Arab peoples as essential for the upbuilding of Palestine and for cooperation between the Jewish world and the Arab world in all branches of life—social, economic, cultural, political—thus making for the revival of the whole Semitic World.
3. The main political aims of the Association Union are as follows:

a. Government in Palestine based upon equal political rights for the two peoples.

b. The agreement of the steadily growing Yishuv and of the whole Jewish people to a Federative Union of Palestine and neighboring countries. This Federative Union is to guarantee the national rights of all the peoples within it.

c. A Covenant between this Federative Union and an Anglo-American Union which is to be part of the future Union of the free peoples. This Union of the free peoples is to bear the ultimate responsibility for the establishment and stability of the international relations in the New World after the war.

4. The Association Union is to cooperate with the league for Jewish-Arab Rapprochement, containing, as it does, representatives of organizations with varying points of view. It is also prepared to cooperate with other organizations and groups in specific projects.

II. UNITED NATIONS SPECIAL COMMITTEE ON PALESTINE, REPORT OF SUBCOMMITTEE TWO (1947), A/AC. 14/32 AND ADD. I

In May 1947, the UN General Assembly established a special committee to develop a plan for resolving the conflict in Mandate Palestine. The committee was composed of representatives from Australia, Canada, Czechoslovakia, Guatemala, India, Iran, the Netherlands, Peru, Sweden, Uruguay, and Yugoslavia. Seven members ultimately endorsed partition; three (India, Iran, and Yugoslavia) favored a federal state (Australia endorsed neither position). The General Assembly then composed itself as a committee of the whole to consider these reports and created one subcommittee to examine partition options and a second to consider other options. The second subcommittee was composed of states representing most Arab or Muslim populations—Afghanistan, Colombia, Egypt, Iraq, Lebanon, Pakistan, Saudi Arabia, Syria, and Yemen. Its full report offered a full legal review of Palestine's status under the 1922 League of Nations' mandate for Palestine, obligations of the mandatory power (Britain) to Palestine's indigenous population, social conditions reflecting mass Jewish immigration, and an appraisal of partition as a solution to the conflict. In its conclusion, the subcommittee offered three draft resolutions. The first referred the entire question of partition—especially regarding the rights of the indigenous population—to the International Court of Justice. The second called for collective efforts to repatriate Jewish refugees to their countries of origin or other "territories of Members of the United Nations," on grounds that Palestine could not take more refugees "without serious injury to the economy of the country and the rights and position of the indigenous population." The third, excerpted here, called for a unitary democratic state in Mandate Palestine: its final provision evades the endemic risk of proportional representation by securing constitutional change regarding minority rights to the will of the minority whatever its size. The full text of the subcommittee report (A/AC.14/32 and Add. I) is reproduced in Walid Khalidi, "63 Binationalism not Partition," in From Haven to Conquest: Readings in Zionism and the Palestinian Problem Until 1948 *(Washington DC: Institute for Palestine Studies, 1987), 645–701.*

Draft Resolution of the Constitution and Future Government of Palestine

The General Assembly,

. . . *Recognizing* that the only solution in consonance with the objectives of the Covenant of the League of Nations and the principles of the Charter of the United Nations is one that is acceptable to the majority of the people of Palestine,

Being satisfied that the partition of Palestine is unjust, illegal and impracticable and that the only just and workable solution is the immediate establishment of a unitary, democratic, and independent State, with adequate safeguards for minorities,

Believing that peaceful and orderly transfer of power from the Mandatory to the government of the people of Palestine is necessary in the interest of all concerned,

Recommends

1. That a provisional government, representative of all important sections of the citizenry in proportion to their numerical strength, should be set up as early as possible in Palestine;
2. That the powers and functions of the present administration of Palestine should be vested in the provisional government as soon as the latter is constituted;
3. That the Mandatory Power should begin the withdrawal of its forces and services from Palestine as soon as the provisional government is installed, and should complete the withdrawal within one year;
4. That the provisional government should, as soon as practicable, enact an electoral law for the setting up of a constituent assembly, prepare an electoral register, and hold elections for the constituent assembly;
5. That the constituent assembly should also function as a legislature and that the provisional government should be responsible to it until elections for a legislature are held under the new constitution;
6. That while the task of framing a constitution for Palestine must be left to the constituent assembly, the following basic principles shall be strictly adhered to:
   a. Palestine shall be a unitary and sovereign State;
   b. It shall have a democratic constitution, with an elected legislature and an executive responsible to the legislature;
   c. The constitution shall provide guarantees for the sanctity of the Holy Places covering inviolability, maintenance, freedom of access and freedom of worship in accordance with the *status quo;*
   d. The constitution shall guarantee respect for human rights and fundamental freedoms without distinction as to race, sex, language or religion, and freedom of religious belief and practice in accordance with the *status quo* (including the maintenance of separate religious courts to deal with matters of personal status);
   e. The constitution shall guarantee the rights of religious bodies or other societies and individuals to maintain, in addition to educational establishments administered by public authority, educational institutions of their own, subject to normal government supervision and inspection;
   f. The constitution shall recognize the right of Jews to employ Hebrew as a second official language in areas in which they are in a majority;

g. The law of naturalization and citizenship shall provide, amongst other conditions, that the applicant should be a legal resident of Palestine for a continuous period to be determined by the constituent assembly;

h. The constitution shall ensure adequate representation in the legislature for all important sections of the citizenry in proportion to their numerical strength;

i. The constitution shall also provide for adequate reflection in the executive and the administration of the distribution of representation in the legislature;

j. The constitution shall authorize the legislature to invest local authorities with wide discretion in matters connected with education, health and other social services;

k. The constitution shall provide for the setting up of a supreme court, the jurisdiction of which shall include, *inter alia*, the power to pronounce upon the constitutional validity of all legislation, and it shall be open to any aggrieved party to have recourse to that tribunal;

l. The guarantees contained in the constitution concerning the rights and safeguards of the minorities shall not be subject to amendment or modification without the consent of the minority concerned expressed through a majority of its representatives in the legislature.

III.   HANNAH ARENDT (1947)

Hannah Arendt (1906–75) became internationally renowned for her insightful and humanitarian philosophical writings and especially her probing analyses of totalitarianism and fascism—most notably for her essays assembled in Eichmann in Jerusalem *(1963), in which she famously identified "the banality of evil." Born in Germany, she openly resisted Hitler's fascism and was arrested in 1933. She later escaped to Paris, where she worked with the Zionist movement to bring Jewish children to Palestine. Fleeing the German occupation, she moved to the United States in 1941, where, from New York, she continued her deep involvement in the Zionist movement. She strongly opposed the extremism that seemed to seize the Zionist movement in 1947 (discussed in chap. 6 of the present study) and particularly such Jewish terrorist organizations as the Irgun, to which she refers in the essay excerpted here, "To Save the Jewish Homeland: There is Still Time," which appeared in the May 1948 issue of* Commentary.

It is true that many non-fanatical Jews of sincere good will have believed in partition as a possible means of solving the Arab-Jewish conflict. In the light of political, military, and geographic realities, however, this was always a piece of wishful thinking. The partition of so small a country could at best mean the petrification of the conflict, which would result in arrested development for both peoples; at worst it would signify a temporary stage during which both parties would prepare for further war. The alternative proposition of a federated state, also recently endorsed by Dr. Magnes [see the program of the Ichud, presented earlier in this appendix], is much more realistic; despite the fact that it establishes a common government for two different peoples, it avoids the troublesome majority-minority constellation, which is insoluble by definition. A federated structure, moreover, would have to rest on Jewish-Arab community councils, which would mean that the Jewish-Arab conflict would be resolved on the lowest and most promising level of proximity and neighborliness. A federated state, finally could be the natural stepping stone for any later, greater federated structure in the Near East and the Mediterranean area. . . .

No matter what the outcome of the present deadlock, the following objective factors should be axiomatic criteria for the good and the bad, the right and the wrong:

1) The real goal of the Jews in Palestine is the building up of a Jewish homeland. This goal must never be sacrificed to the pseudo-sovereignty of a Jewish state.

2) The independence of Palestine can be achieved only on a solid basis of Jewish-Arab cooperation. As long as Jewish and Arab leaders both claim that there is "no bridge" between Jews and Arabs (as Moshe Shertok has just put it), the territory cannot be left to the political wisdom of its own inhabitants.

3) Elimination of all terrorist groups (and not agreements with them) and swift punishment of all terrorist deeds (and not merely protests against them) will be the only valid proof that the Jewish people in Palestine has recovered its sense of political reality and that Zionist leadership is again responsible enough to be trusted with the destinies of the Yishuv.

4) Immigration to Palestine, limited in numbers and in time, is the only "irreducible minimum" in Jewish politics.

5) Local self-government and mixed Jewish-Arab municipal and rural councils, on a small scale and as numerous as possible, are the only realistic political measures that can eventually lead to the political emancipation of Palestine.

It is still not too late.

B. Palestinian Public Opinion
on the One-State Solution

The Jerusalem Media and Communication Centre (JMCC) has conducted regular surveys of Palestinian public opinion since 1993. JMCC polling is done through face-to-face interviews of some twelve hundred people (selected through random sample) in the West Bank and Gaza Strip. (For complete information on methodology and distribution data, see the JMCC Web site at http://www.jmcc.org.) Since 2000, JMCC polls have included the following question regarding a binational state: "Some believe that a two-state formula is the favored solution for the Arab-Israeli conflict, while others believe that historic Palestine cannot be divided and thus the favored solution is a bi-national state on all of Palestine wherein Palestinians and Israelis enjoy equal representation and rights. Which of these solutions do you prefer?"

The results of these polls, tabulated for December 2000 through June 2004 in this appendix, must be read cautiously. Public discussion is lacking in Palestinian communities regarding such options as "bi-national state," "single-nationality state," and "Islamic state," and no consensus clearly pertains among Palestinians about precisely what these terms mean. For example, "Palestinian state" may signify to respondents a state centered on Palestinian ethnonationalism, or it may suggest a territorial designation embracing the secular-democratic formula of formal PLO ideology. Hence, the standing of Jewish identity remains unclear in the support for a "Palestinian state" indicated in the December 2002 and April and October 2003 surveys, which added the provision that such a state embrace "one nationality." Moreover, since options like "Islamic state" were not offered by the interviewer in the question, surveys may significantly undercount support for them. Respondents volunteered "Islamic state" at consistently low rates (normally under 3.5 percent), but in December 2002, 5.6 percent offered the option "Islamic independent state with Jerusalem as its capital," quadrupling support for an Islamic state. Not surprisingly, respondents in Gaza tended to favor an Islamic state in greater proportions.

Results of 2000–2004 JMCC Public Opinion Polls Regarding Israeli-Palestinian Peace Options (percentages of respondents)

Option	Dec 00	Apr 01	Jun 01	Sep 01	Dec 01	Mar 02	Sep 02	Dec 02	Apr 03	Oct 03	Jun 03
Two-state formula	47.0	43.8	47.2	42.9	48.8	41.6	44.0	46.5	51.9	45.7	44.5
Bi-national state	20.0	24.3	22.2	31.8	27.6	31.6	28.9	26.2	25.1	25.3	26.5
Palestinian or single-nationality state		8.2	11.7[a]	13.7	14.4[a]	18.4[b]	8.3	11.2[a]	16.2[a]	13.3	11.1
Islamic state		2.8	1.4[a]	2.9	3.2[a]	3.4	2.1	10.0[a,c]	3.1[a]	3.4	2.3

[a]JMCC explicitly notes that this answer was not included as an option read to the participant, but it does not appear to have been asked in any case.

[b]This answer incorporates three responses: "Sovereign, independent Palestine with Jerusalem as its capital" (5.7 percent); "Palestinian state on all of historic Palestine and return of refugees" (12.5 percent); and "Palestinian state" (0.2 percent).

[c]This answer combines two responses: "Islamic independent state with Jerusalem as its capital" (5.4 percent) and "Islamic state" (4.6 percent).

Notes

CHAPTER 1

1. See, e.g., Don Atapattu, "Interview with Middle East Scholar Avi Shlaim: America, Israel, and the Middle East," *The Nation*, 15 June 2004.

2. *The Complete Diaries of Theodor Herzl* (translated by Harry Zohn, 1960) vol 1, 88. On the expulsion of Palestinians in 1948, see especially Benny Morris's *The Birth of the Palestinian Refugee Problem Revisited* (Cambridge: Cambridge University Press, 2004). See also Ari Shavit's interview of Morris entitled "Survival of the Fittest," in *Ha'aretz*, 19 February 2004.

3. At this writing, the Elon peace plan is available online at www.therightroadtopeace.com. It includes proposals for Israel to "dismantle" the refugee camps forcibly (as crucibles of terror) and deport their populations (a move also proposed to "lessen the poverty and density in the Palestinian Arab towns"). It further proposes that the international community orchestrate the transfer of all Palestinians to "various countries," thereby assisting this "completion of the exchange of populations that began in 1948."

4. For an in-depth critique of historical and political arguments for the claim "Jordan is Palestine," see Daniel Pipes and Adam Garfinkle, "Is Jordan Palestine?" *Commentary*, October 1988, available online at www.danielpipes .org/article/298.

5. Tony Judt, "Israel: The Alternative," *New York Review of Books* 50, no. 16 (October 23, 2003).

6. See, e.g., Sussman, "Is the Two-State Solution Dead?" *Current History* 103, no. 669 (January 2004), 37; "The Challenge to the Two-State Solution," *Middle East Report*, summer 2004.

7. See, e.g., Tony Judt's argument in "Israel: The Alternative."

8. See Sussman, "Is the Two-State Solution Dead?"

9. As I finished writing this book, I was alerted to several monographs in progress, including Ghada Karmi's *Married to Another Man* (London: Pluto Press, in press).

CHAPTER 2

1. The Jewish population of Jerusalem in that year was 464,000. Both figures are from Israel's Central Bureau of Statistics: see *Ha'aretz*, 25 April 2004.

2. Earlier proportions of Christians were higher: the British census of 1931 put the Christian-Arab population at 88,907, or about 9.5 percent of the total Arab population, but at about 50 percent in Jerusalem; by 1944, the total percentage had dropped to 8 percent. Many Christian-Arabs were absorbed into Israel, where the Christian population in 2000 was about 146,000. For one proposal by Jerusalem's Palestinian-Christian community, based on a two-state solution, see "The Jerusalem Sabeel Document: Principles for a Just Peace in Palestine-Israel," *Cornerstone* 19 (summer 2000), available online at www.sabeel.org/old/news/newslt19/princs.htm.

3. Bayit Ne'eman B'Yisrael, "Maale Adumim," *Tehila: A New Dimension of Aliyah,* http://www.tehilla.com/haut/bayit/List%20of%20Communities/maaleadu.html.

4. For one detailed analysis of the Wall and its logistical impact, see Peter Lagerquist, "Fencing the Last Sky: Excavating Palestine after Israel's 'Separation Wall,'" *Journal of Palestine Studies* 130 (winter 2004).

5. A field survey conducted by the Palestinian Central Bureau of Statistics in 1995 assessed the birthrate among the Gaza Strip population at 7.8, with marital fertility at 10. The same project estimated that the Palestinian population in the West Bank and Gaza Strip will reach some 4.2 to 4.3 million by 2010. See Jon Pedersen, Sara Randall, and Marwan Khawaja, eds., *Growing Fast: The Palestinian Population in the West Bank and Gaza Strip,* Fafo Report 353, Fafo Institute for Applied Social Science, 2001, available online at www.fafo.no/pub/rapp/353/353.pdf.

6. The area came briefly under Maccabee rule for only twenty years (167–142 BCE).

7. A recent Jewish National Fund project to build an additional reservoir serving settlement agriculture draws from scarce runoff and will add to the shortage suffered by the Palestinian population.

8. Ibid. The Peace Now survey found that 90 percent of settlers would leave the West Bank and Gaza Strip (with financial compensation) if the government ordered them to. On the potent fusion of secular Jewish thought with ideas of "return," see the letter exchange in the *London Review of Books* (6 May, 20 May, and 3 June 2004 [vol. 26, nos. 9–11]).

9. A 2003 survey of 644 settler households conducted by Peace Now found that 57 percent of settlers thought "hilltop youth" were "extremist and dangerous"; 66 percent thought the hilltop outposts should be removed; and 44 percent supported formation of a Palestinian state in the West Bank and Gaza Strip. See Americans for Peace Now, "Israeli Peace Now Survey of Settlers: Most Reject Extremists, Would Accept Compensation to Leave," press release, 23 July 2003, available online at www.peacenow.org/nia/pr/07232003.html.

10. World Zionist Organization Department for Rural Settlement, "Master Plan for the Development of Settlement in Judea and Samaria, 1979–1983," UN Doc. S./13582 Annex (22 October 1979), reproduced in Tom Mallison and Sally Mallison, *The Palestinian Problem in International Law and World Order* (Essex, England: Longman, 1986), 446–49 (app. 11).

11. Jewish Agency for Israel, Settlement Department, Central District, and World Zionist Organization, Settlement Division, Central District, *Nahal-Eron Project: Five-Year Plan for the Development of the Eron-Reihan Region* (1988).

12. B'Tselem, *Land Grab: Israel's Settlement Policy in the West Bank; Comprehensive Report,* Jerusalem, May 2002.

13. Nehemia Strasler, "The Dear High-Maintenance Sons," *Ha'aretz*, 31 October 2002.

14. *Homecoming* was published primarily to promote *aliyah*, by "showing the quality of life in Judea, Samaria, the Gaza Strip and the Golan Heights." The contents page of the copy in my possession bears an errata sticker to alert readers that the name "Jewish Agency" on given pages "should be read 'World Zionist Organization.'"

15. World Zionist Organization, *New Dimensions: Aliyah to Judaea, Samaria, and Gaza* (1984), 6.

16. *Jerusalem Post*, 1 January 2004, cited in *Middle East Peace Report* 5, no. 23 (5 January 2004).

17. United Nations Conference on Trade and Development, "Transit Trade and Maritime Transport Facilitation for the Rehabilitation and Development of the Palestinian Economy," UNCTAD/GDS/APP/2003/1, 22 March 2004.

18. World Zionist Organization–Jewish Agency for Israel (Status) Law, 5713–1952, app. 13.

19. Israel's Declaration of Independence established Israel as a "Jewish state." Basic Law: Human Dignity and Liberty (1992) reiterates this principle in section 1a: "The purpose of this Basic Law is to protect human dignity and liberty, in order to establish in a Basic Law the values of the State of Israel as a Jewish and democratic state."

20. "Covenant between the Government of Israel (Hereafter the Government) and The Zionist Executive called also the Executive of the Jewish Agency" (1954), cited in Mallison and Mallison, *The Palestinian Problem*, 433.

21. Israel Lands Administration Law, 5720–1960. Cf. Basic Law: Israel Lands (1960), section 1: "Prohibition of transfer of ownership: The ownership of Israel lands, being the lands in Israel of the State, the Development Authority or the Keren Kayemet Le-Israel, shall not be transferred either by sale or in any other manner."

CHAPTER 3

1. Robert Plotkin, "Hamas Would Accept Saudi Peace Plan," *San Francisco Chronicle*, 28 April 2002.

2. "A General Picture: Gaza, Golan, Judea, and Samaria," *Homecoming*, November 1983 (Jerusalem: Ahva Press), 8.

3. David J. Goldberg, *To the Promised Land: A History of Zionist Thought* (London: Penguin Books, 1996), 155.

4. Nadav Shragai, "Split Right Down the Middle," *Ha'aretz*, 18 March 2004.

5. The Jewish National Fund has solicited such funds from the Jewish diaspora for this political purpose since its earliest years; see Yoram Bar-Gal, *Propaganda and Zionist Education* (Rochester: University of Rochester Press, 2004); also Baruch Kimmerling (1983), 76.

6. In the unique worldview of the WZO and its global support networks, West Bank settlements authorized by the Israeli government are "legal," and spending Jewish diaspora donations on them is entirely appropriate. A 2004 revelation that the WZO was also supporting unauthorized "illegal" settlements (outposts) caused a flush of scandal among Jewish-American affiliates of the WZO: see "News Report on Illegal Outposts Prompts Calls for Probe of

WZO," *Forward*, 2 January 2004, available online at www.forward.com/
issues/2004/04.01.02/news4.html.

7. On post- and neo-Zionism, see especially Uri Ram, "From Nation-State
to Nation——State: Nation, History, and Identity Struggles in Jewish Israel,"
and Ilan Pappé, "The Square Circle," both in *The Challenge of Post-Zionism:
Alternatives to Israeli Fundamentalist Politics,* ed. Ephraim Nimni (London:
Zed Books, 2003).

8. A 2003 survey of U.S. Jewish opinion conducted by the American Jewish
Committee found that while 54 percent supported creation of a Palestinian
state, 81 percent believed that the Arabs' true goal was the destruction of Israel.
Only 12 percent supported a full "dismantling" of all settlements, and 34 percent agreed with the statement "The organized Jewish community should pressure the U.S. to let Israel keep its settlements" (23 percent disagreed). See
"2003 Annual Survey of American Jewish Opinion," http://www.us-
israel.org/jsource/US-Israel/ajcsurvey2003.html. A clear majority in several
2003 surveys supported withdrawing "most" settlements, except the "blocs" or
"large" ones (undefined). "Large" here may mean only those not composed of
tents or trailers—that is, all but the outposts. I could find no survey that asked
what should be done with the remaining settlements or if they should be turned
over to Palestinian use. The analysis here is based on interviews.

9. A small Jewish population persisted in Palestine after the Roman attack
in 132, especially in Jerusalem, Jaffa, and some communities around the Sea of
Galilee. The total Jewish population was around 5 to 7 percent in the mid-nine-
teenth century. In 1922, an Ottoman survey reported twenty-two thousand
Jews in Palestine, or about 11 percent. For a good statistical study of population
changes stemming from twentieth-century Zionist immigration, which pushed
the Jewish population to 43 percent (six hundred thousand) by 1948, see Janet
Abu-Lughod, "The Demographic Transformation of Palestine," in *The Transformation of Palestine,* ed. Ibrahim Abu-Lughod (Evanston: Northwestern
University Press, 1971).

10. Americans for Peace Now, "Israeli Peace Now Survey of Settlers."

11. E.g., see Yair Sheleg, "The Settlers and a Binational State," *Ha'aretz,* 31
August 2003; Aharon Megged, "And First of All, the Justice of Our Path,"
Ha'aretz, 26 March 2002.

12. Woodrow Wilson Task Force WWS 401c, "Water Rights in the Jordan
Valley: Geography of Water Resources," http://www.wws.princeton.edu/
~wws401c/geography.html.

13. Thirty-one percent favored forced transfer of Israeli Arabs out of the
country as well. See Asher Arian, *Israeli Public Opinion on National Security,
2003,* Memorandum 26, Jaffee Center for Strategic Studies, Tel Aviv University,
October 2003, available online at www.tau.ac.il/jcss/memoranda/memo
67.pdf.

14. Popular recent compilations of Zionist myths include Alan Dershowitz's
The Case for Israel (Hoboken, NJ: John Wiley and Sons, 2003) and Joan
Peters's *From Time Immemorial: The Origins of the Arab-Jewish Conflict over
Palestine* (New York: Harper and Row). A well-known earlier source, written as
a handbook for activists, is Leonard J. Davis's *Myths and Facts: A Guide to the
Arab-Israel Conflict* (Washington, DC: Near East Report, 1989).

15. For an especially evocative discussion on Arab place-names, see Meron

Benvenisti, *Sacred Landscape: The Buried History of the Holy Land since 1948* (Berkeley: University of California Press, 2000), 11–54.

16. For a concise early history, see Baruch Kimmerling and Joel S. Migdal, *The Palestinian People: A History* (Cambridge: Harvard University Press, 2003). On Palestinian nationalism, see also Rashid Khalidi, *Palestinian Identity: The Construction of Modern National Consciousness* (New York: Columbia University Press, 1997).

17. See especially Morris, *Birth of the Palestinian Refugee Problem Revisited;* Benny Morris, *Righteous Victims: A History of the Zionist-Arab Conflict, 1881–2001* (New York: Vintage, 2001); Shavit, "Survival of the Fittest." For a valuable compilation on the 1948 crisis, see Eugene L. Rogan and Avi Shlaim, eds., *The War for Palestine: Rewriting the History of 1948* (Cambridge: Cambridge University Press, 2001).

18. A report by the International Labor Organization estimated Palestinian unemployment in June 2004 at 35 percent, due mostly to Israeli bans on travel and pass restrictions. A report by the British Commons Select Committee on International Development found much higher rates: "Rates of malnutrition in Gaza and parts of the West Bank are as bad as anywhere one would find in sub-Saharan Africa. The Palestinian economy has all but collapsed. Unemployment rates are in the region of 60–70% and many of those who are employed are dependent upon NGOs [nongovernmental organizations] or international relief organisations for employment" (Third Special Report, 2003–4 [23 March 2004]).

19. See Ephraim Yaar and Tamar Hermann, "The Peace Index: Israeli Jews Fret over the Possibility of a Binational State," *Ha'aretz,* 5 November 2003; "Peace Index: Demographic Fears Favor Unilateral Separation," *Ha'aretz,* 7 January 2004.

20. *Ha'aretz,* 23 February 2004. This logic of ethnic exclusion to protect democracy is not unique to Israel. Aside from the South Africa comparison commonly drawn, a similar strategy was pursued by Australia in the early twentieth century, through the "White Australia" project, which excluded both Aborigines and Asian immigration, with the agenda of preserving white democratic life. See discussions in Geoffrey Stokes, ed., *The Politics of Identity in Australia* (Cambridge: Cambridge University Press, 1997).

21. See Avi Shlaim, *Collusion across the Jordan: King Abdullah, the Zionist Movement, and the Partition of Palestine* (New York: Columbia University Press, 1999).

22. Cited in Avi Shlaim, *The Iron Wall: Israel and the Arab World* (New York: W. W. Norton, 2001), 21.

23. The PLO's Algiers Declaration of 1988 implicitly recognized Israel by endorsing UN Security Council Resolution 181, which established the two-state principle. Explicit language recognizing Israel was missing, however, and the declaration was declared inadequate by Israeli diplomats.

24. *Jerusalem Post,* international ed., 14 October 1995.

25. For critical analyses of the collapse of the Oslo Accords, see Nicholas Guyatt, *The Absence of Peace: Understanding the Israeli-Palestinian Conflict* (London: Zed Press, 1998); Kimmerling and Migdal, *The Palestinian People;* Naseer Aruri, *Dishonest Broker: The U.S. Role in Israel and Palestine* (Cambridge, MA: South End Press, 2003).

26. See, e.g., Hussein Agha and Robert Malley, "Camp David: The Tragedy of Errors," *New York Review of Books* 48, no. 13 (9 August 2001), and the response in Benny Morris and Ehud Barak, "Camp David and After—Continued," *New York Review of Books* 49, no. 11 (27 June 2002).

27. On Sharon's long-standing plans for the Wall and recent local negotiations about its route, see Meron Rappaport, "A Wall in Their Heart," *Yedioh Aharonoth,* 23 May 2003.

CHAPTER 4

1. An additional thirty-nine Security Council resolutions were vetoed by the United States as excessively critical of Israel (the cause of more vetoes than any other topic). For a list of related resolutions, see http://www.us-israel.org/jsource/UN/sctoc.html; for Security Council resolutions vetoed by the United States, see http://www.us-israel.org/jsource/UN/usvetoes.html.

2. On this interpretation, see the April 2004 letter sent by senior diplomats urgently urging British Prime Minister Tony Blair to act on the conflict, which, "more than any other, has for decades poisoned relations between the West and the Islamic and Arab worlds" (*The Independent,* 27 April 2004).

3. In addition to other posts over three decades in government service, George Shultz served as secretary of state under Ronald Reagan, Brzezinski as national security advisor under President Carter, and James Baker as secretary of state under the first President Bush and as White House chief of staff for President Reagan and the first President Bush.

4. I here use the term *realist* in the sense of international relations theory, in which it refers to foreign policy based on rational calculation of state interests understood narrowly as maximizing military and perhaps economic power. In realist policy-making, moral issues are at most, deemed secondary to a state's security and strategic interests; in realist policy analysis, moralistic or idealistic rhetoric does not signal a state's true motives but is seen only as ideological cover.

5. See Hala Jaber's intelligent *Hezbollah: Born with a Vengeance* (New York: Columbia University Press, 1997).

6. The official annual U.S. grant package to Israel is some $3.2 billion, but that is a fraction of the actual total, which is multiplied severalfold by Department of Defense grants, interest from advance loan and grant payments, and myriad unseen trade perks on a dizzying array of exports and imports. One independent assessment put the total at $91 billion between 1948 and 2002; by the 1980s, this support approximated $1000 per Israeli per year (Shirl MacArthur, "A Conservative Total for U.S. Aid to Israel," *Washington Report on Middle East Affairs,* January–February 2001). U.S. military grants to Israel are supposed to rebound to the U.S. arms industry, but special dispensations permit Israel to use some 40 percent of U.S. grants toward buying Israel's own hardware. U.S. materièl is also sold to Israel at a discount, and purchases are tied to reciprocal U.S. purchases of Israeli technology. Thus, the financial return to the United States might be half its intended total. Counting lost interest and investment opportunities, special pricing on arms deals, and other hidden costs, economist Thomas Stauffer has put total U.S. aid to Israel at $241 billion (in 2002 dollars) between 1973 and 2002 (see *Washington Report on Mid-*

dle East Affairs, June 2003). The cost of direct U.S. military involvement in the region puts the figure still higher.

7. The shadow-world partnership of the United States and Israel in Latin America and Africa remains one of the most interesting and underanalyzed strategic alliances shaping politics and regime change in both regions. See, e.g., Jane Hunter, *No Simple Proxy* (Washington, DC: Washington Middle East Associates, 1987); Bishara Bahbah, *Israel and Latin America: The Military Connection* (New York: St. Martin's Press, 1986).

8. This phrase traces to former U.S. national security advisor Zbigniew Brzezinski, who endorsed its logic; see the discussion in Ahmed Rashid, *Taliban: Militant Islam, Oil, and Fundamentalism in Central Asia* (New Haven, CT: Yale University Press, 2001).

9. Rashid, *Taliban.*

10. The number of riot police accompanying Ariel Sharon was later estimated at one thousand. For contemporary accounts, see Suzanne Goldberg, "Rioting as Sharon Visits Islam Holy Site," *The Guardian,* 29 September 2000; "Sharon on Temple Mount Sparks Riot," *Ha'aretz,* 29 September 2000.

11. "The Bush Peace Plan" (24 June 2002), available online at www.jewishvirtuallibrary.org/jsource/Peace/bushplan.html.

12. "The Mitchell Report" (4 May 2001), available online at www.jewishvirtuallibrary.org/jsource/Peace/Mitchellrep.html.

13. "The Bush Peace Plan."

14. Sources on the pro-Israel lobby include Edward Tivnan's historical study *The Lobby: Jewish Political Power and American Foreign Policy* (New York: Simon and Schuster, 1987) and Paul Findlay's *They Dare to Speak Out: People and Institutions Confront Israel's Lobby,* 3rd ed. (Westport, CT: Lawrence Hill, 2003). Cheryl Rubenberg discussed the Israeli lobby in *Israel and the American National Interest* (Urbana: University of Illinois Press, 1986), 329–76. See also Michael Massing, "The Israel Lobby," *The Nation,* 10 June 2002.

15. The International Studies in Higher Education Act (HR 3077), passed by voice vote in the U.S. House of Representatives in March 2004, amended the provisions for Title VI grants (a federal program that provides millions of dollars largely for language training at major universities) by establishing an autonomous seven-member international advisory board to monitor whether recipient institutions are adequately educating and training students "to participate in homeland security efforts." The same act also called for "a study to identify foreign language heritage communities, particularly such communities that include speakers of languages that are critical to the national security of the United States [e.g., Arabic and Farsi]." Data could be garnered from every federal and private resource. Passage of HR 3077 was urged particularly by a coalition of Jewish-Zionist organizations, including the American Jewish Committee, the American Jewish Congress, the Anti-Defamation League, and B'nai B'rith.

16. *Forward,* April 2002, cited in Massing, "The Israel Lobby."

17. James Ennes's *Assault on the Liberty* (New York: Random House, 1979), which chronicled Israel's 1967 attack on a U.S. Navy ship, suffered especially from such a coordinated assault on its distribution. On this case and other such campaigns, see Rubenberg, *Israel and the American National Interest,* 335–44.

18. Oded Yinon, "A Strategy for Israel in the 1980s," *Kivunim* 14 (1982),

ed. and trans. Israel Shahak, available at www.geocities.com/alabasters_archive/zionist_plan.html. Oded Yinon was an Israeli journalist who had once worked with Israel's Foreign Ministry. In the opinion of Israel Shahak, an Israeli-Jewish critic of Zionism with a voluminous body of translations to his credit, Yinon's essay represented "the accurate and detailed plan of the present Zionist regime (of Sharon and Eitan) for the Middle East which is based on the division of the whole area into small states, and the dissolution of all the existing Arab states" (ibid.).

19. Yinon's analysis was hardly unique. Regarding Iraq, such prominent writers as Ze'ev Schiff, military correspondent for *Ha'aretz,* reported a 1982 consensus that Israel's interests would be best served by "the dissolution of Iraq into a Shi'ite state, a Sunni state and the separation of the Kurdish part" (*Ha'aretz,* 5 February 1982).

20. *A Clean Break: A New Strategy for Securing the Realm,* available online at www.israeleconomy.org/strat1.htm. The brief is signed by Richard Perle, American Enterprise Institute, study group leader; James Colbert, Jewish Institute for National Security Affairs; Charles Fairbanks, Jr., Johns Hopkins University/School for Advanced International Studies; Douglas Feith, Feith and Zell Associates; Robert Loewenberg, president, Institute for Advanced Strategic and Political Studies; Jonathan Torop, the Washington Institute for Near East Policy; David Wurmser, Institute for Advanced Strategic and Political Studies; and Meyrav Wurmser, Johns Hopkins University.

21. On this labyrinth of power, see, e.g., Robert Dreyfuss and Jason Vest, "The Lie Factor," *Mother Jones,* January–February 2004; Seymour M. Hersh, "The Debate Within," *The New Yorker,* 11 March 2002, and "Behind the 'Mushroom Cloud,'" *The New Yorker,* 21 March 2003.

22. Business connections among this network also read like an overdrawn thriller. Perle, managing partner in the venture-capital company Trireme Partners L.P., which invested heavily in homeland-security and surveillance technology, had solicited multibillion-dollar security contracts in the Middle East (for which war would be very favorable). He had also faced a scandal in earlier service, for receiving fees as a lobbyist for Israeli arms sales. In the early 1990s, Feith's law firm, Feith and Zell, received hundreds of thousands of dollars from the lobbying firm International Advisors, Inc. (IAI), of which Feith was sole stockholder. IAI was principally concerned with promoting Turkey's interests to the U.S. government and cultivating Turkish-Israeli cooperation.

23. Sherif Hetata, "World Domination, Inc.," *Al-Ahram Weekly,* no. 666 (27 November–3 December 2003).

24. On George W. Bush's understanding of his role in fulfilling divine will, see interviews in Bob Woodward, *Plan of Attack* (New York: Simon and Schuster, 2004). In a *60 Minutes* interview on 17 April 2004, Woodward observed of this messianic self-image that it is "far reaching, and ambitious, and I think will cause many people to tremble."

25. On this logic, see especially Shlaim, *The Iron Wall;* Ian Lustick, "To Build and to Be Built By: Israel and the Hidden Logic of the Iron Wall," *Israel Studies* 1, no. 1 (1996).

26. JINSA and the American Enterprise Institute also cultivated Chalabi, establishing the durable Israeli and Jordanian connections of the Iraqi National Congress (INC). Thus groomed to play its compliant part, the INC was supposed to serve as the new "transition" government of Iraq, guiding the coun-

try toward "democracy"—although a series of bungled coup attempts and some CIA fiascos kept this group waiting uncomfortably in the wings through the decade. See Elizabeth Drew, "The Neo-Cons in Power," *New York Review of Books* 50, no. 10 (12 June 2003); John Dizard, "How Ahmed Chalabi Conned the Neocons," *Salon.com,* 4 May 2004, http://archive.salon.com/news/feature/2004/05/04/chalabi.

27. *A Clean Break: A New Strategy for Securing the Realm,* available online at www.israeleconomy.org/strat1.htm.

28. Ibid.

29. Unfolding in fall 2004, this spy scandal was quickly suppressed by the Bush administration. See, e.g., Robert Dreyfuss, "Agents of Influence," *The Nation,* 4 October 2004.

30. On Israeli involvement in Kurdish areas of Iraq, see Seymour M. Hersh, "Plan B," *The New Yorker,* 28 June 2004.

31. David Hirst, "Wagging Which Way," *Al-Ahram* 661 (23–29 October 2003).

32. The entire Palestinian population is about 7.8 million, of whom about half are registered as refugees with UNRWA (the United Nations Relief Works Agency, which manages the Palestinian refugee camps in the West Bank and the Gaza Strip as well as in the frontline states).

33. Jordan was supposed to participate but withered in the crunch, and Egypt's forces also held back from completing initial plans. For an account of this war from Syria's perspective, see Patrick Seale, *Asad of Syria: The Struggle for the Middle East* (Berkeley: University of California Press, 1990).

34. The Jerusalem Media and Communication Centre survey of Palestinian opinion in June 2004 (available online at www.jmcc.org/publicpoll/results/2004/no51.pdf) found dissatisfaction with Arafat running at about 50 percent.

35. For one close study, see Rex Brynen, *A Very Political Economy: Peacebuilding and Foreign Aid in the West Bank and Gaza* (Washington, DC: United States Institute of Peace Press, 2000).

36. See Uzi Benziman, "Corridors of Power: Whose Freedom Is It Anyway?" *Ha'aretz,* 30 April 2004, available online at www.diak.org/artikelaktuell/ip%20online%2018/Corridors%20of%20Power.htm.

37. Lengthy agreements in the Geneva Accords offered detailed plans for policing, territorial division, and joint authority over borders and Palestinian refugees, but all sensitive questions—including such long-standing deal breakers as water and the disposition of settlements—were referred to a never-published "Annex X." For this reason, although inspiring as dramatic proof of a mutual desire for peace, the accords were seen to lack substance or serious viability. The full text is available from the Foundation for Middle East Peace at http://www.fmep.org/documents/Geneva_Accord.html.

38. "Transcript of Remarks by Bush and Sharon on Israel," *New York Times,* 14 April 2004.

CHAPTER 5

1. International law does not include a "right to exist" ascribed to states. Although seemingly juridical, the formula is a unique figment of Israel's defensive rhetoric.

2. On the Afrikaner civil religion, see Dunbar Moodie, *The Rise of Afrikan-*

erdom: Power, Apartheid, and the Afrikaner Civil Religion (Berkeley: University of California Press, 1975).

3. See http://www.divest-from-israel-campaign.org/index.html.

4. On this early history, see especially Gershon Shafir, *Land, Labor, and the Origins of the Israeli-Palestinian Conflict, 1882–1914* (Berkeley: University of California Press, 1996). Alienation from the land, a condition enforced by centuries of European anti-Semitic restrictions, was considered by early Zionist writers to have "distorted" Jewish culture and even weakened people physically. The mainstream current of "labor Zionism," endorsed by Prime Ministers Ben-Gurion, Peres, and Rabin, took its central inspiration from this idea.

5. The reference to "hewers of wood and drawers of water" comes originally from Joshua 9:21, describing Hittite roles under Jewish rule.

6. See especially debates surrounding the UN World Conference against Racism, held in Durban, South Africa, 31 August–7 September 2001.

7. Many of these arguments were deployed in 1991, in a successful campaign for the UN to repeal its 1975 "Zionism is racism" resolution (UN Resolution 3379); see especially related publications by the Anti-Defamation League.

8. Cited in Shavit, "Survival of the Fittest."

9. Cited in Ari Shavit, "Dear God, this is Effi—A Religious Zionist's Vision of Israel's Future," *Ha'aretz*, 22 March 2002.

10. Cited in Baruch Kimmerling, *Politicide: Ariel Sharon's War against the Palestinians* (London: Verso, 2003), 165.

11. UN Resolution 2106 (XX), 21 December 1965, article 1, paragraph 1.

12. For example, see discussion in Mazin B. Qumsiyeh, *Sharing the Land of Canaan*, 5–17.

13. Edward Said's *Orientalism* (New York: Pantheon Books, 1978) is the foundational work for this analysis.

14. For a useful regional development profile, see Abdulatif Y. Al-Hamad, "The Dilemmas of Development in the Arab World," paper presented at Arab World 2000 Symposium: Transformation and Challenges, Center for Contemporary Arab Studies (Washington, DC), n.d., available online at www.ccasonline.org/symposium/Al-Hamad.htm.

15. See, e.g., Deborah Gerner, *One Land, Two Peoples: The Conflict over Palestine* (Boulder: Westview Press, 1991); Daniel Elazar, *Two Peoples—One Land: Federal Solutions for Israel, the Palestinians, and Jordan* (Lanham, MD: University Press of America, 1991); Ilan Pappé, *A History of Modern Palestine: One Land, Two Peoples* (New York: Cambridge University Press, 2003).

16. Ethnic legislation in Islamic states (e.g., Malaysia, Pakistan, and Iran) and Catholic states (e.g., Italy and Spain) proscribes discrimination among citizens based on religion or ethnicity but, in identifying the state with one religion, creates various configurations of unequal advantages among religiously diverse populations. Among the world states, Malaysia stood out in this study for securing special rights to one ethnic group (Malays, 53 percent of the population) in its constitution, restricting landholding in certain districts to Malays ("Malay reservations") and restricting service in the special Malay Regiment to Malays. In Latin America (e.g., Brazil, Bolivia, Ecuador, and Peru), constitutional provisions for territorial and cultural rights among indigenous peoples also reflect state measures to accommodate ethnic needs. In no state but Israel, however, is the state's "nation" defined as one ethnic group within the state.

17. Israel's High Court has explicitly rejected appeals to claim an "Israeli" nationality (see discussion in chap. 6). A relevant case is *George Rafael Tamarin v. State of Israel*, 20 January 1972, in *Decisions of the Supreme Court of Israel* (Jerusalem: Supreme Court, 1972), vol. 25, pt. 1, 197 (in Hebrew). In December 2003, a group appealed again to the High Court to permit registration as an "Israeli" national but was rejected: "State Refuses to Register 'Israeli' Nationality," *Ha'aretz*, 19 May 2004.

18. Roselle Tekiner has been a major voice illuminating this distinction: see "On the Inequality of Israeli Citizens," *Without Prejudice* 1, no. 1 (1988), 9–48. For a summary, see her "Israel's Two-Tiered Citizenship Law Bars Non-Jews from 93 Percent of Its Lands," *Media Monitors Network*, 13 February 2001, available online at www.mediamonitors.net/tekiner1.html.

19. Eugen Weber's *Peasants into Frenchmen: The Modernization of Rural France, 1870–1914* (Stanford, CA: Stanford University Press, 1979) remains the classic study of this history.

20. Israel was freshly reaffirmed as a "Jewish and democratic state" in article 1a of Basic Law: Human Dignity and Liberty (1992).

21. Benedict Anderson, *Imagined Communities: Reflections on the Origins and Spread of Nationalism* (London: Verso, 1991). A rich literature exists on nationalist symbology: see, inter alia, Anthony D. Smith, *Myths and Memories of the Nations* (New York: Oxford University Press, 1999).

22. Ram, "From Nation-State to Nation—State."

23. On metaconflict, see René Lemarchand's discussion in chapter 2 of his *Burundi: Ethnic Conflict and Genocide* (New York: Cambridge University Press, 1996).

24. This narrative is assembled from my own experience of public Zionist polemics over two decades. Popular codified versions include Joan Peters's *From Time Immemorial* and Alan Dershowitz's *The Case for Israel*, but in the United States, the component tenets are disseminated through a multiplier effect employing a very wide range of outlets, drawing especially on WZO publications and, more recently, the WZO official Web site.

25. This narrative is drawn from my personal experience of public polemics by the Palestinian solidarity movement and diplomacy over two decades. Many fine scholarly studies support details of this account, but I do not draw on them here.

26. Ilan Pappé, "The Square Circle: The Struggle for Survival of Traditional Zionism," in *The Challenge of Post-Zionism: Alternatives to Israeli Fundamentalist Politics*, ed. Ephraim Nimni (London: Zed Books, 2003), 46.

27. Ibid., 54.

28. Walter Laqueur, *A History of Zionism: From the French Revolution to the Establishment of the State of Israel* (New York: Schocken Books), xx.

29. Regarding the history of Israel's relationships with the Arab world, the most well-known works include Avi Shlaim's *Collusion Across the Jordan: King Abdullah, the Zionist Movement, and the Partition of Palestine* (New York: Columbia University Press, 1999) and *The Iron Wall: Israel and the Arab World* (New York: W. W. Norton, 2001). On the expulsion of the Palestinians in 1948, Benny Morris's *The Birth of the Palestinian Refugee Problem Revisited* (New York: Cambridge University Press, 2004) has had the biggest impact. Morris's views about his own role were illuminated in an interview with Ari Shavit, "Survival of the Fittest," *Ha'aretz*, 19 February 2004. On post-Zionism and the role

of the "new historians," see Ilan Pappé's three-part "Post-Zionist Critique on Israel and the Palestinians" in *Journal of Palestine Studies* 26, especially "Part I: The Academic Debate" (no. 2); also Laurence J. Silberstein's *Postzionism Debates: Knowledge and Power in Israeli Culture* (New York: Routledge, 1999) and Ephraim Nimni's especially engrossing collection in *The Challenge of Post-Zionism: Alternatives to Israeli Fundamentalist Politics* (2003). For a portrait of post-Zionism and an in-depth critical response, see Yoram Hazony, *The Jewish State: The Struggle for Israel's Soul* (New York: Basic Books, 2001).

30. E.g., see Shavit, "Survival of the Fittest"; Laqueur, *History of Zionism,* xx–xxi.

31. Cited in Shlaim, *The Iron Wall,* 14.

32. This claim is indeed one of the oldest Zionist tenets. The "father of modern Zionism," Theodor Herzl, was principally inspired by it, believing that nothing really united the culturally diverse and geographically dispersed Jewish people except their vulnerability to anti-Semitic persecution, an enduring condition that required a "state for the Jews" (*Der Judenstaat,* the title of Herzl's 1896 thesis). Actual physical danger to Jews, however, was a minor theme in Zionist writings of this period, when the primary concern was Jewish-nationalist and cultural fulfillment.

33. Although common in U.S. parlance, the term *Holocaust* is controversial, because some have argued that its Greek etymology ("burnt offering") can be read to suggest that Jews "offered" themselves for sacrifice. While respecting this reason for using the alternative term *Shoa,* I have chosen to use *Holocaust* here because it is the term most familiar to U.S. readers.

34. Norman Finkelstein's *The Holocaust Industry* (London: Verso, 2000) is the most famous example.

35. Aside from among the "post-Zionists," these arguments have appeared since the early twentieth century in anti-Zionist writings, discussed in chap. 6.

36. Cf., e.g., Walter Laqueur's denunciation in the preface to his *History of Zionism,* xx: "The contemporary post-Zionists belong to a generation of academics that has never personally experienced anti-Semitism, for whom the Holocaust is not a real historical experience, who did not have to face the danger of destruction and to flee Europe to save their lives."

37. For one formulation of these arguments, see, e.g., Abraham Foxman, *Never Again? The Threat of the New Anti-Semitism* (San Francisco: HarperSanFrancisco, 2003). On views of Israeli Arabs as a fifth column, see also Arial Shenbol, "The Only Democracy in the Middle East," *Maariv International,* 17 June 2004; Moshe Gorali, "Second-Class Status and the Fear of a Fifth Column," *Ha'aretz,* 24 May 2004.

38. Seth Tillman, *The United States in the Middle East: Interests and Obstacles* (Bloomington: Indiana University Press, 1982), 123–71.

39. See Foxman, *Never Again?*

40. Much of this view appears in Web sites and oral addresses: for example, "A View from the Eye of the Storm," a widely reproduced piece by nuclear theorist Haim Harari, which affirmed that "The root of the trouble is that this entire Moslem region is totally dysfunctional, by any standard of the word." For a Christian-Zionist equivalent, see Hal Lindsey, *The Everlasting Hatred: The Roots of Jihad* (Murrieta, CA: Oracle House, 2002).

41. Aside from The Other Israel and Peace Now, outspoken Israeli peace

groups who endorse this assumption are mostly small in formal membership, but their proliferation, "supporter" networks, and philosophical diversity suggest the spectrum of sentiment contributing to the leftist-liberal camp, which assumes the possibility of good relations with Palestinians. Better-known organizations supporting these groups include Ariga, B'Tselem, Gush Shalom, Bat-Shalom, ICHAD (the Israeli Committee against House Demolition), Ta'ayush, and, for Israeli soldier refuseniks, Courage to Refuse/Seruv (the last has a support list of over fourteen thousand).

42. Indigenous peoples consistently fail to meet awful settler-society predictions of vengeful native massacre. For instance, in Guatemala in the 1980s, some ladinos openly feared massacres by vengeful Maya should the "Indians" ever gain any power. After the Peace Accords in the mid-1990s, the long-abused Maya—predictably, to all who knew those communities—promptly formed political parties and lobbied for educational reforms. On democratic Mayan politics in the transition period, see Santiago Bastos and Manuela Camus, *Entre el mecapal y el cielo: Desarrollo del movimiento maya en Guatemala* (Guatemala: Facultad Latinoamericana de Ciencias Sociales, 2003).

43. See, e.g., Lenni Brenner's chronicle of these complicated relations, *Zionism in the Age of the Dictators,* at http://www.onestate.org.

44. *New York Times,* 23 December 1969; *Der Spiegel,* 5 November 1969.

45. "Senator John Kerry Addresses ADL's National Leadership Conference," 10 May 2004, available online at www.adl.org/adl_in_action/conference_2004_kerry.asp.

46. A press release from the Steinmetz Center on 7 January 2004 explains: "The Peace Index project is conducted at the Tami Steinmetz Center for Peace Research of Tel Aviv University, headed by Prof. Ephraim Yaar and Dr. Tamar Hermann. The telephone interviews were conducted by the B. I. Cohen Institute of Tel Aviv University from December 29–31, and included 579 interviewees who represent the adult Jewish and Arab population of Israel (including the territories and the kibbutzim). The sampling error for a sample of this size is about 4.5% in each direction."

47. The Jerusalem Program (1968), adopted at the Twenty-Seventh World Zionist Congress, was "aimed to redefine aims, ideals and principles of Zionism." The text of the program is available online at www.wzo.org.il/en/resources/view.asp?id=497&subject=43.

48. Translation by Israel's Ministry of Foreign Affairs.

49. On ultra-Orthodox thoughts about Zionism and other related controversies, see especially Aviezer Ravitsky's *Messianism, Zionism, and Jewish Religious Radicalism,* trans. Michael Swirsky and Jonathan Chipman (Chicago and London: University of Chicago Press, 1993); see also Elmer Berger, "Zionist Ideology: Obstacle to Peace," in *Anti-Zionism: Analytical Reflections,* ed. Roselle Tekiner, Samir Abed-Rabbo, and Norton Mezvinsky (Brattleboro, VT: Amana Books, 1988).

50. Joan Peters's *From Time Immemorial* is possibly the best-known source for this argument, but it well predates her book. Census data offers a very different explanation of Arab population growth—natural increase, resulting from better living conditions stemming from expanding trade, beginning in the nineteenth century. From census records, Charles Kamen found that Arab immigration during the entire British Mandate was about fifty-eight thousand, or

only 7 percent of the total increase in the Arab population during the period: see *Little Common Ground* (Pittsburgh: Pittsburgh University Press, 1991), 231, cited in Benvenisti, *Sacred Landscape* (2000), 82.

51. Exodus 3:8, Revised Standard Version. Despite extensive Israeli excavations, the sudden Hebrew conquest recounted in the Old Testament has not been supported by archaeological evidence, which instead indicates a slower process of ethnic arrival and mixing, with cities conquered (by various agents) in different centuries.

52. See Benvenisti, *Sacred Landscape,* chap. 1.

53. One related current of Zionist thought, marked by theorists from Ber Borochov to Harold R. Isaacs, made much of these "primordial" connections. See Isaacs, *Idols of the Tribe* (New York: Harper and Row, 1977).

54. Martin Buber, *Israel and Palestine: The History of an Idea* (London: East and West Library, 1952), xi. See also Buber's "The Land and Its Possessors" [a letter to Mahatma Gandhi], in *Israel and the World: Essays in a Time of Crisis* (New York: Schocken Books, 1948), 228–29.

55. Ariel Sharon, address to the Jewish Agency assembly, Jerusalem, 23 June 2002.

56. Cited in Goldberg, *To the Promised Land,* 180–81.

57. Cited in Shahak, "Zionism as a Recidivist Movement," in *Anti-Zionism: Analytical Reflections,* ed. Roselle Tekiner, Samir Abed-Rabbo, and Norton Mezvinsky (Brattleboro, VT: Amana Books, 1988), 292.

58. Law of Return, Amendment 5714–1954, passed in 1970. This definition does not accord with Halacha law, which holds that a person remains Jewish even after converting to another religion.

59. Anti-Defamation League, "The Conversion Crisis: The Current Debate on Religion, State, and Conversion in Israel," n.d., http://www.adl.org/ Israel/Conversion/crisis.asp.

60. Eliezer Rauchberger, "United Torah Judaism Rejects High Court's Conversion Decision," *Dei'ah veDibur,* 27 February 2002, available online at http://chareidi.shemayisrael.com/KS62aconvrt.htm.

CHAPTER 6

1. Tony Judt, "Israel: The Alternative."

2. Avi Shavit, "Cry, the Beloved Two-State Solution," *Ha'aretz,* 6 August 2003.

3. Daniel Gavron, *The Other Side of Despair: Jews and Arabs in the Promised Land* (New York: Rowman and Littlefield, 2004).

4. Shavit, "Cry, the Beloved Two-State Solution."

5. Tony Judt, "Israel: The Alternative."

6. See especially Morris, *Birth of the Palestinian Refugee Problem Revisited.*

7. Shavit, "Survival of the Fittest."

8. Yoram Hazony, *The Jewish State: The Struggle for Israel's Soul* (New York: Basic Books, 2001), xvii.

9. Yoel Esteron, "Who's in Favor of Annihilating Israel?" *Ha'aretz,* 28 November 2003.

10. Ibid.

11. Cited in Ruthie Blum, "ONE on ONE: It's the Demography, Stupid," *Jerusalem Post,* 20 May 2004.

12. Cited in Shavit, "Cry, the Beloved Two-State Solution."

13. Edward Said, "Truth and Reconciliation," in *The End of the Peace Process: Oslo and After* (New York: Vintage, 2001), 318.

14. Cited in Peter Hirschberg, "Hello, I'm Israeli-Palestinian," *Mideast*, 9 February 2004.

15. Wafa Amr, "Palestinian PM Says Two-State Solution in Danger," Reuters, 8 January 2004, available at www.one.state.org/articles/2004/amr.htm.

16. Cited in Ali Abunimah, "Palestine/Israel: The End of the Road for the Two-State Solution?" paper presented at a seminar of the Middle East Centre, St. Anthony's College, Oxford, 20 February 2004.

17. Cited in David Landau, "Maximum Jews, Minimum Palestinians," *Ha'aretz*, 19 February 2004.

18. Musa Al-Hindi, "The Road to Palestine," *Al-Ahram Weekly* 690, 13–19 May 2004.

19. Ibrahim Kazerooni, "A One-State Solution in the Mideast," *Denver Post*, 24 April 2004.

20. Raja Halwani, "Palestinian Options: The One-State Solution," *Palestine Report*, 31 March 2004.

21. Khalid Amayreh, "Controversial Move," *Al-Ahram Weekly* 673, 15–21 January 2004.

22. Abunimah, "Palestine/Israel." The breadth of Zionist sentiment toward "transfer" may challenge this idea; as noted earlier, a 2002 survey found that 46 percent of Jewish Israelis favor the Palestinians' forced expulsion, and 31 percent favor expulsion even of Israeli Arabs. But real-life politics would likely play out differently, and the Wall itself suggests some acceptance of a permanent (if distanced) Palestinian presence. See Asher Arian, *Israeli Public Opinion on National Security 2003*, Memorandum 67, Jaffee Center for Strategic Studies, Tel Aviv University.

23. Abunimah, "Palestine/Israel."

24. Gavron, *The Other Side of Despair*, 235.

25. Haim Bresheeth, "Two States, Too Little, Too Late," *Al-Ahram Weekly* 681, 11–17 March 2004.

26. See discussion in Ephraim Nimni, "From *Galut* to *T'futsoth:* Post-Zionism and the Dis><location of Jewish Diasporas," in *The Challenge of Post-Zionism: Alternatives to Israeli Fundamentalist Politics,* ed. Ephraim Nimni (London: Zed Books, 2003).

27. This interpretation of Palestinian thought is based to some extent on writings and public statements by PA and Hamas officials but primarily on my own impressions taken from conversations with Palestinians—intellectuals, activists, and cultivators—in the United States and in towns and villages in the West Bank and the Gaza Strip. Serious professional surveys on these questions are obviously needed.

28. This thesis has been freshly compiled in recent books: see, e.g., Phyllis Chesler, *The New Anti-Semitism* (San Francisco: Jossey-Bass, 2003); Gabriel Shoenfeld, *The Return of Anti-Semitism* (San Francisco: Encounter Books); Foxman, *Never Again?*

29. "An Alternative Future: An Exchange," *New York Review of Books,* 50, no. 19 (4 November 2003). In an email, Dr. Judt informed me that he received some six hundred emailed responses and some 150 hard-copy letters to his article—not counting some hundred responses he discarded as "too dumb or obscene" or that were copied from some organizer Web site.

30. Brian Klug, "The Myth of the New Anti-Semitism," *The Nation*, 15 January 2004.

31. Gidon Remba, "Anti-Semitism—New or Old?" *The Nation*, 24 March 2004.

32. See, e.g., Zionist Organization of America, "Saudi 'Peace' Plan Would Reduce Israel to Indefensible Pre-1967 Borders," news release, 21 February 2002, available online at www.zoa.org/pressrel2002/20020227a.htm.

33. *Report to the General Assembly by the United Nations Special Committee on Palestine* (Official Records of the Second Session of the General Assembly, 1947, Supplement No. 11), cited in Walid Khalidi ed., *From Haven to Conquest: Readings in Zionism and the Palestinian Problem Until 1948* (Washington, DC: Institute for Palestine Studies), 645–99. The special committee included Australia, which endorsed neither position.

34. Khalidi, *From Haven to Conquest,* 695. See app. A for the full text of the subcommittee's final draft resolution.

35. Ibid., 683.

36. On these early Arab philosophers, see John Esposito, *The Islamic Threat: Myth or Reality?* 3rd ed. (New York: Oxford University Press). On Israeli Arab politics, see especially research by As'ad Ghanem, Nadim Rouhana, and Ian Lustick.

37. Gavron, *The Other Side of Despair,* 236.

38. See especially Mallison and Mallison, *Palestine Problem.*

39. Among several important titles, see Rashid Khalidi's *British Policy towards Syria and Palestine, 1906–1914: A Study of the Antecedents of the Hussein-McMahon Correspondence, the Sykes-Picot Agreement, and the Balfour Declaration* (Ithaca, NY: Ithaca Press, 1980) and David Fromkin's *A Peace to End All Peace* (New York: Henry Holt, 2001). A shorter excellent analysis is W. Thomas Mallison's "The Balfour Declaration: An Appraisal in International Law," in *The Transformation of Palestine,* ed. Ibrahim Abu-Lughod (Evanston: Northwestern University Press, 1987).

40. On drafts of the Balfour Declaration and its controversies, see especially Mallison, "The Balfour Declaration."

41. "Letter from President Bush to Prime Minister Sharon on Sharon's Disengagement Plan," (14 April 2004), Foundation for Middle East Peace, available on-line at www.fmep.org/documents/Bush_letter_to_Sharon_Disengagement_Plan.html.

42. "Sharon Letter to Bush on Disengagement Plan," Foundation for Middle East Peace, available on-line at www.fmep.org/documents/Sharon_letter_to_Bush_Disengagement_Plan.html.

43. "Letter from President Bush to Prime Minister Sharon."

44. Jerusalem Program, "The Unity of the Jewish People," adopted at the Twenty-Seventh World Zionist Congress, Jerusalem, 1968.

45. See Nimni, "From *Galut* to *T'futsoth,*" 133.

46. A Web log maintained by self-described "opinionated scientists" cited "grim numbers": "In *Reexamining Intermarriage: Trends, Textures, Strategies,* the most comprehensive study to date of intermarried couples, sociologist Bruce Phillips found that *only 14% of intermarried couples could be classified as 'Judaic,'* in the sense that the balance of religious observance in the home is Jewish. And even in such homes, 60% had x-mas trees. Close to 90% of the children of intermarriages will themselves marry non-Jews. Due to the pervasiveness of intermarriage, American Jewry is too emotionally compromised to even oppose it. A 2001 study by the American Jewish Committee found that *only 12%*

of Jewish parents strongly oppose their children intermarrying (a figure only slightly higher than the percentage of Orthodox Jews). Well over half responded that they would not be troubled at all by their children intermarrying." The Web log also recognized the link of these trends to liberal democracy: "To oppose intermarriage today, points out historian Jonathan Sarna, means going against the entire modern American ethos by placing group identity over social integration, individualism, and liberal values. . . . Half of those polled in the American Jewish Committee study go so far as to term opposition to intermarriage 'racist'" (Gene Expression, "Jewish Assimilation," available online at www.gnxp.com/MT2/archives/000740.html).

47. On the distinction between *Galut* and *T'futsoth,* see especially Nimni, "From *Galut* to *T'futsoth.*"

48. Responding to a lawsuit brought by Uzi Ornan and others in 2004, the Israeli Prosecutor's Office rejected their petition to register their nationality as "Israeli," affirming that "the dictionary definition of a nationality is 'a nation, a people; a large group of people of a joint origin, common destiny and history and usually a shared spoken language.'" The prosecutor's office thus maintained that registering as "Israeli" would not reflect the true "national and ethnic identity" of the petitioners. See Yuval Yoaz, "State Refuses to Register 'Israeli' Nationality," *Ha'aretz,* 19 May 2004; see also n. 17 of chap. 5 in the present study.

49. Hazony, *The Jewish State.*

50. Albert Einstein, *Ideas and Opinions* (New York: Crown Publishers, 1954), 190, cited in Hazony, *The Jewish State,* 213.

51. Cited in Hazony, *The Jewish State,* 203.

52. Martin Buber, "The Bi-national Approach to Zionism," in *Towards Union in Palestine: Essays on Zionism and Jewish-Arab Cooperation,* ed. M. Buber, J. L. Magnes, and E. Simon (Westport, CT: Greenwood Press, 1947), 10.

53. Martin Buber, "The Ichud," in *A Land of Two Peoples: Martin Buber on Jews and Arabs,* ed. Paul R. Mendes-Flohr (New York: Oxford University Press, 1983), 149. For the full program of the Ichud, see app. A.

54. Hannah Arendt, "To Save the Jewish Homeland: There is Still Time," *Commentary,* May 1948, 399.

55. Ibid., 402.

56. Ibid., 400.

57. Ibid.

58. Ibid., 403

59. Israeli and U.S. lobbyists pressured the Soviet government for many years to allow Jewish emigration from the Soviet Union. When restrictions were loosened, the vast majority of Russian Jews chose to migrate to the United States. Viewing with dismay this loss of emigrés so valuable to its demographic project, Israel then lobbied successfully for the United States to cease providing visas and for the Russian government to grant exit visas only to Jews who held Israeli visas, which were attached to travel arrangements to Israel. Initially covered through Israeli loans, the Russians' travel costs to Israel were converted to grants for Jews who then remained in Israel at least five years; otherwise, the loan was called, totaling many thousands of dollars per person. The intent and effect was to lock Russian immigrants financially within Israel until they had established personal ties to the country.

60. Will Kymlicka is one theorist noted for addressing this shift, especially in his *Multicultural Citizenship: A Liberal Theory of Minority Rights* (New York: Oxford University Press, 1996). The literature has expanded greatly in the past decade.

61. Thirty-Fourth Zionist Congress Resolutions, "A. Israel as a Jewish and Democratic state, based on Zionist Principles," Hagshama Department, World Zionist Organization, available online at www.wzo.org.il/en/resources/view.asp?id=1149.

62. The continued relevance of the Jerusalem Program is also indicated by its prominent position under the "Zionism" link on the Web site of the WZO's Hagshama Department: see http://www.wzo.org.il/en/resources/view.asp?id=1707&subject=28.

63. Cited in Ari Shavit, "Elective Affinities/Reality Bites," *Ha'aretz*, 16 January 2003.

64. Cited in Peter Hirschberg, "One-State Awakening," *Ha'aretz*, 10 December 2003.

65. Bresheeth, "Two States."

66. See As'ad Ghanem, "Zionism, Post-Zionism, and Anti-Zionism in Israel: Jews and Arabs in Conflict over the Nature of the State," in *The Challenge of Post-Zionism: Alternatives to Israeli Fundamentalist Politics,* ed. Ephraim Nimni (London: Zed Books, 2003).

67. The quoted phrase is from a decision (cited in n. 44) in which the Israeli Prosecutor's Office rejected "Israeli" nationality. Daniel Gavron (*The Other Side of Despair,* 234) has suggested renaming the new state the "State of Jerusalem/al-Quds."

68. Daniel Barenboim, "On Israel," speech to the Israeli Knesset upon receiving the Wolf Prize, 9 May 2004, reprinted in *The Nation,* 24 May 2004.

APPENDIX A

1. See Susan Lee Hattis, *The Bi-National Idea in Palestine during Mandatory Times* (Haifa: Shikmona Publishing, 1970), 222, cited in Paul R. Mendes-Flohr, ed., *A Land of Two Peoples: Martin Buber on Jews and Arabs* (New York: Oxford University Press, 1983), 134.

Bibliography

Abu-Lughod, Janet. 1971. "The Demographic Transformation of Palestine." In *The Transformation of Palestine*, ed. Ibrahim Abu-Lughod. Evanston: Northwestern University Press.

Abunimah, Ali. 2004. "Palestine/Israel: The End of the Road for the Two-State Solution?" Paper presented at Middle East Centre, Seminar Series: Palestinians on Palestine: The Way Forward, St. Anthony's College, Oxford, UK, 20 February.

Al-Hamad, Abdulatif Y. N.d. "The Dilemmas of Development in the Arab World." Paper presented at Arab World 2000 Symposium: Transformation and Challenges, Center for Contemporary Arab Studies, Washington, DC. Available online at http://www.ccasonline.org/symposium/Al-Hamad.htm.

Al-Hindi, Musa. 2004. "The Road to Palestine." *Al-Ahram Weekly* 690 (13–19 May).

Amayreh, Khalid. 2004. "Controversial Move." *Al-Ahram Weekly* 673 (15–21 January).

Americans for Peace Now. 2003. "Israeli Peace Now Survey of Settlers: Most Reject Extremists, Would Accept Compensation to Leave." Press release, 23 July. Available online at http://www.peacenow.org/nia/pr/07232003.html.

Anderson, Benedict. 1983. *Imagined Communities: Reflections on the Origins and Spread of Nationalism*. London: Verso.

Anti-Defamation League. N.d. "The Conversion Crisis: The Current Debate on Religion, State, and Conversion in Israel." http://www.adl.org/Israel/Conversion/crisis.asp.

Arendt, Hannah. 1948. "To Save the Jewish Homeland: There Is Still Time." *Commentary*, May.

Arian, Asher. 2003. *Israeli Public Opinion on National Security, 2003*. Memorandum 67. Jaffee Center for Strategic Studies, Tel Aviv University, October. Available online at http://www.tau.ac.il/jcss/memoranda/memo67.pdf.

Aruri, Naseer. 2003. *Dishonest Broker: The U.S. Role in Israel and Palestine*. Cambridge, MA: South End Press.

Bahbah, Bishara. 1986. *Israel and Latin America: The Military Connection*. New York: St. Martin's Press.

Barenboim, Daniel. 2004. "On Israel." Speech to the Israeli Knesset upon receiving the Wolf Prize, 9 May. Reprinted in *The Nation*, 24 May.

Bar-Gal, Yoram. 2004. *Propaganda and Zionist Education: The Jewish National Fund 1924–1947*. Rochester, NY: University of Rochester Press.

Bastos, Santiago, and Manuela Camus. 2003. *Entre el mecapal y el cielo: Desarrollo del movimiento maya en Guatemala*. Guatemala: Facultad Latinoamericana de Ciencias Sociales.

Bayit Ne'eman B'Yisrael. N.d. "Maale Adumim." *Tehila: A New Dimension of Aliyah.* http://www.tehilla.com/haut/bayit/List%20of%20Communities/maaleadu.html.

Benvenisti, Meron. 2000. *Sacred Landscape: The Buried History of the Holy Land since 1948*. Berkeley: University of California Press.

Benziman, Uzi. 2004. "Corridors of Power: Whose Freedom Is It Anyway?" *Ha'aretz*, 30 April. Available online at http://www.diak.org/artikelaktuell/ip%20online%2018/Corridors%20of%20Power.htm.

Berger, Elmer. 1988. "Zionist Ideology: Obstacle to Peace." In *Anti-Zionism: Analytical Reflections*, ed. Roselle Tekiner, Samir Abed-Rabbo, and Norton Mezvinsky. Brattleboro, VT: Amana Books.

Bishara, Azmi. 2004. "Separation Spells Racism." *Al-Ahram* 697 (1–7 July). Available online at http://weekly.ahram.org.eg/print/2004/697/op2.htm.

———. 2004. "Jewishness versus Democracy." *Al-Ahram* 714 (23 October–3 November). Available online http://weekly.ahram.org.eg/2004/714/op63.htm.

Blum, Ruthie. 2004. "ONE on ONE: It's the Demography, Stupid." *Jerusalem Post*, 20 May.

Bresheeth, Haim. 2004. "Two States, Too Little, Too Late." *Al-Ahram Weekly* 681 (11–17 March).

Brynen, Rex. 2000. *A Very Political Economy: Peacebuilding and Foreign Aid in the West Bank and Gaza*. Washington, DC: United States Institute of Peace Press.

B'Tselem. 2002. *Land Grab: Israel's Settlement Policy in the West Bank; Comprehensive Report*. Jerusalem; May.

Buber, Martin. 1947. "The Bi-national Approach to Zionism." In *Towards Union in Palestine: Essays on Zionism and Jewish-Arab Cooperation*, ed. M. Buber, J. L. Magnes, and E. Simon. Westport, CT: Greenwood Press.

———. 1948. "The Land and Its Possessors." *Israel and the World: Essays in a Time of Crisis*. New York: Schocken Books.

———. 1952. *Israel and Palestine: The History of an Idea*. London: East and West Library.

Chesler, Phyllis. 2003. *The New Anti-Semitism*. San Francisco: Jossey-Bass.

Cohen, Asher, and Bernard Susser. 2000. *Israel and the Politics of Jewish Identity*. Baltimore: Johns Hopkins University Press.

Coon, Anthony. 1992. *Town Planning under Military Occupation*. Aldershot: Dartmouth.

Davis, Leonard J. 1989. *Myths and Facts: A Guide to the Arab-Israel Conflict*. Washington, DC: Near East Report.

Dershowitz, Alan. 2003. *The Case for Israel*. Hoboken, NJ: John Wiley and Sons.

Dizard, John. 2004. "How Ahmed Chalabi Conned the Neocons." *Salon.com*, 4 May. http://archive.salon.com/news/feature/2004/05/04/chalabi.

Drew, Elizabeth. 2003. "The Neo-Cons in Power." *New York Review of Books* 50, no. 10 (12 June).

Dreyfuss, Robert. 2004. "Agents of Influence." *The Nation*, 4 October.

Dreyfuss, Robert, and Jason Vest. 2004. "The Lie Factor." *Mother Jones*, January–February.

Elazar, Daniel. 1991. *Two Peoples—One Land: Federal Solutions for Israel, the Palestinians, and Jordan.* Lanham, MD: University Press of America.

Ennes, James. 1979. *Assault on the Liberty.* New York: Random House.

Esposito, John. 1999. *The Islamic Threat: Myth or Reality?* 3rd ed. New York: Oxford University Press.

Esteron, Yoel. 2003. "Who's in Favor of Annihilating Israel?" *Ha'aretz*, 28 November.

Findlay, Paul. 2003. *They Dare to Speak Out: People and Institutions Confront Israel's Lobby.* 3rd ed. Westport, CT: Lawrence Hill.

Finkelstein, Norman. 2000. *The Holocaust Industry.* London: Verso.

Foundation for Middle East Peace. 2004. "Sharon's Enduring Agenda: Consolidate Territorial Control, Manage the Conflict." *Report on Israeli Settlement in the Occupied Territories* 14, no. 1 (January–February).

Foxman, Abraham. 2003. *Never Again? The Threat of the New Anti-Semitism.* San Francisco: HarperSanFrancisco.

Fromkin, David. 2001. *A Peace to End All Peace: The Fall of the Ottoman Empire and the Creation of the Modern Middle East.* New York: Henry Holt.

Gavron, Daniel. 2004. *The Other Side of Despair: Jews and Arabs in the Promised Land.* New York: Rowman and Littlefield.

Gerner, Deborah. 1991. *One Land, Two Peoples: The Conflict over Palestine.* Boulder: Westview Press.

Ghanem, As'ad. 2003. "Zionism, Post-Zionism, and Anti-Zionism in Israel: Jews and Arabs in Conflict over the Nature of the State." In *The Challenge of Post-Zionism: Alternatives to Israeli Fundamentalist Politics,* ed. Ephraim Nimni. London: Zed Books.

Goldberg, David J. 1996. *To the Promised Land: A History of Zionist Thought.* London: Penguin Books.

Gorali, Moshe. 2004. "Second-Class Status and the Fear of a Fifth Column." *Ha'aretz*, 24 May.

Gresh, Alain. 1985. *The PLO: Towards an Independent Palestinian State.* London: Zed Books.

Guyatt, Nicholas. 1998. *The Absence of Peace: Understanding the Israeli-Palestinian Conflict.* London: Zed Press.

Halper, Jeff. 2004. "Beyond Road Maps and Walls." *The Link* 37, no. 1 (January–March).

Halpern, Ben, and Jehuda Reinharz. 1998. *Zionism and the Creation of a New Society.* New York: Oxford University Press.

Halwani, Raja. 2004. "Palestinian Options: The One-State Solution." *Palestine Report*, 31 March.

Hazony, Yoram. 2001. *The Jewish State: The Struggle for Israel's Soul.* New York: Basic Books.

Hersh, Seymour M. 2002. "The Debate Within." *The New Yorker*, 11 March.

———. 2003. "Behind the 'Mushroom Cloud.'" *The New Yorker*, 21 March.

———. 2004. "Plan B." *The New Yorker*, 28 June.

Herzl, Theodor. 1988. *The Jewish State.* Trans. Sylvie d'Avigdor. New York: Dover Publications. (Orig. pub. 1896.)

Hetata, Sherif. 2003. "World Domination, Inc." *Al-Ahram Weekly* 666 (27 November–3 December).

Hirschberg, Peter. 2003. "One-State Awakening." *Ha'aretz*, 10 December.

———. 2004. "Hello, I'm Israeli-Palestinian." *Mideast,* 9 February.

Hirst, David. 2003. "Wagging Which Way." *Al-Ahram* 661 (23–29 October).

Hunter, Jane. 1987. *No Simple Proxy.* Washington, DC: Washington Middle East Associates.

Isaacs, Harold R. 1977. *Idols of the Tribe.* New York: Harper and Row.

Jaber, Hala. 1997. *Hezbollah: Born with a Vengeance.* New York: Columbia University Press.

Jewish Agency for Israel Settlement Department, Central District, and World Zionist Organization Settlement Division, Central District. 1988. *Nahal-Eron Project: Five-Year Plan for the Development of the Eron-Reihan Region.*

Judt, Tony. 2003. "Israel: The Alternative." *New York Review of Books* 50, no. 16 (23 October).

Kazerooni, Ibrahim. 2004. "A One-State Solution in the Mideast." *Denver Post,* 24 April.

Khalidi, Rashid. 1980. *British Policy towards Syria and Palestine, 1906–1914: A Study of the Antecedents of the Hussein-McMahon Correspondence, the Sykes-Picot Agreement, and the Balfour Declaration.* Ithaca, NY: Ithaca Press.

———. 1997. *Palestinian Identity: The Construction of Modern National Consciousness.* New York: Columbia University Press.

Khalidi, Walid. 1987. *From Haven to Conquest: Readings in Zionism and the Palestinian Problem Until 1948.* Washington, DC: Institute for Palestine Studies.

Kimmerling, Baruch. 2003. *Politicide: Ariel Sharon's War against the Palestinians.* London: Verso.

Kimmerling, Baruch, and Joel S. Migdal. 2003. *The Palestinian People: A History.* Cambridge: Harvard University Press.

Klug, Brian. 2004. "The Myth of the New Anti-Semitism." *The Nation,* 15 January.

Kymlicka, Will. 1996. *Multicultural Citizenship: A Liberal Theory of Minority Rights.* New York: Oxford University Press.

Lagerquist, Peter. 2004. "Fencing the Last Sky: Excavating Palestine after Israel's 'Separation Wall.'" *Journal of Palestine Studies* 130 (winter).

Landau, David. 2004. "Maximum Jews, Minimum Palestinians." *Ha'aretz,* 19 February.

Laqueur, Walter. 2003. *A History of Zionism: From the French Revolution to the Establishment of the State of Israel.* New York: Schocken Books.

Lemarchand, René. 1996. *Burundi: Ethnic Conflict and Genocide.* New York: Cambridge University Press.

Lustick, Ian. 1980. *Arabs in the Jewish State: Israel's Control of a National Minority.* Austin: University of Texas Press.

———. 1996. "To Build and to Be Built By: Israel and the Hidden Logic of the Iron Wall." *Israel Studies* 1, no. 1.

MacArthur, Shirl. 2001. "A Conservative Total for U.S. Aid to Israel." *Washington Report on Middle East Affairs,* January–February.

Mallison, Tom, and Sally Mallison. 1986. *The Palestinian Problem in International Law and World Order.* Essex, England: Longman.

Mallison, W. Thomas. 1987. "The Balfour Declaration: An Appraisal in International Law." In *The Transformation of Palestine,* ed. Ibrahim Abu-Lughod. Evanston: Northwestern University Press.

Massing, Michael. 2002. "The Israel Lobby." *The Nation,* 10 June.

Megged, Aharon. 2002. "And First of All, the Justice of Our Path." *Ha'aretz*, 26 March.

Mendes-Flohr, Paul R., ed. 1983. *A Land of Two Peoples: Martin Buber on Jews and Arabs*. New York: Oxford University Press.

Moodie, Dunbar, 1975. *The Rise of Afrikanerdom: Power, Apartheid, and the Afrikaner Civil Religion*. Berkeley: University of California Press.

Morris, Benny. 2001. *Righteous Victims: A History of the Zionist-Arab Conflict, 1881–2001*. New York: Vintage.

———. 2004. *The Birth of the Palestinian Refugee Problem Revisited*. Cambridge: Cambridge University Press.

Netanyahu, Benjamin. 1993. *A Place among the Nations: Israel and the World*. New York: Bantam Books.

Nimni, Ephraim, ed. 2003. *The Challenge of Post-Zionism: Alternatives to Israeli Fundamentalist Politics*. London: Zed Books.

———. 2003. "From *Galut* to *T'futsoth*: Post-Zionism and the Dis><location of Jewish Diasporas." In *The Challenge of Post-Zionism: Alternatives to Israeli Fundamentalist Politics*, ed. Ephraim Nimni. London: Zed Books.

Pappé, Ilan. 1992. *The Making of the Arab-Israeli Conflict, 1947–51*. New York: I. B. Tauris.

———. 1997. "Post-Zionist Critique on Israel and the Palestinians. Part I: The Academic Debate." *Journal of Palestine Studies* 26, no. 2.

———. 2000. "Israel at a Crossroads between Civic Democracy and Jewish Zealotocracy." *Journal of Palestine Studies* 29, no. 3.

———. 2003. *A History of Modern Palestine: One Land, Two Peoples*. New York: Cambridge University Press.

———. 2003. "The Square Circle." In *The Challenge of Post-Zionism: Alternatives to Israeli Fundamentalist Politics*, ed. Ephraim Nimni. London: Zed Books.

Peace Now. 2003. "Israeli Peace Now Survey of Settlers." Press release, 23 July. Available online at http://www.peacenow.org/nia/pr/07232003.html.

Pederson, Jon, Sara Randall, and Marwan Khawaja, eds. 2001. *Growing Fast: The Palestinian Population in the West Bank and Gaza Strip*. Fafo Report 353. Fafo Institute for Applied Social Science. Available online at http://www.fafo.no/pub/rapp/353/353.pdf.

Peters, Joan. 2001. *From Time Immemorial: The Origins of the Arab-Jewish Conflict over Palestine*. New York: Harper and Row.

Qumsiyeh, Mazin. 2004. *Sharing the Land of Canaan: Human Rights and the Israeli-Palestinian Struggle*. London: Pluto Press.

Ram, Uri. 2003. "From Nation-State to Nation——State: Nation, History, and Identity Struggles in Jewish Israel." In *The Challenge of Post-Zionism: Alternatives to Israeli Fundamentalist Politics*, ed. Ephraim Nimni. London: Zed Books.

Rappaport, Meron. 2003. "A Wall in Their Heart." *Yedioh Aharonoth*, 23 May.

Rashid, Ahmed. 2001. *Taliban: Militant Islam, Oil, and Fundamentalism in Central Asia*. New Haven, CT: Yale University Press.

———. 2003. *Jihad: The Rise of Militant Islam in Central Asia*. New York: Penguin Books.

Rauchberger, Eliezer. 2002. "United Torah Judaism Rejects High Court's Conversion Decision." *Dei'ah veDibur*, 27 February. Available online at http://chareidi.shemayisrael.com/KS62aconvrt.htm.

Ravitsky, Aviezer. 1993. *Messianism, Zionism, and Jewish Religious Radicalism.* Trans. Michael Swirsky and Jonathan Chipman. Chicago: University of Chicago Press.

Remba, Gidon. 2004. "Anti-Semitism—New or Old?" *The Nation*, 24 March.

Rogan, Eugene L., and Avi Shlaim, eds. 2001. *The War for Palestine: Rewriting the History of 1948.* Cambridge: Cambridge University Press.

Rubenberg, Cheryl. 1986. *Israel and the American National Interest.* Urbana: University of Illinois Press.

Said, Edward. 1978. *Orientalism.* New York: Pantheon Books.

———. 2001. "Truth and Reconciliation." In *The End of the Peace Process: Oslo and After.* New York: Vintage. First published in *New York Times Magazine*, 10 January 1999.

Schoenfeld, Gabriel. 2003. *The Return of Anti-Semitism.* San Francisco: Encounter Books.

Schöpflin, George. 1997. "The Functions of Myths and a Taxonomy of Myths." In *Myths and Nationhood*, ed. Geoffrey Hosking and George Schöpflin. New York: Routledge.

Seale, Patrick. 1990. *Asad of Syria: The Struggle for the Middle East.* Berkeley: University of California Press.

Segev, Tom. 2000. *One Palestine, Complete: Jews and Arabs under the British Mandate.* Trans. Haim Watzman. New York: Henry Holt.

Shahak, Israel. 1988. "Zionism as a Recidivist Movement." In *Anti-Zionism: Analytical Reflections*, ed. Roselle Tekiner, Samir Abed-Rabbo, and Norton Mezvinsky. Brattleboro, VT: Amana Books.

Shafir, Gershon. 1996. *Land, Labor, and the Origins of the Israeli-Palestinian Conflict, 1882–1914.* Berkeley: University of California Press.

Shavit, Avi. 2003. "Elective Affinities/Reality Bites." *Ha'aretz*, 16 January.

———. 2003. "Cry, the Beloved Two-State Solution." *Ha'aretz*, 6 August.

———. 2004. "Survival of the Fittest." *Ha'aretz*, 19 February.

Sheleg, Yair. 2003. "The Settlers and a Binational State." *Ha'aretz*, 31 August.

Shenbol, Arial. 2004. "The Only Democracy in the Middle East." *Maariv International*, 17 June.

Shlaim, Avi. 1999. *Collusion across the Jordan: King Abdullah, the Zionist Movement, and the Partition of Palestine.* New York: Columbia University Press.

———. 2001. *The Iron Wall: Israel and the Arab World.* New York: W. W. Norton.

Shragai, Nadav. 2003. "Split Right Down the Middle." *Ha'aretz*, 18 March.

Silberstein, Lawrence J. 1999. *Postzionism Debates: Knowledge and Power in Israeli Culture.* New York: Routledge.

Sternhall, Zeev. 1998. *The Founding Myths of Israel: Nationalism, Socialism, and the Making of the Jewish State.* Princeton: Princeton University Press.

Stokes, Geoffrey, ed., 1997. *The Politics of Identity in Australia.* Cambridge: Cambridge University Press.

Sussman, Gary. 2004. "Is the Two-State Solution Dead?" *Current History* 103, no. 669 (January).

———. 2004. "The Challenge to the Two-State Solution." *Middle East Report*, summer.

Tekiner, Roselle. 1988. "On the Inequality of Israeli Citizens." *Without Prejudice* 1, no. 1.

———. 2001. "Israel's Two-Tiered Citizenship Law Bars Non-Jews from 93

Percent of Its Lands." *Media Monitors Network*, 13 February. Available online at http://www.mediamonitors.net/tekiner1.html.

Tilley, Virginia. 2004. "The One-State Solution." *London Review of Books* 25, no. 21 (6 November).

———. 2004. "Unfair to Revenants." *London Reviews of Books* 26, no. 11 (3 June).

Tillman, Seth. 1982. *The United States in the Middle East: Interests and Obstacles*. Bloomington: Indiana University Press.

Tivnan, Edward. 1987. *The Lobby: Jewish Political Power and American Foreign Policy*. New York: Simon and Schuster.

Weber, Eugen. 1979. *Peasants into Frenchmen: The Modernization of Rural France, 1870–1914*. Stanford, CA: Stanford University Press.

Woodrow Wilson Task Force WWS 401c. 1999. "Water Rights in the Jordan Valley: Geography of Water Resources." http://www.wws.princeton.edu/~wws401c/geography.html.

Woodward, Bob. 2004. *Plan of Attack*. New York: Simon and Schuster.

Yaar, Ephraim, and Tamar Hermann. 2003. "The Peace Index: Israeli Jews Fret over the Possibility of a Binational State." *Ha'aretz*, 5 November.

———. 2004. "Peace Index: Demographic Fears Favor Unilateral Separation." *Ha'aretz*, 7 January.

Yinon, Oded. 1982. "A Strategy for Israel in the 1980s." *Kivunim* 14. Available, ed. and trans. Israel Shahak, at http://www.geocities.com/alabasters_archive/zionist_plan.html.

Index

Nakba (Palestinian), 97, 131, 149
Naming Committee. *See* Jewish
    National Fund
Nasr, Gamal, 118
Nationalism, 173, 182, 190, 193;
    Arab, 90, 118, 142; Christian, 177;
    ethnic, 13, 215, 232; Hindu, 177;
    Islamic, 177; Jewish, 75, 136, 155;
    Northern Ireland, 23, 128, 133–34,
    143–44, 146; one-state solution,
    configuration in, 204; Palestinian,
    5, 9, 32–33, 68, 71, 122, 144, 203,
    247n. 16; racial thought in, 173–74;
    religious, 177–79, 252n. 16
National Religious Party, 45, 138
National Union Party, 45
Nazi Germany, 159–60, 164–65, 195,
    216, 218
Neoconservatives. *See* United States
Netanyahu, Benjamin, 34, 110, 155,
    158; neoconservative connection
    of, 108; settlement policy of, 52
New Zealand, 126
Nimni, Ephraim, 156

Office of Special Plans (U.S. Penta-
    gon), 109–11, 113
Olmert, Ehud, 6, 189, 194
One-state solution, 9–16, 45, 88, 91,
    220; Arab interests in, 115, 165,
    168; implications for Golan
    Heights, 19; Israeli-Jewish views
    and fears of, 80, 163, 168–69; mod-
    els for, 220–25; objections to, gen-
    eral, 192–94; objections to, regard-
    ing anti-Semitism, 17, 194–97, 218;
    objections to, regarding Arab
    threat, 197–205; objections to,
    regarding international opinion,
    205–9; Palestinian views of, 142,
    188–91, 203, 241–42; post-Zionist
    thought regarding, 184–86; water
    as driving factor of, 64. *See also*
    Binational state; Post-Zionism
Oslo Accords, 16, 17, 28, 32, 34, 49,
    54, 64, 104, 121, 145, 154, 199, 207,
    247n. 25; impact on Palestinian
    politics of, 121–22, 128, 193; nego-
    tiation process of, 20, 76–77, 86,
    156; provisions of, 54, 65, 80–82;

settlement policy during, 28, 52;
    two-state premise in, 76–77, 205,
    208
Other Israel, The, 163
Ottoman Empire, 70, 108, 141; popu-
    lation and trade statistics in, 172,
    246n. 9

Palestine Liberation Organization
    (PLO), 72, 94, 95, 119, 190; cor-
    ruption in, 97; democratic charac-
    ter of, 54, 119, 153, 203–4; Israeli
    perceptions of, 152; leadership of,
    71, 120–21, 124; position on one-
    and two-state solutions, 54, 77, 79,
    165, 191, 198, 241
Palestine National Council (PNC),
    203
Palestinian Communist Party, 203
Palestinian Interim Self-Government
    Authority (PA), 52, 120, 124, 190;
    destruction of offices, by Israel,
    122–23; position on one- and
    two-state solutions, 11, 54, 76, 77,
    188–89, 193; position on West
    Bank, 71; weakness of, 123–25
Palestinian nationalism, 33, 68, 71–72,
    247n. 16; configuration of, during
    the Oslo era, 122, 190; democratic
    currents in, 202–4; prospects in a
    two-state solution, 5, 9, 32, 188;
    shifts regarding one-state solution,
    193–94. *See also* Palestine Libera-
    tion Organization
Pappé, Ilan, 153–56, 158, 246n. 7
Peace Index, 167, 255n. 46
Peace Now, 244nn. 8–9, 254n. 41
Perle, Richard, 102, 108–11, 250nn.
    20–22
Peters, Joan, 255n. 50
Popular Front for the Liberation of
    Palestine (PFLP), 203
Population in Israel-Palestine, 10, 65;
    Christian, 244n. 2; demographic
    engineering in Nahal Eron and
    Rehan bloc, 38–40; "demographic
    threat" (of an Arab majority in a
    one-state solution), 9–10, 74–76,
    88, 167–69, 186, 199, 219, 223–24;
    Jewish, in historic Palestine, 246n.

tional policy toward, 16, 181; as
model for Israel, 10, 128, 133,
135–36, 139–40, 143, 145, 164, 181,
187, 196, 200, 204, 223–24
Status Law (World Zionist Organization–Jewish Agency), 48
Stauffer, Thomas, 248n. 6
Sulzberger, Arthur Hays, 213
Sussman, Gary, 12
Syria, 115, 116, 119, 151, 166, 207;
early support for one-state option,
201, 236; and Golan Heights, 21,
94; Israeli policy toward, 107–8;
U.S. policy toward, 96, 108,
111–13, 115
Syria Accountability Act (S-982), 112
Szold, Henrietta, 235

Ta'ayush, 255n. 41
Temple Mount, 22, 97, 122
Terrorism: in Iraq, 114; Islamic, 93;
as Israeli rationale for Wall, 167;
Jewish, 152–53, 157, 216; Nazi,
159, 218; Palestinian, 46, 53, 96,
163, 193, 121, 186; Palestinian,
Jewish perceptions of, 101, 152,
243n. 3; potential for, in two-state
solution, 5–6; regional threat of,
12, 88, 103, 126, 112, 117, 120, 127;
suppression of, as Israeli condition
for talks, 98, 122, 133; war on, 93,
105, 114
T'futsoth, 212, 259n. 47
Trade: as factor guaranteeing
one-state solution, 224;
Israeli-Palestinian interdependence,
11; Middle East regional, 89, 115,
118; Palestinian, 5, 32, 45, 54, 65–66,
73–74, 169; provisions in Oslo
Accords, 81; United States with
Israel, 248n. 6. *See also* Boycott
Transfer (of Palestinians), 6, 13,
64–65; in early Zionist thought,
157–58, 181; in Elon Plan, 243n. 3;
"hard" (forced), 6–7, 9, 120, 126,
137, 184; in Israeli-Jewish opinion,
246n. 13, 257n. 22; "soft"
(induced), 5, 7
Trireme Partners, 250n. 22
Twain, Mark, 182

Two-state solution, 76–77, 79–81, 91,
106, 132, 140, 143, 184, 191, 194,
205, 207–9; dangers to Israel of,
163, 167, 186; dangers to peace of,
12; Geneva Accords, endorsement
of, 123; Jewish statehood, need
for, 10; logistical impossibility of,
1, 3, 6; obsolescence of, 14, 129,
185; Sharon version of, 65, 86, 188,
208

United Jewish Appeal, 36
United Nations, 77, 90, 99, 111; General Assembly Resolution 181
("partition resolution"), 77, 79, 81,
151, 153, 201–7, 216, 247n. 23;
Israeli endorsement of principles
of, 232; resolutions on
Israeli-Palestinian conflict, 89, 99,
153, 205, 248n. 1; Security Council
Resolution 242 (1967), 99, 207;
Security Council Resolution 338
(1973), 99; World Conference
against Racism, 252n. 6; "Zionism
is racism" resolution, 252n. 7
United Nations Relief Works
Agency, 251n. 32
United States, 147; aid to Israel,
248n. 6; divestment campaign in,
136; foreign policy toward Israel
and Middle East, 90–114, 126–27,
135, 150, 153, 168, 173; International Studies in Higher Education
Act (HR 3077), 249n. 15; involvement in Russian Jewish emigration, 259n. 59; Israeli attack on,
249n. 17; Israeli dependence on,
90, 224; Jewish diaspora life in,
210, 246n. 8; neoconservative foreign policy of, 106–14; occupation
of Iraq, 125, 131, 165; policy on a
two-state solution, 208; pro-Israeli
(Zionist) lobby in, 100–106, 143,
166, 253n. 24; relations with Arab
states, 117, 119; relations with
Europe, 125–27; relations with
Palestinians, 120, 124; relations
with Turkey, 250n. 22; "road map
for peace" (of George W. Bush),
34, 76, 128, 184, 208; role in